Science, Reason, and Faith

SCIENCE, REASON, AND FAITH

DISCOVERING THE BIBLE

FR. ROBERT SPITZER, SJ

Our Sunday Visitor
Huntington, Indiana

Nihil Obstat
Msgr. Michael Heintz, Ph.D.
Censor Librorum

Imprimatur
✠ Kevin C. Rhoades
Bishop of Fort Wayne-South Bend
May 26, 2023

The *Nihil Obstat* and *Imprimatur* are official declarations that a book is free from doctrinal or moral error. It is not implied that those who have granted the *Nihil Obstat* and *Imprimatur* agree with the contents, opinions, or statements expressed.

Our Sunday Visitor Publishing Division
Our Sunday Visitor, Inc.
200 Noll Plaza
Huntington, IN 46750
www.osv.com
1-800-348-2440

ISBN: 978-1-63966-057-5 (Inventory No. T2802)
1. RELIGION — Biblical Studies — General.
2. RELIGION — Religion & Science.
3. RELIGION — Christianity — Catholic.

eISBN: 978-1-63966-058-2
LCCN: 2023939217

Cover design: Tyler Ottinger
Interior design: Amanda Falk
Cover and interior art: AdobeStock

PRINTED IN THE UNITED STATES OF AMERICA

In memory of my mother, who was a chemist and daily communicant, and my father, who blended science, reason, and faith in his life and teachings.

To my many good professors of Scripture and theology at the Gregorian University and the Weston School of Theology, who inspired me for a lifetime, especially Fr. John Navone, SJ.

Contents

Part One

Questions about the Old Testament

The purpose of this book is to answer the great questions of science, reason, and faith arising out of the Bible in its dialogue with modern science, history, and scriptural interpretation. Some of the topics that generate the most questions are:

- The existence of God in light of science
- The existence of a transphysical soul (made in the image and likeness of God) in light of science
- The veracity of the Bible in light of science, contemporary Scripture scholarship, and history
- The veracity of the Genesis account of creation in light of

the scientific view of big bang cosmology and evolution
- The possibility and reality of miracles in light of contemporary scientific, philosophical, and historical criticism

As will be seen, scientific, historiographical, and exegetical research do not run contrary to the existence of God, the soul, and the Bible, but rather support them probatively, allowing each pursuit — reason and faith — to complement and elucidate the other. Science and reason can tell us much about *how* the observable world operates, but Revelation alone (seen through the eyes of faith) can tell us *why* we and the world exist. Each area uses its own specific methods to achieve its distinctive yet complementary goals. The objective of Scripture is to reveal sacred truths needed for salvation, while the objective of science is quite different — to give an empirical-mathematical explanation of the physical universe.

There are certainly differences in the truths of Scripture and science, but this is because they are looking at different aspects of the same reality — Scripture looking at God's revelation of the path to salvation, and science looking at the mathematical-physical intelligibility of the observable universe. As we shall see, seemingly irreconcilable differences between these two pursuits come more from misunderstandings than reality. Most of them are attributable to the fallacy of making Scripture do science, and science interpret Divine Revelation.

In part 1 of this book, we will explore five groups of questions concerned with science, reason, history, and faith in the Old Testament:

1. **Chapter 1 (OT#1–OT#4):** Foundational Questions Concerned with the Methods of Science, Scriptural Interpretation, and History
2. **Chapter 2 (OT#5–OT#12):** Questions Concerned with Evidence for God and the Soul from Contemporary Science, Medicine, and Philosophy
3. **Chapter 3 (OT#13–OT#17):** Questions Concerned with the Relationship Between Science and the Bible
4. **Chapter 4 (OT#18–OT#21):** Questions Concerned with

CHAPTER 1
Foundational Questions Concerned with the Methods of Science, Scriptural Interpretation, and History

OT#1: What Does the Catholic Church Say about Science and Faith?

The *Catechism of the Catholic Church* states the Church's general position on faith and reason/science as follows:

> "Though faith is above reason, there can never be any real discrepancy between faith and reason. Since the same God who reveals mysteries and infuses faith has bestowed the light of reason on the human mind, God cannot deny himself, nor can truth ever contradict truth." "Consequently, methodical research in

all branches of knowledge, provided it is carried out in a truly scientific manner and does not override moral laws, can never conflict with the faith, because the things of the world and the things of faith derive from the same God."[1]

This position was first articulated in Catholic doctrine in the First Vatican Council in 1870 (*Dei Filius*, par. 4), but it was developed much earlier, before the age of science, by Saint Augustine (about AD 412)[2] and later by St. Thomas Aquinas (in 1260).[3] Priests of the Roman Catholic Church were foundational in the incremental move from Aristotelian physics to modern physics initiated by Galileo Galilei in 1583 and Sir Isaac Newton in 1687. Some of these priests were Robert Grosseteste (c. 1200), St. Albert the Great (c. 1250), Roger Bacon (initial formulation of empirical method and testing, c. 1260), and Jean Buridan (c. 1330). All of them contributed to the development of inductive reasoning (generalizations of particular observable data), measurement of observational data, experimental verification, and mathematical expression of generalizations. Nicolaus Copernicus (a non-ordained Catholic cleric) formulated the first mathematical justification of heliocentrism, called "the Copernican Revolution," which was at the center of the Galilean controversy.

Since the time of Galileo, there have been about 286 priests and clerics instrumental in the development of most branches of physics, chemistry, biology, and applied mathematics.[4] Some of the most well-known priest scientists are:

- Gregor Mendel, an Augustinian monk and abbot, who is acknowledged to be the founder of modern quantitative genetics[5]
- Nicolas Steno, a Danish Catholic bishop, who is acknowledged to be one of the founders of modern stratigraphy and palaeontology[6]
- Georges Lemaître, a Belgian diocesan priest with a Ph.D. in physics from MIT, who is acknowledged to be the founder of contemporary cosmology after discovering the big bang theory in 1927 — a revolutionary, rigorously established,

comprehensive theory of universal origin[7]
- The Jesuits, who were integral to the development of seismology throughout the world, made a substantial number of organizational, experimental, and theoretical contributions to the discipline and started thirty-eight seismographic stations, some of which were the only stations in vast regions (e.g., South America, Africa, and Asia)[8]

The Catholic Church is the only church to have an Academy of Sciences, with Nobel Prize winners from every area of science. It currently has eighty members (twenty of whom are Nobel laureates), and throughout its history has had ninety Nobel laureates.

The Catholic Church also supports departments of natural science in eighteen hundred universities and supports contemporary science departments in over forty-three thousand Catholic secondary schools. She also supports scientific research institutes and astronomical observatories and seismological stations around the world.

The Church's fundamental view of faith and science is summarized in the *Catechism of the Catholic Church*:

> The question about the origins of the world and of man has been the object of many scientific studies which have splendidly enriched our knowledge of the age and dimensions of the cosmos, the development of life-forms and the appearance of man. These discoveries invite us to even greater admiration for the greatness of the Creator, prompting us to give him thanks for all his works and for the understanding and wisdom he gives to scholars and researchers. (283)

OT#2: Are There Conditions of Inerrancy in Biblical Statements Concerned with Science, History, and Religious/Moral Matters?

The assertion of biblical inerrancy in all of Scripture has been nuanced by the Catholic Church since the time of Saint Augustine. Some of the most important nuances have come from St. Robert Bellarmine, Pope Pius XII, the Second Vatican Council, and Joseph Ratzinger (prior to becoming Pope Benedict XVI). The essential distinction between divine inspiration and inerrancy (which entails the Holy Spirit's intention to reveal an *infallible* truth) allows for some passages of Scripture to be inspired but not inerrant, and other passages to be inspired and inerrant. This is particularly important in three areas:

1. Established scientific truths that may differ from the literal meaning of biblical passages
2. Established historical facts from archaeological evidence, records, and convergent testimony that may differ from biblical accounts of those events
3. Religious/moral matters in the Old Testament that may be superseded by later Old Testament passages or by the teaching of Jesus Christ as interpreted by His living Presence in the Catholic Church

In the discussion that follows, we will examine how such conflicts might arise, how the Catholic Church interprets them, and why they do not affect the reliability of the Scriptures or the *general* historicity of the Old and New Testaments. We will begin the discussion with scientific matters (section 1), then proceed to an explanation of the Catholic Church's rationale for distinguishing divine inspiration from inerrancy (section 2), and finally additional considerations from Pope Pius XII on inspiration, literary genre, and science (section 3).

1. Science, Scriptural Revelation, and the Catholic Church

The Catholic Church has tried, since the time of Saint Augustine, to respect the distinct methods and objectives of natural philosophy and Scripture-Revelation. Saint Augustine states it bluntly in his work *On the Literal Interpretation of Genesis*:

Often a non-Christian knows something about the earth, the heavens, and the other parts of the world, about the motions and orbits of the stars and even their sizes and distances … and this knowledge he holds with certainty from reason and experience. It is thus offensive and disgraceful for an unbeliever to hear a Christian talk nonsense about such things, claiming that what he is saying is based in Scripture. We should do all that we can to avoid such an embarrassing situation, lest the unbeliever see only ignorance in the Christian and laugh to scorn.[9]

After the advent of empirical-mathematical science, the Church found herself in conflict with Galileo concerning the problem of geocentrism (the earth at the center of the solar system) and heliocentrism (the sun at the center of the solar system). The Church was certainly not against natural science (see OT#1) or heliocentrism (since its first mathematical proponent was Nicolaus Copernicus, a Catholic cleric). So, what was the problem? The *proof* of heliocentrism. At that time, the only way to prove the truth of either heliocentrism or geocentrism was a technique called *stellar parallax*, but this technique requires accurate astronomical observations of distant stars, which the telescopes of the time were unable to make. Friedrich Bessel was the first to make this conclusive confirmation with much more accurate astronomical instrumentation in 1839 — more than two hundred years after Galileo.

Since Pope Urban VIII was being pressured by both Catholics and Protestants to maintain the seemingly correct geocentric interpretation of Genesis, he asked Galileo to refrain from publishing heliocentrism *as fact* until conclusive proof had been given.[10] The pope's request was consistent with St. Robert Bellarmine's principle of scriptural interpretation:

I say that if there were a true [scientific] demonstration that the sun is at the center of the world and the earth in the third heaven, and that the sun does not circle the earth but the earth circles the sun, then one would have to proceed with great care in explaining the Scriptures that appear contrary; and say rather that we do not understand [the Scriptures] than that what is [scientifically] demonstrated is false.[11]

In agreement with Augustine, Bellarmine advocated that scientifically demonstrated fact must take precedence over scriptural interpretation to the contrary.

Unfortunately, Galileo did not have the proof because of the inadequacy of astronomical instruments to achieve stellar parallax. Nevertheless, he proclaimed heliocentrism to be fact, contrary to his promise to the pope, and indicated that the Church's interpretation of Scripture was wrong. The famous trial resulted, in which Galileo was given too harsh a penalty (exile to his villa in Florence), and for which Pope St. John Paul II later apologized. Essentially, Pope John Paul said that since the Church was also uncertain about the truth of heliocentrism, she should not have accused Galileo of theological error, because this led her to "transpose into the realm of the doctrine of the faith, a question which in fact pertained to scientific investigation."[12]

Since the First Vatican Council, the Church has respected Bellarmine's principle of scriptural interpretation: Scriptural interpretation cannot contradict what has been conclusively scientifically demonstrated.

2. Biblical Inerrancy in the Areas of Science, History, and Religion/Morality

In 1943, Pope Pius XII formalized Bellarmine's principle as a standard of Catholic biblical interpretation in his encyclical *Divino Afflante Spiritu*: "The sacred writers, or to speak more accurately — the words are St. Augustine's — the Holy Spirit, Who spoke by them, *did not intend* to teach men these things — that is the essential nature of the things of the universe — things in no way profitable to salvation."[13]

This is a significant condition of biblical inerrancy, which Pope Leo XIII asserted applied to the whole of Scripture insofar as it was inspired by the Holy Spirit: "For all the books which the Church receives as sacred and canonical, are written wholly and entirely, with all their parts, at the dictation of the Holy Ghost; and ... that inspiration ... is essentially incompatible with error."[14]

Pope Pius XII acknowledges Pope Leo XIII's teaching that all the books of Sacred Scripture are inspired by the Holy Spirit and that this inspiration is incompatible with error, yet he adds that the Holy Spirit did not intend to inspire scientific truths or truths not profitable for salvation. This distinction between the inspiration of the Holy Spirit and the intention of the Holy Spirit to speak inerrantly has given rise to considerable theological reflection. A general statement of Pope Pius XII's teaching is that the Holy Spirit inspires Scripture with the intention of teaching inerrant truth only when such truth affects our salvation ("is profitable for salvation").

Some theologians concluded from this that Scripture teaches inerrantly only in the areas of faith and morals but not in the areas of science and history. Joseph Ratzinger, among other notable theologians, asserted that this restriction of scriptural inerrancy was too simple.[15] God's self-revelation includes aspects of both science and history that are necessary for salvation — for example, that human beings are not explicable solely in terms of science (which is restricted to observable data within our universe) and that God can and does influence history — though this dimension of history is beyond the strictly academic disciplines of history and historiography.[16] We may conclude from this that the Holy Spirit intends to inspire inerrantly not only in faith and morals but also in science and history when those disciplines touch upon truths necessary for salvation (e.g., the prohibition of scientific reductionism, materialistic reductionism, or secular historical reductionism). However, where science and history do not touch upon truth necessary for salvation, and there is conflict between established scientific fact and the Bible (or documented historical fact and the Bible), then we should give preference to established scientific or historical fact because the Holy Spirit did not intend to inspire this passage of Scripture inerrantly.

Ratzinger goes beyond the disciplines of science and history and applies the condition of inerrancy to moral and religious matters. This is because moral and religious truths in Scripture are conditioned by the transitoriness of the culture and the worldview of the historical-social milieu in which they were conceived and formulated: "The Bible, venerated by faith as the word of God, has been disclosed to us, by historical-critical scholarship, as a thoroughly human book. Not only are its literary forms those of the world that produced it, but its manner of thought, even in respect to religious topics, has been determined by the world in which it arose."[17]

Ratzinger distinguishes between two aspects of the word of God: the "outward form of the message" and the "real message of the whole," noting that the real message of Scripture, which is inerrant, is often accompanied by merely human, accidental features that are interwoven with the real message. Inasmuch as this "outward form of the message" is merely human and may be conditioned by frameworks of thought that have been superseded by more comprehensive and precise frameworks and methods, it cannot automatically be viewed as inerrant but must await a judgment of inerrancy by the Catholic Church, seeing it through the lens of the fullness of Revelation — Jesus Christ.[18]

The justification for this distinction between merely human frameworks (the outward form of the message) and the real message of the whole (inerrantly inspired by the Holy Spirit) is based on Jesus' treatment of the Old Testament as interpreted by the Pharisees:

> [Jesus] answered them, "And why do you transgress the commandment of God for the sake of your tradition? ... So, for the sake of your tradition, you have made void the word of God. You hypocrites! Well did Isaiah prophecy of you, when he said:
>
> > 'This people honors me with their lips,
> > but their heart is far from me;
> > in vain do they worship me,
> > teaching as doctrines the precepts of men.'" (Matthew 15:3, 6–9)

Distinguishing between the divinely revealed message in Scripture and the merely human outward expression of that Revelation is a very complex matter. It requires not only scholarly competence but also purity of motive and above all the guidance of Jesus Christ, the fullness of Revelation, through the Holy Spirit. Evidently, this task cannot be accomplished by any scholar or set of scholars. Only one institution is capable of doing this: the Catholic Church initiated by Jesus himself, acting as His living Presence and interpreter in the world. As Ratzinger puts it:

What is [divine] revelation and what is [merely human outward expression] can never be ascertained by the individual theologian — from his own perspective — on the basis of scholarly methods. In the end, this can only be decided by the living community of faith, which, as the Body of Christ, is the abiding presence of Christ, who does not let his charge over his work slip from his grasp.[19]

Ratzinger insists that human scholarly methods alone — no matter how comprehensive and precise — cannot be an adequate judge for what is divinely revealed and what is merely human outward expression of that Revelation. Only the Son of God, Jesus Christ, the fullness of Revelation, living and present in the Church He initiated, is capable of doing this. Thus we might say that religious and moral teachings in the Bible are also subject to the same restriction of inerrancy as scientific truths and historical truths. They are inerrant only insofar as they teach what is necessary or profitable for salvation and only insofar as the Catholic Church — manifesting the living Presence of Christ — determines what is truly divinely revealed versus what is the merely human outward expression of that Revelation. This teaching will be central to the analysis of moral development in the Old and New Testaments (in OT#22).

The implication of Ratzinger's solution to the question of what is biblically inerrant (and what is not) is that Scripture alone, without the Church, is powerless to make this critical judgment by itself. Those who hold that Scripture alone is sufficient are therefore forced to say either that every passage of Scripture is wholly biblically inerrant or that the question of what is biblically inerrant (or not) can be resolved by human agency that is not divinely ordained and given the grace to do this. Both options inevitably lead to serious misinterpretations of Scripture that are incommensurate with the teaching of Jesus Christ.

The first option requires that passages in which God commands the Israelites to kill every living being in conquered Canaanite countries, including innocent women and children (see Dt 20:16–18), be judged as equally inerrant as Jesus' command, "See that you do not despise one of these little ones; for I tell you that in heaven their angels always behold the face of my Father who is in heaven. … It is not the will of my Father who is in heaven that one of these little ones should perish" (Mt 18:10, 14). The second of the above inadequate options puts the judgment of what is biblically inerrant into the hands of theologians and scholars, who do not have an authoritative office originating in Jesus (e.g., Peter's supreme teaching office signified by "the keys to the kingdom of heaven"). Without this authoritative office, these theologians and scholars are not given the grace to make a definitive judgment about biblical inerrancy for the people of God. This human inadequacy can only be overcome by God's intervention to establish an authoritative office to make a definitive interpretation about biblical inerrancy.

Jesus Christ is that "divine intervention." He is the incarnate Son of God, who could bestow the Holy Spirit (who can read the mind and heart of God) on the Church and those holding her authoritative teaching offices (see NT#18). Evidently, Jesus anticipated the need for a supreme, definitive authority to make these judgments on His behalf. This is precisely what is intended in Matthew 16:19: "I will give you the keys of the kingdom of heaven, and whatever you bind on earth shall be bound in heaven, and whatever you loose on earth shall be loosed in heaven."

As will be shown in NT#18, the term "keys to the kingdom" refers to a prime minister's office, which is precisely to speak on behalf of the king in his absence (see Is 22:22). The primacy of the office of Peter is not restricted to earthly authority, for Jesus commissions the holders of Peter's office to bind on His behalf *in the kingdom of heaven.* As such, Jesus gives the holders of this supreme office the authority and grace not only to decide on His behalf what is Divine Revelation (inerrant) versus what is merely human outward expression (not inerrant) but also to determine the canon of the Bible (which books should be included in the Bible). It seems therefore that Jesus anticipated the need for a supreme authority not only to make definitive judgments to resolve theological and juridical controversies in His Church (Mt 16:18–19) but also to decide on the books of Scripture (canonicity), as well as what is biblically inerrant in the passages of those books of Scripture.

Therefore, a divinely initiated Church with the office of supreme authority and the Holy Scriptures are necessarily complementary, for without the Church, a divinely inspired canon of Scripture would not be able to exist. It would be merely a humanly (arbitrarily) chosen group of "scriptural" writings. A divinely inspired Church, designated by Jesus Christ, had to come first in time, and then the divinely inspired Scriptures. After that, the Church had to remain as Jesus' living Presence[20] in which the Holy Spirit would act, through her legitimate authorities, to make definitive interpretation of those Scriptures until the end of time.

We will address the extent of biblical inerrancy in three areas later in this book:

1. Scientific Truths and Scripture (chapter 3)
2. Historical Truths and Scripture (chapter 4)
3. Religious and Moral Truths in Scripture (OT#22)

The section on Old Testament miracles (OT#23) concerns both science and history in Scripture.

3. Other Contributions of Pope Pius XII on Inspiration, Literary Genre, and Science

Let us now return to Pope Pius XII's distinction between Scripture and science. Recall that Scripture teaches sacred truths needed for salvation, while science gives empirical-mathematical explanations of the physical universe. We should not force Scripture to do science or force science to give Divine Revelation. Each discipline has its proper purpose, its method to accomplish that purpose, and its criteria for correctness in its conclusions. If we let science do science, and biblical interpretation discern Revelation, both disciplines can be correct without contradiction.

Pope Pius XII also made another important clarification. He indicated that God's inspiration of the various human biblical authors was intertwined with the thoughts and capacities of those authors. God and the biblical authors were "co-participators," so to speak, in the writing of the biblical text:

> For having begun by expounding minutely the principle that the inspired writer, in composing the sacred book, is the living and

reasonable instrument of the Holy Spirit, [Catholic authorities and exegetes] rightly observe that, impelled by the divine motion, [the biblical author] so uses *his* faculties and powers, that from the book composed by him all may easily infer "the special character of each one and, as it were, *his personal traits.*" Let the interpreter then, with all care and without neglecting any light derived from recent research, endeavor to determine the peculiar character and circumstances of the sacred writer, the age in which he lived, the sources written or oral to which he had recourse and the forms of expression he employed.[21]

God is clearly the source of inspiration, and so the primary source of Revelation, but He uses the biblical author to produce a work that can be understood by the biblical author's audience, situated within a particular culture and time.

Notice that this "co-participative" theory of inspiration is quite different from the "dictation" theory. The dictation theory holds that God simply spoke to the mind of the biblical author, who in turn wrote down what he "heard" — verbatim. In this view, the biblical author plays only a transcriber's role, while God does everything else, so that every word in the Bible is the literal truth of God, which must in turn be taken literally. Though some Christian denominations hold this view, Catholicism does not.

So, can there be a conflict between the proper interpretation of Scripture and science? According to the Catholic Church, there can be no contradiction, because if the interpretation of Scripture *seems* to contradict scientifically demonstrated fact, the scientific viewpoint, if properly established, should be given preference, and scriptural interpretation must be adjusted to it.

OT#3: Is the Old Testament Historical?

As may by now be clear, Scripture is the divinely inspired word of God to give His people sacred truths necessary for salvation. God did not dictate the Scriptures to the biblical authors but *inspired* the biblical authors to formulate these sacred truths in the categories, worldview, and perspectives of their time, culture, and religious traditions. Thus Scripture is not science (see OT#1 and OT#2) or history (as we conceive it today). The initial books of the Old Testament (i.e., the five books of the Pentateuch, Judges, and Joshua),[22] though not a continuous historical narrative, are nevertheless grounded in authentic historical traditions.[23] Other books of the Old Testament are more solidly grounded in history (i.e., 1 Samuel, 2 Samuel, 1 Kings, 2 Kings, 1 Chronicles, 2 Chronicles, Ezra, Nehemiah, 1 Maccabees, and 2 Maccabees). The Gospel narratives (see NT#1–NT#4) are even more strongly grounded in history,[24] and, as Cambridge University's Richard Bauckham shows, they are based on eyewitness accounts formulated within living memory of Jesus.[25] Many of these eyewitnesses are mentioned in the Gospel narratives themselves (see NT#2).[26] The New Testament epistles are situated within history, for they are addressed to contemporary audiences within living memory of Jesus. (The issue of "living memory" is discussed in NT#2.)

Let us now return to the first five books of the Old Testament (the Pentateuch or the Torah). According to the Documentary Hypothesis, these books are a synthesis of previous traditions woven together by four editor-authors: the Yahwist, the Elohist, the Deuteronomist, and the Priestly Author. The Documentary Hypothesis is generally, but not universally, accepted among scholars.[27] It holds that the Yahwist editor finished his narratives around 950 BC, that the Elohist editor produced his narratives around 850 BC, that the Deuteronomist editor produced his narrative slightly after the reform of Josiah, around 600 BC, and that the Priestly Author produced his narrative around 500 BC. The whole consolidated Pentateuch was probably composed between 450 and 330 BC.

Each of the four major author-editors has several identifiable distinguishing features. For example, the Yahwist uses *Yahweh* for God, while the Elohist uses *Elohim* for God. The Deuteronomist is concerned with the law in Israel's history, while the Priestly Author is concerned with priestly rituals and the temple.[28]

There are other kinds of writing in the Old Testament beyond the twenty-one historical books (in the Catholic list). They are grouped into three general categories: prophecy, prayer/psalms, and wisdom. We will briefly describe each in turn:

1. **Prophecy:** A divine oracle or message given to the prophet to proclaim to Israel and her leaders. It is intended to motivate Israel's reconversion and fidelity to the Lord by revealing that failure to do so will have bitter consequences. During the times of these consequences, the Lord speaks through the prophets to give an oracle of future restoration and consolation. The prophetic books are split into major prophets (Isaiah, Jeremiah, Ezekiel, and Daniel) and minor prophets (Hosea, Joel, Amos, Obadiah, Jonah, Micah, Nahum, Habakkuk, Zephaniah, Haggai, Zechariah, and Malachi).[29]

2. **Prayer/The Psalms:** The five books of the Psalms (constituting 150) are meant for individual prayer as well as group prayer. They still form the foundation of the breviary and Christian common daily prayer. There are several excellent exegetical commentaries on the Psalms,[30] as well as many spiritual interpretations of them.

3. **Wisdom Literature:** The objective of wisdom literature is to give advice on how to achieve the "good life." It gives proper rules of conduct, practical advice on achieving virtue and piety, and ways to avoid vice and excess. It does not have as its objective historical themes or prophetic oracles or prayers.[31] The five books of wisdom literature are Proverbs, Job, Ecclesiastes, Sirach, and Wisdom. Though some have implied the historicity of the Book of Job, the author did not intend it this way but rather as a story to address the question of why just people suffer.

We may now return to the Old Testament books that address Israel's history. As noted above, the biblical authors did not write history as we do today. The patriarchal narratives express traditions formed well before the written narratives of Genesis, and their historical content is most difficult to identify with certainty.[32] The historical content of the periods of the exodus and desert wandering are the next most difficult to identify, then the period of the judges, then the period of conquest, then the period of the consolidation of the kingdom, and so forth as we move further down the historical line to the Babylonian exile, the return to Israel, and the rebuilding of the temple.[33] In general, the later the narrative (and the shorter the gap between events and the formulation of the narrative), the greater the accuracy and detail of the historical content of the narrative.

As may be evident, the record of ancient Israel's history in the Old Testament is filled with interpretations of the events from the perspective of God, His fidelity, Israel's obedience or disobedience, God's fulfillment of His covenant and promises (despite Israel's infidelity), and God's forgiveness and love of Israel. Sometimes, the biblical author gives this interpretation as a part of the narrative; often, it is given through the words of prophets (e.g., Moses, Samuel, Nathan, Elijah, Elisha, etc.), and sometimes through the words of judges, kings, and other historical figures. For those who are unfamiliar with historiography and theological interpretation in ancient Israel's historical books, it is best to turn to a biblical historian (such as John Bright), to get a clearer sense of Israel's history and faith. A brief summary of Bright's analysis of the historicity of the Old Testament from the patriarchal period through the conquest of Canaan and the confederation will be given in OT#18–OT#21. For the moment, suffice it to say that there is considerable historical accuracy in these narratives, but we will have to use the expertise of historians such as John Bright to separate the history from theological interpretation.

OT#4: How Do We Interpret the Primeval Narratives (Genesis 1–11)?

By now it may be evident that Genesis 1–3 is neither science nor history. We have already implied in OT#2 that the scientific picture of creation is quite different from the biblical account, and this will be explained in much greater detail in OT#13–OT#16. We also discussed the Catholic Church's acceptance of science and Bellarmine's principle — scientifically demonstrated fact should take precedence over scriptural interpretation to the contrary (see OT#2). Furthermore, Genesis 1–11 could not have been written as history because the events of the narrative vastly predate the authors of the narratives.

As we shall see, the primeval narratives are likewise not, strictly speaking, *historical* but, rather, the biblical author's reinterpretation of several major cosmogonies (origin myths) from surrounding nations. The biblical author integrates the Lord's Revelation to Israel into the structure of these well-known origin myths so that they conform to Israel's sacred doctrine rather than the false doctrines of surrounding cultures. There are six narratives in Genesis that interpret ancient origin myths through the theological lens of the Yahwist and Priestly Author:

- Creation of the heavens, the earth, and human beings (priestly account) — Genesis 1
- The creation of Adam and Eve (Yahwist account) — Genesis 2
- The original sin of Adam and Eve (Yahwist) — Genesis 3
- Cain's murder of Abel (Yahwist) — Genesis 4
- The flood and Noah's ark (Yahwist) — Genesis 6–9
- The tower of Babel (Yahwist) — Genesis 11

The Yahwist and the Priestly Author reinterpreted three major predecessor myths: the Gilgamesh Epic,* the Enuma Elish Epic,† and the Atrahasis Epic.[34] Genesis 1–11 should be taken as an integral unit on origins, which responds to the "competitor myths" of Israel's neighbors. The biblical author has a primary *theological* purpose and, like every other epic or myth of the time, uses metaphorical and literary form (not scientific or historical method) to convey these theological truths. This is precisely what Pope Pius XII recognized in *Divino Afflante Spiritu*.[35]

So, what were the biblical authors' *theological* intentions when they were refashioning the rival myths of the cultures around them? We will consider each of the six primeval narratives.

1. The Creation Narrative (Genesis 1)

This creation narrative was written by the Priestly Author (see OT#3), who was responding to the Babylonian origin myth, the Enuma Elish. This Babylonian myth was written on seven clay tablets and had divi-

---

* The Gilgamesh Epic was written around 2100 BC in ancient Mesopotamia. It contains stories about the conflict between men and gods and would have been known by many in ancient Israel.
† The Enuma Elish was written in Babylon about 1700 BC (over one thousand years earlier than Gn 1) on seven tablets that are similar to the seven days of creation in Genesis 1.

sions roughly similar to the seven days of creation. The biblical author first replaces the god Marduk, who is one among many gods, with the God of Israel, who is supreme over everything.[36] Marduk is in conflict with other gods as well as humans and the natural elements. The biblical author asserts that everything is a creation of God, who is superior and prior to them. In the Enuma Elish, the natural world is filled with evil, but the biblical author asserts that creation is good because the all-good God created it.

Furthermore, in the Enuma Elish, Marduk fashions man out of the blood of a slain rival god (Kingu). He made men to be the slaves of the gods.[37] The biblical author refashions this by revealing that the one supreme God created human beings in His own image and likeness — not as slaves to Him but as free persons to fill and subdue the earth (see Gn 1:28).

The biblical account, though similar in structure to the Enuma Elish, gives a vastly different portrayal of God, creation, humankind, good, and evil than its religious rival. Every one of these differences is very significant for understanding God, ourselves, and the path to salvation. Though the biblical account is not scientific, every one of its salvific truths (in contradistinction to those in the Enuma Elish) is just as relevant today as it was in 500 BC.[38] What would the world be like if we believed ourselves to be slaves to God rather than free agents created in His all-good image and likeness?

2. The Creation of Our First Parents (Genesis 2)

The Yahwist author was correcting and refashioning the well-known Akkadian‡ myth called the Atrahasis, written around the eighteenth century BC. This myth was the foundation of three of the primeval narratives (see Gn 2–9): the creation of our first parents (Gn 2), the original sin of our first parents (Gn 3), and the story of Noah and the flood (Gn 6–9). With respect to the creation of our first parents, the Atrahasis describes primeval humans as springing from a mix of the blood of a rival god and dust of the earth, but the Yahwist changes this to Yahweh fashioning man from the dust of the earth and filling him with the divine breath.

---

‡ Akkad was the successor civilization to Sumer in the region of Mesopotamia — the northwestern division of Babylon, which would be roughly equivalent to central Iraq today.

Evidently, the Atrahasis sees enmity between the gods and primeval men, while the Yahwist sees man created through the very breath (life force) of Yahweh himself. Primeval humans in the Atrahasis are meant to be slaves of the gods, but the Yahwist changes this to Adam (*ha-'ādām*), to whom God gives His garden to care for.

The creation of woman in Genesis 2 distinctively emphasizes the complementarity between the sexes — "bone of my bones and flesh of my flesh" (Gn 2:23). This is used to justify the covenant union ("new family") of marriage: "Therefore a man leaves his father and his mother and cleaves to his wife, and they become one flesh" (Gn 2:24). The garden in the Atrahasis is similar to the Garden of Eden, but the Yahwist places two "special" trees in the garden to introduce his unique central *moral* theme (eating the forbidden fruit): the tree of life and the tree of the knowledge of good and evil (see Gn 2:9). The Yahwist intends that the creation of our first parents (Gn 2) should be read as a single narrative with the original sin of our first parents (Gn 3). Hence, the significance of the trees is not made known until Genesis 3.

Though the narratives have a similar structure and take place in a similar garden, the differences between the narratives go beyond mono-theism versus polytheism. The starkest difference is the intrinsic rival-ry between the gods and primeval humans in the Atrahasis, versus the closeness and friendship between Yahweh and Adam in Genesis 2. The Yahwist sets up the story so that the sin does not result from a rebel-lion against *harsh* conditions (as in the Atrahasis) but rather that Adam wishes for more than the *good* conditions into which God created him. It should be noted that the Yahwist is not relating these salvific truths to give a description of the physical universe (science) but rather to correct the theological errors of surrounding cultures.

3. Original Sin of Adam and Eve (Genesis 3)

The Yahwist continues his refashioning of the Atrahasis, which portrays a rebellion of primeval men against the gods because of the harsh con-ditions and natural rivalry in which they have been created. The Yahwist now takes the story in a significantly different (and extended) direction by developing the *moral* theme of the forbidden fruit. Recall that Adam and Eve are born into very good conditions and have no real needs in the divine garden. Nevertheless, they fall prey to the temptation of a serpent (an evil rival to the one God), who essentially tells them that they deserve — are entitled to — *more*. The implicit message of God's evil rival is that Yahweh is withholding something very important from them because He does not want them to be equal to Him:

> [The serpent] said to the woman, "Did God say, 'You shall not eat of any tree of the garden'? And the woman said to the serpent, "We may eat of the fruit of the trees of the garden; but God said, 'You shall not eat of the fruit of the tree which is in the midst of the garden, neither shall you touch it, lest you die.'" But the serpent said to the woman: "You will not die. For God knows that when you eat of it your eyes will be opened, and you will be like God, knowing good and evil." (3:1b–5)

The biblical author has framed the moral theme as a contest between the unrestrained desire and ego of human beings and the command of God. Adam and Eve no longer see God and His commandment as something good and helpful to them but as constraints to prevent them from getting the more they deserve. Their free choice to treat God as a rival rather than a benevolent and loving Creator is born out of pride — unrestrained autonomy and self-assertion of the creature before his Creator. This pride leads not only to their fall but also to a life of harsh conditions compounded by the recognition of death (see OT#17).

4. Cain and Abel (Genesis 4)

There are many myths and stories about brotherly rivals in ancient Mesopotamia and nearby regions, so it is difficult to know which, if any, was the Yahwist's source. Whatever the case, the Yahwist is using this story to emphasize that the effects of the original sin extend into the next generation of human beings. As in the original sin of Adam and Eve, the Yahwist attributes suffering to sin — in this case, sin against our neighbor.

The Yahwist emphasizes God's mercy rather than strict justice throughout the passage. First, God warns Cain that terrible consequences will come not only to Abel but to him if he does not master his anger and hatred: "If you do well, will you not be accepted? And if you do not do well, sin is couching at the door; its desire is for you, but you must master it" (Gn 4:7). Secondly, after Cain ignores God's warning and pitilessly murders his innocent brother in anger, God has mercy on him when he asks for His protection:

> Cain said to the LORD, "My punishment is greater than I can bear. Behold, thou hast driven me this day away from the ground; and from thy face I shall be hidden; and I shall be a fugitive and a wanderer on the earth, and whoever finds me will slay me." Then the LORD said to him, "Not so! If any one slays Cain, vengeance shall be taken on him sevenfold." And the LORD put a mark on Cain, lest any who came upon him should kill him. (4:13–15)

This emphasis on the mercy of God even in the midst of egregious injustice and rebellion toward God is unique to Israel's Scriptures, reflecting a tradition that continues through the prophets and the late Book of Maccabees (around 100 BC). As will be seen, Jesus reveals that this attribute of God is unconditional and central to His nature (e.g., the father of the prodigal son — Lk 15:11–32).

5. The Flood and Noah (Genesis 6:9—9:29)

In view of the proliferation of flood stories from ancient Mesopotamia,§ it is likely that there was a historical event that inspired these stories. This event may have been a gigantic flood around 5500 BC, near the Black Sea.[39] The Yahwist[40] is reliant on the myth of Atrahasis, which he might have borrowed from the later Gilgamesh Epic.[41] The Atrahasis frames the event as rivalry between the gods, a rebellion of lower gods, and the fashioning of human beings to help the lower gods with their labors.[42] Many of the gods are disturbed by the tumult and noise of the rapidly growing human population and decide to wipe out the human race. One of the high gods, Enki, reveals the plot of the gods to his human friend,

---

§ The flood story can be found in the eleventh tablet of the Gilgamesh Epic (from Sumer), and a considerably expanded version, from which the Yahwist borrows, is found in the Atrahasis.

Atrahasis, who builds a ship and survives the flood because of his friendship with Enki.

The Yahwist borrows the structure of the story but edits it to integrate God's Revelation to Israel. There are not many gods but one God, who is in relationship with all human beings who have become disobedient, unjust, and wicked, which incites God to destroy the human race. Notice that the Atrahasis emphasizes the bothersomeness of human beings (i.e., the tumult, noise, and fast-growing population) as the gods' motive for their destruction, while the Yahwist changes this to a distinctively *moral* problem: They have become disobedient and wicked to one another (following from Adam, Eve, Cain, and Abel). The Yahwist says that God selects Noah because he is a *just and pious* man. Atrahasis, on the other hand, has the good fortune of having the high god Enki's friendship — a nonmoral rationale. After the flood, God allows Noah to become the new father of the human race, gives him power over all the creatures of the world, and establishes a covenant with him to protect his progeny. Before establishing the covenant, God proclaims that every *individual* will be accountable for what he does — particularly with respect to unjustly taking the life of another: "Whoever sheds the blood of man, by man shall his blood be shed; for God made man in his own image" (Gn 9:6).

The following point must be emphasized. The Noah story concerns neither science nor history (strictly speaking). Though there probably was a great flood near the Black Sea (around 5500 BC), the story of Noah is meant not to record a historical event that occurred four thousand years before the Yahwist wrote about it (950 BC) but rather to make modifications and additions to the Atrahasis (or perhaps the Gilgamesh Epic).

6. Tower of Babel (Genesis 11:1–9)

The Yahwist is the probable author of the Tower of Babel story.[43] It has a loose connection to a Sumerian predecessor myth, Enmerkar and the Lord of Aratta, written around 2000 BC. The predecessor myth's basic theme is to show that Sumerian/cuneiform — one of the first written languages — is necessary to unify peoples in commerce and political relationships, as they are divided by their diverse languages.[44] It includes sections on the building of temples and towers, which are suggestive of the

Tower of Babel story. Regardless of whether the Yahwist was responding to it, the Yahwist's basic question is why there should be diversification of language when human beings have a common origin in Adam and Eve and later in Noah. Once again, the Yahwist turns to a moral theme (quite distinct from the practical theme of Enmerkar and the Lord of Aratta): the arrogance of human beings and their desire to elevate themselves to the status of a god. "Then they said, 'Come, let us build ourselves a city, and a tower with its top in the heavens, and let us make a name for ourselves, lest we be scattered abroad upon the face of the whole earth'" (Gn 11:4). In order to bring human beings back to reality, the Lord diversifies and confuses their language and scatters them over the earth, at which point they cease to build their city and towers into the sky.

Conclusion to the Primeval Narratives

The primeval narratives are neither science nor history (in our conception of it), and they depart significantly from contemporary scientific and historical accounts in the events that they portray. The narratives are biblically important not because of their scientific or historical content but for the salvific truths they present — truths about God, creation, human beings, human purpose and destiny, disobedience and sin, and God's mercy — all of which are needed for salvation. In view of this, we may conclude that the primeval narratives are some of the most important pieces of God's Revelation to the world, which have had a great effect on the development of culture throughout the world.

CHAPTER 2

Questions Concerned with Evidence for God and the Soul from Contemporary Science, Medicine, and Philosophy

OT#5: What Do Scientists and Physicians Say about God and Religion?

There is an unfortunate misconception in popular culture that most scientists are atheists. This is factually untrue. The Pew Research Center, surveying the membership of the American Association for the Advancement of Science, determined the following:

- Fifty-one percent of scientists profess belief in God or a higher spiritual reality, and only 41 percent self-identify as either agnostics or atheists (about 21 percent agnostics and about

20 percent atheists if the split is even as it is with physicians).[1]

- Sixty-six percent of young scientists profess belief in God or a higher spiritual reality, while only 32 percent are agnostic or atheist — two-thirds are believers, while less than one-third are either agnostics or atheists.[2]
- Seventy-six percent of physicians are believers in God or a higher spiritual power, while only 12.4 percent are agnostic and 11.6 percent are atheist.[3]
- Seventy-four percent of physicians believe that miracles have occurred in the past, and 73 percent believe they occur in the present.[4]

Most of the originators of modern physics were religious believers, including Galileo Galilei, the father of observational astronomy and initial laws of dynamics and gravity; Sir Isaac Newton, father of calculus, classical mechanics, and quantitative optics; James Clerk Maxwell, father of the classical theory of electromagnetic radiation; Max Planck, father of quantum theory and cofounder of modern physics; Albert Einstein, father of the theory of relativity and cofounder of modern physics; Kurt Gödel, modern mathematician and logician and originator of the incompleteness theorems; Werner Heisenberg, father of the matrix theory of quantum mechanics and the uncertainty principle; and Freeman Dyson, originator of multiple theories in contemporary quantum electrodynamics.[5]

There are many other contemporary Nobel Prize-winning physicists, chemists, and biologists who have openly professed belief in God and a transphysical soul.[6] In view of the above, it seems that science and religion are not opposed to one another and that scientists and physicians have considerable openness to religion and the supernatural.

Sir Arthur Eddington, father of the nuclear fusion explanation of stellar radiation, summarizes the viewpoint of scientific theism as follows:

We all know that there are regions of the human spirit untrammeled by the world of physics. In the mystic sense of the creation around us, in the expression of art, in a yearning towards God, the soul grows upward and finds the fulfillment of something implanted in its nature. The sanction for this development is within us, a striving born with our consciousness or an Inner Light proceeding from a greater power than ours. Science can scarcely question this sanction, for the pursuit of science springs from a striving which the mind is impelled to follow, a questioning that will not be suppressed. Whether in the intellectual pursuits of science or in the mystical pursuits of the spirit, the light beckons ahead and the purpose surging in our nature responds.[7]

OT#6: Can Science Disprove the Existence of an Intelligent, Transcendent Creator?

In the current age, some skeptics and scientists have flooded social and traditional media with the contention that science can and has disproved God. As we shall see, science, by the constraints of its own method, cannot possibly disprove God, and so this cultural myth should be vigorously resisted. The rationale for this may be set out in three steps:

1. Science, according to the constraints of its method, must be grounded in observational data.
2. Observational data must come from within our universe because we cannot observe anything beyond the event horizon of our universe. We might be able to infer from our universe's limits (e.g., a proven limit to past time) that the universe needs a cause beyond itself, but we cannot directly observe such a cause.
3. God, defined as a "unique, uncaused, unrestricted Creator of everything else in reality," is beyond our universe.

Therefore, God is beyond observational data and thus cannot be disproved by science. How can science, which is restricted to observational data within our universe, disprove a reality that is beyond our observational universe (God)? Obviously, this is beyond the capacity of science, according to its own method.

Some scientists have also contended that we now know enough

about the universe to know that it does not require a Creator — that is, that it can explain itself. This is also false according to the constraints of science's own method. We can see this in three steps:

1. Since science must be grounded in observational data, scientists cannot know what they do not know until they have discovered it in observational data.
2. Now if this is the case, no scientist can know whether or not he knows everything about the universe. How could he possibly know whether he knows everything about the universe if he does not know what he does not know until he has discovered it in observational data?
3. If scientists cannot know whether or not they know everything about the universe, they cannot know if the universe needs or does not need a Creator — they cannot know whether the universe is self-explanatory.

What does this mean? It means that there can be no scientific justification for atheism. It is beyond the possible scope of scientific method.

Though science cannot disprove God, might it be able to give evidence for God — evidence for a cause outside of the limits of past time? As we shall see in OT#8 and OT#9, there are three ways of showing the probable existence of an intelligent, causative force beyond physical reality: space-time geometry proofs, entropy, and fine-tuning for life in our universe.[8]

OT#7: Can the Existence of God ("A Unique Uncaused Unrestricted Creator") Be Rationally Disproved?

If *God* means "a unique, uncaused, unrestricted Creator," then such a being cannot be disproved, because the unrestricted nature of God renders all methods of disproof fruitless. There are only three ways of proving the truth or falsity of any claim:

1. Observable evidence

2. Intrinsic contradiction
3. A proposition that can be shown to be contradictory to fact

We will examine each. First, observational evidence refers to any form of observational verification. The greater the number of people who agree with this observational verification, the better. It includes not only direct sensory observation but deductions from multiple observations, experimental (scientific) evidence derived from observation, and deductions from measurements of observations.

Our second method is intrinsic contradiction. This method is based on the principle of noncontradiction, which is the most fundamental principle in formal logic. It goes like this: Any particular reality cannot be both X and not X in the same respect at the same place and time. For example, John cannot be both six feet, two inches tall and six fee, three inches tall in the same respect at the same place and time. Similarly, there cannot be a square circle of the same area in the same respect at the same place and time. As the vast majority of logicians agree, intrinsic contradictions (like square-circles) are impossible (and therefore false) in all universes, dimensions, spaces, and times — without exception. Thus, if you can show that a particular proposition is a contradiction, then you can prove its falsity.

Our third method, contradiction of fact, means that if any proposition contradicts observable data, then that proposition is false. This method is particularly helpful in science.

None of the three above methods can be used to disprove God. The first method (observable evidence) is quite useful for proving the *existence* of a reality but useless for proving the *nonexistence* of a reality. If, for example, I wish to prove the existence of dogs, I need only observe one and have other people corroborate that observation. However, if I wish to prove the nonexistence of, say, unicorns, I would have to experience everything that there is to experience in this universe, and any other possible universe, and any other state of existence beyond physical universes, to be certain that I had exhausted the entire range of possible realties in all these universes (and beyond) and notice that unicorns are not there. This would seem to be rather daunting, if not impossible.

Since God is beyond our universe, and we cannot obtain observational data from beyond our universe, this method of disproving hypotheses cannot be successfully applied to God.

The second method (proving falsity through intrinsic contradiction) is equally fruitless. Recall that intrinsic contradictions occur when one or more characteristics of a particular entity contradict one another, making the combination (in the same respect at the same place and time) impossible. Remember the square circle. Now let's look at the characteristics intrinsic to God as defined above: a unique, uncaused, unrestricted Creator. Is there any intrinsic contradiction among these characteristics that would preclude them from existing? As we shall see (OT#10), there cannot be such a contradiction, because unrestrictedness, uniqueness, and Creator of everything else are necessarily entailed by an uncaused reality existing through itself. Therefore, these characteristics do not and cannot contradict "existence through itself" (an uncaused reality). This means we cannot use the second method to disprove God.

The third method, contradiction of fact, cannot be applied to an unrestricted reality. Why? What causes a contradiction? Contradictions are caused by boundaries or restrictedness. It is the boundary of a square that contradicts the boundary of a circle in the same respect at the same place and time. Similarly, it is the restrictedness of an electron's activities (attracting protons and repelling electrons) that contradicts the restrictedness of a proton's activities (attracting electrons and repelling other protons) at the same place and time. In short, in order to have a contradiction, there must be at least two restricted (bounded) realities. Here is the problem. Since God is unrestricted and has absolutely no boundaries or restrictions, He cannot come into contradiction with anything because He has absolutely no exclusionary properties — no boundaries or restrictedness. Therefore, no reality in this universe or anywhere else can come into contradiction with God, and so the third method for disproving God is fruitless.

Inasmuch as these three methods exhaust the scope of formal proof or disproof, it follows that the existence of God (defined as a unique, uncaused, unrestricted Creator of all else that exists) cannot be disproved through any method.

OT#8: What Is the Evidence of a Beginning/Creator from Science?[9]

Contemporary cosmology and astrophysics have shown very probatively that the universe is 13.8 billion years old (± one hundred million years). This is based on several mutually corroborating sets of evidence: the red shifting of distant galaxies, the 2.7°k uniformly distributed radiation throughout the universe, measurements from the two COBE satellites, measurements from the WMAP probe, and measurements from the Planck satellite. Was the big bang the beginning of our universe? It might have been, but scientists have theorized five other possible pre-big bang states that might be extendable to infinite past time:

1. A multiverse — a mega inflationary universe that is producing trillions of bubble universes, one of which is our own
2. A bouncing (oscillating) universe — expanding then contracting then re-expanding, and so on
3. A universe in the higher dimensional space of string theory (a model of quantum gravity)
4. A universe that has been in a quantum gravitational state for an infinite past time, which became metastable and exploded 13.8 billion years ago
5. An infinite fractal multiverse within eternal inflation

There are two physical discoveries that require that options one through three have a beginning:

- The Borde-Vilenkin-Guth theorem (proof — hereafter "B-V-G theorem"), which proves that every universal (or multiversal) system with an average Hubble expansion greater than zero must have a beginning of past time[10]
- The second law of thermodynamics (entropy), which shows that every physical system will move from order to disorder (effectively "running down") until it becomes a dead physical system incapable of physical change and activity[11]

Both the B-V-G theorem and the second law of thermodynamics are widely applicable. The former applies to all universes (or multiverses) with average Hubble expansion greater than zero, and the latter applies to all physical systems. So how do the B-V-G theorem and entropy apply to our universe and options one through three above?

- **Our universe:** Our universe is an inflationary system, which means that it has average Hubble expansion greater than zero, and so it must have a beginning. Furthermore, our universe is a closed physical system (in the standard model), which means that entropy must have been affecting it since its inception. If our universe had existed for an infinite time in the past, it would now be dead (incapable of physical change and activity). However, it is far from dead — on the contrary, it is very active — and therefore had a beginning in the finite past.

- **A non-fractal multiverse:** A non-fractal multiverse is an inflating system, meaning that it has an average Hubble expansion greater than zero and must therefore have a beginning, according to the Borde-Vilenkin-Guth theorem.[12] Entropy applies to all physical systems and, as such, applies to an inflating multiverse. Sean Carroll has postulated a model of multiverse to elude the consequences of entropy, but it is highly problematic.[13] Thus, in standard (non-fractal) inflating multiverse models, it is highly likely that these multiverses have a beginning. There is a hypothetical *fractal* multiverse model, which could be infinite and eternal. This is disproved below.

- **Bouncing (oscillating) universes of all kinds (in standard space and the higher dimensional space of string theory):** Borde, Vilenkin, and Guth apply their theorem to both standard and higher dimensional space bouncing universes, showing that both must have a beginning.[14] Entropy also applies to bouncing universes, because each bounce produces an increase in entropy. Thus, going back into the past, every previous cycle must have a lower entropy. As Sean Carroll shows, in the infinite past, the universe would have had an infinitesimally low entropy (implying infinite fine-tuning, which implies an intelligent Creator).[15] In view of this, bouncing universes of any kind must have a beginning and/or a Creator.

- **Universes in the higher dimensional space of string theory:** Borde, Vilenkin, and Guth show all nucleating and other universes in the higher dimensional space of string theory must have an average expansion rate greater than zero, implying a beginning.[16]

The above means that every universal and multiversal system (in standard space and higher dimensional space) requires a beginning. There are only two options left:

- An eternally static universe
- An infinite fractal multiverse

The eternally static universe is a contradiction. If it is eternally static, it would be perfectly stable, which means that it would not have exploded in a big bang 13.8 billion years ago. If the universe is not perfectly static/stable (that is metastable), allowing it to explode, then it could not have been eternally static. William Lane Craig (an American analytic philosopher and research professor of philosophy at Biola University) shows this on a logical basis,[17] and Vilenkin and Mithani show this on a quantum physics basis.[18] This means that the eternally static hypothesis is not plausible or even possible.

This leaves only one option for avoiding a beginning of physical reality: an eternally inflating fractal multiverse. Though this hypothesis (postulated by Andre Linde and Leonard Susskind,[19] among others) held out a possibility for an eternal multiverse with literally infinite possibilities, it fell prey to three irresolvable problems:

1. Stephen Hawking and Thomas Hertog showed that the in-

finite fractal multiverse could not have spawned a universe like our own, because there is no indication of fractal origins in our universe and also because our universe's division between quantum and classical physics prohibits it.[20] They go on to show that any multiverse that could have spawned our universe would have to have a beginning, a finite number of bubble universes, and very probably only a small number of bubble universes, most of which would be similar to our universe.[21] As Hawking and Hertog assert: "Now we're saying that there is a boundary in our past [a *beginning of any* multiverse that could generate our universe]. ... We are not down to a single, unique universe, but our findings imply a significant reduction of the multiverse, to a much smaller range of possible universes."[22]

2. Thomas Banks also shows that the eternal inflation hypothesis (and the string theory landscape) disagrees violently with experimental/observational evidence.[23]

3. The vexing problem of Boltzmann Brains and Brief Brains: The implication of an infinite multiverse, according to theoretical physicists and cosmologists, is that there would be a virtually 100 percent chance that every human being would not be a physical-organic body in a universe like ours, but rather a Boltzmann Brain/Brief Brain that has fluctuated into existence fully loaded with a memory of being in a universe like ours. If we are not a Boltzmann Brain or a Brief Brain, then it is virtually certain that we did not originate in an infinite/eternal multiverse.[24] It should be noted that the Boltzmann Brain/Brief Brain problem occurs in every model of an infinite/eternal multiverse.

In view of the above, it is highly likely, on the basis of scientific evidence alone, that physical reality itself (whether it be just our universe, a multiverse of any kind, a bouncing universe of any kind, or a string universe) would have to have a beginning. What is the consequence of a beginning of physical reality itself? This implies a Creator of physical reality, which is beyond physical reality itself (including physical time and space). Why? This can be set out in three steps:

1. If physical reality itself had a beginning, then "prior" to that beginning, physical reality would have been nothing — this would include not only its mass-energy but its laws and constants, physical space and time, and any other physical-organic component.
2. Nothing is literally nothing, and as such, can only do nothing.[25]
3. If "prior" to the beginning, physical reality itself was nothing, it could only do nothing. If physical reality could only do nothing, then it could not have moved itself from nothing to something when it was nothing.

Therefore, something beyond physical reality had to move physical reality from nothing to something. Since this entails an act of creation *ex nihilo* (creation out of nothing), the transcendent cause of physical reality must have the power to create something out of nothing. Therefore, a Creator with a power to create out of nothing very likely exists. This is consistent with the Genesis narrative's implication that God created out of nothing the whole of physical reality in the finite past.

OT#9: What Is the Evidence for an *Intelligent* Creator from Fine-Tuning for Life in Our Universe?

Though the evidence of a beginning of physical reality implies a transcendent Creator, it does not speak explicitly about the intelligence of this Creator. Contemporary science has identified a considerable number of initial conditions and constants of our universe that make life possible. However, these initial conditions and constants are not prescribed or required by our laws of physics. As it turns out, each of the values for these initial conditions and constants is exceedingly, exceedingly tiny in comparison with other possible values, which do not allow *any* life form to develop. This means that the occurrence of life in our universe by pure chance is exceedingly, exceedingly unlikely. It is about the same odds as a monkey typing the entire corpus of English literature perfectly by random tapping of the keys in a single try — virtually impossible. Three examples of these fine-tuning coincidences[26] are:

1. **The low entropy of our universe at the big bang:** According to Oxford mathematical physicist Roger Penrose, the odds against low entropy at the big bang (necessary for the development of organic life in our universe) is $10^{10^{123}}$ to one.[27] This fine-tuning coincidence alone is like a monkey typing the corpus of Shakespeare perfectly in a single try. Therefore, it is virtually impossible that our low entropy could have occurred by pure chance.

2. **Fine-tuning of the cosmological constant:** According to Nobel laureate Steven Weinberg, the cosmological constant, which controls the precise acceleration of our universe in the past and the present, must be fine-tuned to 1 part in 10^{120}.[28] If the value of this constant diverged by only one part in a trillion trillion trillion trillion trillion trillion trillion trillion trillion trillion (higher or lower), then the universe would have expanded too rapidly to form galaxies and stars — or it would have collapsed upon itself into a black hole. In either case, life in our universe would be impossible.[29] This is like trying to hit a one-square-inch spot in a million trillion trillion trillion trillion trillion trillion trillion trillion square miles — virtually impossible.

3. **The critical density of mass-energy one nanosecond after the big bang** must be highly fine-tuned to produce the "nearly flat" geometry of our universe needed for any life form to develop in our universe — fine-tuned to one part in 10^{24} kg per cubic meter (one part in a trillion trillion). If the mass-energy had been only one kilogram per cubic meter more out of a trillion trillion, the universe would have collapsed in on itself by now, inhibiting the formation of life. If it had been one kilogram per cubic meter less out of a tril-

lion trillion kilograms per cubic meter, the universe would have expanded so rapidly that it would have never formed stars or galaxies necessary for life.[30] This is like trying to hit one square centimeter in an area which is a trillion trillion square centimeters — exceedingly, exceedingly improbable.

There are only two possibilities to explain this exceedingly improbable fine-tuning:[31]

1. A multiverse — either infinite or finite
2. A highly intelligent Creator that infused these initial conditions and constants into physical reality at the big bang

As noted in OT#8, the infinite fractal multiverse was shown to be exceedingly unlikely by Stephen Hawking and Thomas Hertog, as well as Thomas Banks. Furthermore, *any* model of an infinite multiverse was shown to be exceedingly unlikely because it requires that all of us be either Boltzmann Brains or Brief Brains rather than the organic life forms we perceive ourselves to be. As such, the infinite multiverse is not a plausible explanation for fine-tuning for life. How about a finite multiverse with $10^{10^{123}}$ (or more) bubble universes? This is also highly unlikely, according to Hawking and Hertog's conclusion that any multiverse that could generate our universe would have to have a *small* number of bubble universes much like our own. Thus, this hypothesis cannot possibly explain the low entropy of our universe, the value of the cosmological constant, and/or the critical density of mass-energy at the big bang — or any of the other instances of fine-tuning in our universe.[32] If Hawking and Hertog are correct about a small number of bubble universes in a multiverse, then a finite multiverse will fall very far short of explaining the exceedingly improbable fine-tuning for life in our universe.

In view of the high unlikeliness of an infinite multiverse and the deficiency of a finite multiverse to explain our universe's exceedingly improbable fine-tuning for life, the most reasonable option that remains is a highly intelligent transcendent Creator.[33] Therefore, there is a strong likelihood of a super intelligent, transcendent Creator of our universe as well as any multiverse from which it may have originated.

In light of this, we are compelled to agree with Sir Fred Hoyle, the former director of astronomy at Cambridge University and the father of the theory of stellar nucleosynthesis, who abandoned his atheism after investigating the exceedingly high improbability of life forms in our universe:

> Would you not say to yourself. … Some supercalculating intellect must have designed the properties of the carbon atom, otherwise the chance of my finding such an atom through the blind forces of nature would be utterly minuscule. … A common sense interpretation of the facts suggests that a superintellect has monkeyed with physics, as well as with chemistry and biology, and that there are no blind forces worth speaking about in nature. The numbers one calculates from the facts seem to me so overwhelming as to put this conclusion almost beyond question.[34]

OT#10: Can the Existence of God ("A Unique Uncaused Unrestricted Creator") Be Proved? — Philosophical Proof of God

As we have seen in OT#6 and OT#7, science gives considerable probative evidence for an intelligent Creator. Reason can go beyond scientific evidence by using what is called *a priori synthetic* evidence, that is, noncontradictory evidence that is grounded in fact. This kind of evidence for God was used by Aristotle, Saint Augustine, and St. Thomas Aquinas, and today, by philosophers such as Bernard Lonergan, Mortimer Adler, Jacques Maritain, Étienne Gilson, Alvin Plantinga, and Emerich Coreth — to name just a few. These individuals have formulated what might be called metaphysical proofs for God, which, because they use *a priori* evidence, obtain a broader conclusion than scientific evidence. Typically, such proofs argue to a unique, uncaused, unrestricted, Creator of everything else in reality. Below is a summary of a proof in four steps:[35]

Step 1: There Must Be at Least One Uncaused Reality *in the Whole of Reality*

The basic argument follows: If there is not at least one uncaused reality in the whole of reality, then there are only caused realities in the whole of reality — that is, realities that need to be caused by something extrinsic to themselves in order to exist. Now if the whole of reality is composed of realities that need to be caused in order to exist, then the whole of reality *itself* must also be a reality that needs to be caused in order to exist. Now since there is literally nothing outside the whole of reality, and if the whole of reality needs to be caused in order to exist, then the whole of reality cannot possibly exist, because its cause does not exist (it is outside the whole of reality). This is counterfactual, because presumably you and I exist. Therefore, there must be at least one uncaused reality in the whole of reality.

Step 2: An Uncaused Reality Must Be Unrestricted

This part of the proof has four sub-steps:

1. An uncaused reality exists through itself, and if it exists through itself, it is the pure power of actualization, and if it is the pure power of actualization, it can actualize anything which is not self-contradictory, because there is nothing in non-contradictory states of affairs opposed to being actualized.

2. Every restricted way of existing (e.g., the way of existing like an electron) excludes other restricted ways of existing from itself (e.g., the way of existing like a proton). Note that there cannot be a single reality existing like both a proton and an electron in the same respect at the same time — like a proton-electron — because their activities exclude one another. If every restricted way of existing excludes other restricted ways of existing from itself (in the same respect at the same time), then no restricted way of existing can actualize every non-contradictory state of affairs, meaning that every restricted way of existing cannot be the pure power of actualization, and therefore, is not existence through itself (an un-

caused reality).

3. If no restricted way of existing is an uncaused reality, then no restricted way of existing exists through itself, and therefore, it must be caused — ultimately, brought into existence by an uncaused reality.

4. If an uncaused reality must bring every restricted way of existing into existence, then an uncaused reality must exist prior* to every restricted way of existing. If an uncaused reality is prior to every restricted way of existing, it must in all ways be unrestricted.

Step 3: An Unrestricted Reality Must Be Unique (One and Only One)

This has four sub-steps:

1. In order to have multiplicity, there must be difference. For example, if there are to be two of anything, there must be some difference between the one and the other — such as a difference of space-time point, activity/power, qualities, magnitudes, or dimensions, and so forth. If there is no difference of any kind, then the two realities are the self-same — that is, they are only one. Hence, multiplicity requires difference.

2. If there is a difference between one reality and another, then one of the realities would have to be restricted. Why? For example, if there is a difference in space-time point between two realities, then one of those realities would have to be in a space-time point that the other one was not. However, if that other reality is not in the space-time point that the other is in, then it must be spatially *restricted*. The same thing applies to a difference of activity. So, if one of the realities acts in a way that the other one does not, then the reality

---

* An uncaused reality must be both ontologically prior and temporally prior to every restricted way of existing. "Ontologically prior" means that it is necessary for restricted ways of existing to exist; that is, an uncaused reality can exist without restricted ways of existing, but restricted ways of existing cannot exist without an uncaused reality. "Temporally prior" means that an uncaused reality would have to be prior in time to every restricted reality. This does not imply that an uncaused reality is in time, because an uncaused reality would have to exist even before time itself (a non-contemporaneous continuum — time — is a restricted way of existing.

that does not act in this way must be restricted in its activity. The same holds true for qualities, magnitudes, other dimensions, and any other difference. Therefore, difference entails restriction.

3. If multiplicity requires difference, and difference entails restriction, then multiplicity entails restriction in every differentiated reality.

4. Now let's apply the above general principle to two supposedly unrestricted realities. Inasmuch as there are two hypothetical unrestricted realities, then there would have to be a difference between them; and if there were a difference between them, one of them would have to have something, be something, be somewhere, or be in another dimension that the other unrestricted reality was not. But if that other unrestricted reality does not have something or is not somewhere or is not in a dimension that the other one is, then the other unrestricted reality would have to be restricted. Evidently, a restricted-unrestricted reality is an intrinsic contradiction and is therefore impossible in any possible universe, dimension, conceptual thought, and the like. Therefore, every second, third, and so on hypothetical unrestricted reality would have to be an intrinsic contradiction (i.e., a restricted-unrestricted reality), meaning that it is impossible in every place, time, universe, dimension, and the like. This means that there can only be one unrestricted reality.

Step 4: The One Uncaused, Unrestricted Reality Must be the Creator of *Everything Existing in Reality*

This has three sub-steps:

1. If an uncaused reality (existing through itself) must be unrestricted, and if every unrestricted reality must be unique (one and only one), then there can be only one uncaused reality (existing through itself) in the whole of reality.

2. If there is only one uncaused reality in the whole of reality,

then everything else in the whole of reality must be caused realities — realities that need to be caused in order to exist.

3. Since every caused reality must ultimately depend on an uncaused reality to exist, and there can be only one uncaused reality in the whole of reality, then the one uncaused reality must be the ultimate cause of everything else in the whole of reality. As such, it is the Creator of everything else that exists.

Conclusion

Since there must be at least one uncaused reality in the whole of reality, and that one uncaused reality must be unrestricted, unique, and the Creator of everything else in reality, then the one uncaused, unrestricted Creator of everything else must exist. If this unique, uncaused, unrestricted reality did not exist, there would be nothing in the whole of reality. Since the one, uncaused, unrestricted reality meets the general definition of *God*, then *God* as defined must exist.

Please note, denial of this conclusion (God exists) entails one or both of the following consequences:

- **Denying the existence of the whole of reality (including oneself):** Recall that denying the existence of an uncaused reality entails the denial of everything in the whole of reality, which is contrary to fact.
- **Arguing an intrinsic contradiction on one or more of the following three levels:**

    1. In order to deny the unrestricted nature of an uncaused reality, one would have to say that a restricted way of existing can actualize every restricted way of existing (including those that are excluded by it) — a contradiction.
    2. In order to deny the uniqueness of an unrestricted reality, one would have to either affirm that there can be multiplicity without difference or that there can be difference without one of the realities being

somewhere or something that the other is not. Both assertions are self-contradictory (as shown in step 3, "An Unrestricted Reality Must Be Unique," above).

3. In order to deny that the one uncaused, unrestricted reality is the Creator of everything else, one would have to either affirm that there is some other possibility beyond caused or uncaused realities (which there is not) or that the one uncaused reality was not the cause of the caused realities in the whole of reality. (This would mean that the whole of reality is a caused reality without something to cause it, implying that the whole of reality is nothing.)

In conclusion, if one is unwilling to deny one's own existence or argue one of the above contradictions, then it is reasonable and responsible to affirm the existence of God defined as a unique, uncaused, unrestricted Creator of everything else in reality.[36]

OT#11: What Is the Evidence for a Transphysical Soul and Life after Death from Peer-Reviewed Medical Studies?

The rational and scientific validation of a transphysical soul is important to bring the light of reason to four biblical revelations:

1. That human beings are transcendent realities made in the image and likeness of God (not merely physical/material realities)
2. That human beings were created by God for eternal life with Him — not merely for this life alone
3. That human beings are categorically different from all other animals on the face of this earth in their rationality and self-consciousness
4. That human beings are genuinely free and are endowed by God with a conscience for moral reflection

The first two points will be taken up in this question (OT#11), and the second two points will be taken up in the following question (OT#12).

1. Peer-Reviewed Medical Studies Giving Evidence of a Transphysical Soul and Life After Death

The New York Academy of Sciences recently published a consensus statement of scientists and physicians based on a review of the extensive peer-reviewed medical and scientific studies indicating that it is likely that consciousness and cognitive processes do not end with death.[37] They further elucidated five points that are overwhelmingly attested in peer-reviewed medical studies:

> (a) separation from the body with a heightened, vast sense of consciousness and recognition of death; (b) travel to a destination [in this world or in another worldly domain]; (c) a meaningful and purposeful review of life, involving a critical analysis of all actions, intentions, and thoughts towards others; (d) a perception of being in a place that feels like "home," and (e) a return back to [bodily] life.[38]

Many other careful, longitudinal, peer-reviewed studies done by Dr. Samuel Parnia (2014),[39] Dr. Pim van Lommel (2001),[40] Dr. Bruce Greyson (2010),[41] Dr. Kenneth Ring (1999),[42] and the University of Virginia Medical School Department of Perceptual Studies[43] give further explanation of the likelihood that consciousness and cognitive processes will survive bodily death in this or otherworldly destinations. Three additional factors (beyond those mentioned in the *Annals of the New York Academy of Sciences*) are important:

1. **Veridical data:** There are several hundred cases of confirmed, unique, veridical data reported by patients during their near-death experiences. These data could not have been known if the patients were not conscious, thinking, seeing, hearing, and remembering when they were clinically dead — flat EEG, absence of gag reflex, fixed and dilated

pupils. For example, a woman floated out of her body, went outside the operating room, and then outside the hospital walls and hovered above a third-floor ledge of the hospital. She reported seeing a tennis shoe that had been there for many years with a shoelace under the heel and a worn left toe. A researcher crawled out onto the ledge of the hospital and found the shoe there, precisely as described.[44] Many of these reports concerned technical activities inside the operating room (hitherto unknown by patients), and many report data occurring outside the operating room — in the waiting room next door, outside the hospital, on the roof of the hospital, and so forth.

2. **Blind patients:** Dr. Kenneth Ring's study of the near-death experiences of blind people indicates that 80 percent of blind people were able to see (many of them for the first time) during their near-death experience.[45] These testimonies also have veridical confirmation. For example, one sixteen-year-old boy, Bradley Burroughs, blind from birth, moved through the operating room and then through hospital walls and found himself outside in the snow. He gave an accurate description of the train tracks, the snow, and a moving train (with a sign indicating the direction of the train on the back) passing by the hospital at the exact moment of his clinical death.[46] This is important, because he described the train with the sign correctly, and the time of the train was confirmed to be coincident with Bradley's clinical death. Since Bradley was blind from birth, he did not have any pre-existing visual images in his physical brain, which virtually eliminates hallucination by the physical brain as an explanation for the phenomenon.

3. **Encounters with deceased relatives:** Many near-death experiences in which the soul moves from this world/universe to an otherworldly domain have a phase in which patients encounter deceased relatives. Dr. Bruce Greyson and Dr. Emily Kelly of the University of Virginia Medical School have catalogued many of these encounters in which the

deceased relative was not previously known by the patient. When these accounts were checked with living relatives, it was confirmed that the clinically dead patients had very precise information about the deceased relatives they had not previously known.[47]

Dr. Pim van Lommel summarizes the data from his peer-reviewed longitudinal study as follows:

> How could a clear consciousness outside one's body be experienced at the moment that the brain no longer functions during a period of clinical death with flat EEG? … Furthermore, blind people have described veridical perception during out-of-body experiences at the time of this experience. NDE pushes at the limits of medical ideas about the range of human consciousness and the mind-brain relation. In our prospective study of patients that were clinically dead (flat EEG, showing no electrical activity in the cortex and loss of brain stem function evidenced by fixed dilated pupils and absence of the gag reflex) the patients report a clear consciousness, in which cognitive functioning, emotion, sense of identity, or memory from early childhood occurred, as well as perceptions from a position out and above their "dead" body.[48]

Van Lommel found that about 18 percent of adults undergoing clinical death had a near-death experience of the kind mentioned above. There are many possible explanations for why patients did not experience or remember their experiences.[49]

2. Physicalist/Materialist Hypotheses to Explain Near-Death Experiences

There are several physicalist/materialist hypotheses formulated to explain near-death experiences:[50]

- Narcotically induced hallucination
- Stimulation of the angular gyrus of the parietal lobe

- Anoxia (oxygen deprivation) producing hallucinations of a white light at the end of a tunnel
- "Dreamlets" produced in a stressed brain
- Production of weak transcranial magnetic stimulation of the temporal lobe

There are several inadequacies in all physicalist explanations. First and foremost, *none* of these physicalist hypotheses can explain the accounts of 100 percent accurate veridical data or the accurate veridical perception of blind people. Secondly, as Dr. Mario Beauregard[51] (a professor of neuroscience at the University of Arizona), Pim van Lommel,[52] Samuel Parnia,[53] Bruce Greyson,[54] Edward Kelly,[55] and Emily Kelly[56] show, all of these physicalist explanations differ physiologically and experientially from near-death experiences. For example, they all give rise to inaccurate, weird, and often unpeaceful visual experiences. However, near-death experiences are accurate, clear, and peaceful. Thirdly, physicalist explanations occur through a functioning brain (electrical activity in the cerebral and frontal cortices), while near-death experiences occur through a non-functioning brain (flat EEG — no electrical activity in the cerebral cortex and exceedingly limited brain stem function). In view of these significant discrepancies between physicalist explanations and near-death experiences, as well as the complete incapacity of physicalist hypotheses to explain the 100 percent accurate veridical data of blind and sighted people, the New York Academy of Sciences (cited above) believes that it is reasonable to conclude that consciousness and cognitive processes would likely continue after physical death.[57]

3. Peer-Reviewed Medical Studies of Other Evidence for a Transphysical Soul

Medical studies of a phenomenon called *terminal lucidity* and studies of intelligence in hydrocephalic patients confirm the likelihood of a transphysical soul capable of surviving bodily death. These phenomena may be described as follows:[58]

- **Terminal lucidity:** Patients who have severe brain trauma or atrophying (caused by severe injury, genetic problems, advanced Alzheimer's, or dementia) suddenly become lucidly conscious and verbally proficient one to two hours before death, when their brain capacity cannot possibly produce these cognitive functions.

- **Intelligent hydrocephalic individuals:** Patients with 95 percent of their brain replaced by spinal fluid in the cranial cavity manifest intelligence between ninety and genius-level IQ in multiple cases. With less than 5 percent of a functioning brain, such cognitive activities cannot have been caused by it.[59]

OT#12: What Is the Rational and Scientific Evidence for Human Freedom and the Uniqueness of Human Intelligence and Self-Consciousness?

As noted in OT#11, peer-reviewed medical evidence is important for bringing the light of reason not only to the transcendent soul of human beings, but also to life after physical death. This section will provide evidence not only for a transphysical soul but also for the uniqueness (within the animal kingdom) of human conceptual intelligence, self-consciousness, and freedom.

We will examine three themes concerned with philosophical and anthropological studies of human transphysical activities:

1. The immateriality of conceptual (abstract) intelligence and human self-consciousness (section 1)
2. The uniqueness of human conceptual (abstract) intelligence and self-consciousness (section 2)
3. The soul (and its powers) as the source of human freedom (section 3)

1. The Immateriality of Conceptual (Abstract) Intelligence and Human Self-Consciousness

Catholic philosophers for centuries have shown the immateriality of human intelligence, particularly in the abstraction of conceptual ideas that can be used for predicates, direct and indirect objects, and syntactically significant language.[60] These excellent arguments have been amplified today by several philosophical and scientific studies of human self-consciousness and intellection.[61]

- Bernard Lonergan's argument for the transcendental nature of human intellection manifest in our tacit awareness of complete intelligibility standing behind every question (and our pure, unrestricted desire to know)[62]
- David Chalmers's analysis of the "hard problem of consciousness," in which he argues to a *transphysical* dimension of self-consciousness[63]
- Sir John Eccles's (Nobel laureate in physiology) argument for the immateriality of human self-identity and its quantum unification with embodiment[64]
- Robert Berwick and Noam Chomsky's implication of a "mysterious" (seemingly nonphysical) dimension of syntactically significant language[65]

2. The Uniqueness of Human Conceptual (Abstract) Intelligence and Self-Consciousness

The above four studies show the immateriality of both human self-consciousness and abstract intellection (leading to conceptual ideas). There are other studies that show that these seemingly immaterial powers of the soul are completely absent in other animals (specifically, higher primates, such as apes, gorillas, and chimpanzees):[66]

- The studies of Herbert Terrace showing that higher primates do not have syntactically significant language, indicating they do not formulate abstract ideas that can be used as predicates for indirect or direct objects[67]
- The studies of Noam Chomsky and Robert Berwick of the uniqueness of human syntax and its absence in higher primates[68]

- The studies of Endel Tulving implying that autonoetic episodic memory (self-consciousness that can project itself into the continuous memory of the past and into the imaginative anticipation of the future) is unique to human beings — not in higher primates or even in pre-Homo sapien hominids[69]

Now here is the point: Inasmuch as contemporary philosophical and scientific studies show that human self-consciousness and abstract intellection are transphysical (immaterial), and these two immaterial powers are unique to human beings (absent in higher primates), then these studies also imply that nonhuman animals *do not have a soul* — they are not made in the image and likeness of God like human beings.

3. The Soul (and Its Powers) as the Source of Human Freedom

The above two immaterial powers/activities (self-consciousness and abstract intelligence) are also the linchpins of human freedom. In addition to these two powers, there are four transcendental activities coming through our transphysical soul that lift us out of physical determinism (being restricted by merely physical processes, sensorial images, and perceptual ideas):[70]

1. The interior awareness of the mysterious, numinous (spiritual), fascinating, overwhelming, and sacred ("wholly other"), which is the ground of religious experience, the mystical, and the desire to worship[71]
2. The felt awareness of good and evil coming through conscience[72]
3. The awareness of and enchantment by beauty, pointing to supreme beauty[73]
4. Five kinds of transcendental awareness and desire — the tacit awareness of perfect truth, perfect love, perfect goodness/justice, perfect beauty, and perfect being/home, which incite us to move toward greater creativity and perfection in these five areas[74]

If we hold that we are restricted to physical processes, sensorial images, and perceptual ideas alone, we will inevitably argue to determinism (the absence of freedom). However, if we acknowledge that we have a transphysical soul (giving rise to the transcendental awareness of perfect truth, love, goodness, beauty, and being, as well as the interior awareness of God and good and evil), then we need not be locked into the closed world of stimulus-response — the world of physical processes and individuated sensorial images and desires. See the studies of Bernard Lonergan,[75] Karl Rahner,[76] and Paul Ricoeur.[77]

Our awareness of God (the numinous), the intelligibility of the world around us, and the five kinds of transcendental awareness lifts us into a world of ideas and reality beyond merely physical sensations and perceptual ideas — out of the world of mere stimulus-response and into a world of higher purpose. This world of higher purpose gives us a choice to act not just according to physical-egotistical stimuli and desires, but for the sake of God's will, the good (and highest good), the truth, and love (care for others). Sometimes, acting for a higher purpose can be at odds with physical and egotistical stimuli and desires. When we self-consciously and rationally decide to choose a higher purpose when it disagrees with our physical and egotistical desires, our freedom becomes apparent, because we are breaking out of physical and egotistical determinism by choosing a higher purpose that is not intrinsic to either physical processes or egotistical instincts.

Thus it might be said that our soul — our spiritual or transphysical dimension — unfetters us from domination by our physical and egotistical dimensions. Without a soul enabling us to be rationally self-conscious and transcendentally aware of God, the good, self-sacrificial love, and the intelligibility of the world, we would be mere physical machines devoted to self-interest — radically unfree. Thanks to our soul, we become aware of three choices available to us as we act in the world:[78]

1. To choose between acting for the highest good *or* the strongest instinctive or egotistical desire
2. To choose against evil (recognized through conscience and religion) *or* to do evil (which is egotistically or sensually

      pleasing)

3. To choose between what is pleasing to God (which may be recognized through the numinous experience, conscience, and religion) *or* what is pleasing to one's sensuality or ego-centricity (which may be in conflict with God's will)

If we begin our analysis of freedom with the powers of the soul as well as with the powers of the body and allow our rational self-consciousness (a power of the soul) to mediate between our transcendental awareness and our bodily/egotistical desires, then freedom is truly a reality. And if freedom is truly a reality, then we can use it for obedience or disobedience to God, for adherence to or rejection of our conscience, for living for the highest good or living for the greatest pleasure.

Human freedom is the condition necessary for the possibility of both original sin and personal sin, and given the high likelihood of a human transphysical soul (shown in the above studies), it is highly likely that human beings are uniquely capable of such free choice. This will be important when we consider original sin (in OT#17) and development of moral doctrine in the Old Testament (in OT#22).

CHAPTER 3
Questions Concerned with the Relationship Between Science and the Bible

OT#13: What Is the Scientific Picture of Creation and Its Unfolding?

As noted in OT#8 and OT#9, physical reality (whether conceived as only our universe, a multiverse, a string universe, etc.) very likely had a beginning of past time. This means that physical reality did not exist before that beginning and was literally nothing. As such, there would have to be a creative power transcending physical reality who created space-time, mass-energy, and all the laws and constants of physical reality out of nothing. As noted in OT#9, this would require a highly mathematically ordered plan so that the laws and constants would be coordinated with space-time and mass-energy to give rise to an exceedingly improbable life-permitting universe. This highly complex plan implies, as Hoyle called it, a "supercalculating intellect." The following is a summary of the scientific account of how the intelligent Creator chose to unfold this life-permitting universe over several billion years.[1]

1. The Evolution of Our Physical Universe

1. **The initial quantum gravity epoch:** The universe likely had a quantum gravitational form in which all four forces (the electromagnetic force, the strong nuclear force, the weak force, and the gravitational force — in a quantized form) were completely unified. Since this epoch is prior to the big bang, it is hard to judge the duration, but since it has to be metastable (in order to explode in the big bang), it would have to be finite in duration. Many physicists believe it was very short in duration.

2. **The space-time epoch:** Gravity moves from a quantum configuration to a space-time configuration describable by Einstein's general theory of relativity. This is coincident with the big bang between 10^{-42} seconds and 10^{-36} seconds.

3. **The inflationary epoch:** This is an exceedingly brief period of exponentially increasing inflation, in which the universe grew from a singularity to a radius of ten centimeters between 10^{-36} seconds and 10^{-32} seconds after the big bang.

4. **Electroweak epoch:** The strong nuclear force separates from the electroweak force, leaving the electroweak symmetry in place (between 10^{-32} seconds and 10^{-15} seconds after the big bang).

5. **The Higgs epoch:** The electroweak symmetry breaks up, and the Higgs field imparts rest mass to formerly massless energy (between 10^{-15} seconds and 10^{-12} seconds after the big bang).

6. **The quark, baryon, and hadron epochs:** Quarks (the constituents of baryons — protons and neutrons) predominate and, when temperatures become lower, fuse into protons and neutrons. At this juncture, baryons become more numerous than antibaryons (antimatter particles), and the predomi-

nance of matter in the universe begins. This ultimately results in 10^{80} baryons in the universe (between 10^{-5} seconds and 1 second after the big bang).

7. **The lepton epoch:** When the baryon and antibaryon particles annihilate one another, they give rise to leptons and anti- leptons (the precursor to electrons and antielectrons — positrons). Eventually the leptons and antileptons annihilate each other, leaving a comparatively small number of non-annihilated leptons as well as high-energy photons (from 1 second to 10 seconds after the big bang). At this point, particle formation is almost complete.

8. **The nucleosynthesis epoch:** As the temperature falls, protons and neutrons begin to fuse into light elements, such as deuterium and helium (between 2 minutes and 20 minutes after the big bang). At the end of the process, about 75 percent of the particles in the universe are hydrogen and 25 percent helium, with some residual deuterium and lithium. Heavier elements have to await fusion in supernovae and stars.

9. **Large-scale structure epoch:** As the universe cools, it goes into what is known as the "Dark Ages," where there is very little visible light. About 100 million to 150 million years after the big bang, clusters of hydrogen begin to form, which give rise to initial stars. About 300 to 400 million years ago, the first galaxies begin to form. Supernovae and stars fuse most of the other elements on the periodic table. The process of cluster formation and stellar nucleosynthesis continues to this day.

The complexity and extent of mathematical preprogramming needed to allow this universe to smoothly emerge into one that was life-permitting is virtually inestimable, truly requiring a "supercalculating intellect."[2]

2. The Evolution of Life
With respect to the development of life, most scientists believe that it probably exists on other exoplanets (those having similar life-permitting

qualities as the earth) throughout the universe. Currently, scientists estimate that there are about 10^{20} (one hundred million trillion) exoplanets in our universe. If the laws of biology were not infused in the universe at the big bang, and as a consequence are not universal, then there might not be life on other planets (including exoplanets). This possibility of life does not imply that there is *intelligent* life on other planets, because, as shown in OT#11 and OT#12, such life requires a soul, which is incapable of evolving through a merely physical evolutionary process. This means that if there is intelligent life on other planets, it would have to have a transphysical cause — like God. Therefore, if intelligent life exists on other planets, it would have to be through the creative will of that transphysical cause (Creator).

The movement from nonliving to living substances is incredibly complex and requires yet another level of preprogramming at the big bang to infuse the laws of biology into the universe — laws that are not reducible to the laws of physics and chemistry. The introduction of these laws into the universe cannot be explained by a merely physical evolutionary process because they are irreducible (see the explanation of Michael Polanyi[3] below in OT#15). Again, this implies a highly intelligent Creator present at the big bang to infuse these biological laws and operators into our universe.

With respect to life on earth, the earth is approximately 4.6 billion years old.[4] A consensus of evolutionary biologists believe that life emerged on earth about four billion years ago.[5] The development of life occurred in an evolutionary fashion[6] through thousands of stages. Some of the major ones are:

- 4 billion years ago — Emergence of the precursors of single-celled organisms
- 2 billion years ago — Eukaryotic cells emerge (with interior organelles), the precursors of multi-celled organisms[7]
- 900 million years ago — First multicellular life emerges
- 535 million years ago — Cambrian explosion (the generation of the precursors to most modern species)
- 489 million years ago — First terrestrial plants

- 460 million years ago — First bony and cartilaginous fish
- 400 million years ago — First insects
- 397 million years ago — Tetrapods conquer the land and give rise to all amphibians, reptiles, birds, and mammals
- 385 million years ago — First fossilized tree
- 250 million years ago — Dinosaurs emerge
- 275–100 million years ago — A group of therapsids, called *cynodonts*, evolve into the first mammals
- 55 million years ago — First primates emerge[8]
- 6 million years ago — First hominids emerge[9]

There are two mysteries surrounding this remarkable, four-billion-year-old process that perplex the majority of today's scientists:

1. How did the laws of biology necessary for the emergence and development of life occur? Recall that the laws of biology are not reducible to the laws of chemistry and physics.[10] This implies the same kind of intelligence needed to preplan the mathematical laws and constants needed for the unfolding of the universe described above.

2. The above evolutionary process has literally trillions of "programming" steps of complexification between the precursors to a single-cell organism and the emergence of the first hominid. As nonreligious philosophers and scientists have admitted, four billion years is not nearly enough time to complete this process in a purely naturalistic, neo-Darwinian fashion.[11] This again implies some kind of transcendent mind to explain the exceedingly high improbabilities.

3. Human Evolution

The final stage of evolution is the emergence of human beings from our early ancestors (hominids). As noted above, the first hominids emerged about six million years ago (Sahelanthropus tchadensis).[12] The major developments in human evolution are as follows:

1. 4 million to 3 million years ago — Australopithecus emerges and develops (may have had some primitive tools)
2. 2.5 million years ago — Homo habilis emerges and develops (more developed stone tools for butchering, skinning animals, and crushing bones; scavenger — not hunter)
3. 2 million years ago — Homo erectus emerges and develops (more sophisticated multipurpose stone tools, such as hand axes and two-sided knives; fire-making tools; a hunter of large animals — for example, elephants — indicating organized hunting parties)
4. 430,000 years ago — Homo neanderthalensis emerges and develops (more sophisticated tools, including bone tools, fire-making tools, fashioned ornaments — i.e., primitive aesthetic sense; buried their dead — but without grave goods for an afterlife)
5. 300,000 years ago — Homo sapiens, anatomically modern humans, emerge and develop (fire-controlling tools, more sophisticated tools, ornaments, and burial of dead)
6. 200,000 years ago — Our genetic ancestors Mitochondrial Eve and Y Chromosome Adam. Though they are our *genetic* ancestors, they do not appear to be *ensouled* because of the absence of seven distinctly human characteristics (see OT#16)
7. 60,000 — Our first ensouled ancestors ("the great leap forward" — seven distinctly human characteristics: the development of syntactically significant language, mathematics, religion and life after death, sophisticated art and music, explosive technological innovation, domestication of animals and cultivation of land, and worldwide geographical expansion out of coastal Africa — see OT#16)

As we shall see in OT#15 and OT#16, this picture of human evolution is consistent with Church teaching because it entails a transphysical soul, which must be caused by a transphysical Creator — like God (see Pope Pius XII, *Humani Generis*, discussed in OT#15). Though most of the evolutionary process can be explained through naturalistic causes, a purely materialistic neo-Darwinian evolutionary view "is almost certainly false,"[13] because of the following four enigmas:

1. How are we to explain the incredibly complex, precise mathematical ordering of the unfolding of our universe that appears to have been preplanned and infused in our universe at its inception? The idea that this could arise either by pure chance (or even through a limited multiverse described by Hawking and Hertog) is exceedingly improbable. Along with the values of initial conditions and constants fine-tuned for life (see OT#9), this mathematically precise integration of physical and chemical laws, constants, spatio-temporal separation, and mass-energy distribution strongly implies the presence of a transcendent intelligence.

2. The laws of biology (which are not reducible to the laws of physics and chemistry and seem to be infused in the laws and operators of the universe at the big bang) have no physical-chemical explanation, implying the presence of a transcendent intelligence in the precise preplanning of the universe at the big bang.

3. The evolutionary process from the precursors of unicellular life to the emergence of the first hominid requires trillions of intricate improbable transitions. If these complexifications are to be explained by a purely materialistic evolutionary process, it would take hundreds of billions of additional years (beyond the four billion years of life on earth) to occur. This very short time in which the complexification of life occurred on earth implies that something like a transcendent intelligence facilitated the process either through preplanned laws of execution at the big bang (nomogenesis) or has been acting throughout the evolutionary process to bring it to its higher level of development (orthogenesis).*

4. As shown in OT#12, the seven distinctively human characteristics exemplifying transphysical activities (going beyond

---

* Nomogenesis and orthogenesis will be explained more fully below in OT#15.

physical processes) require a transphysical soul, which must be caused by a transphysical Creator — like God. (This is explained in detail in OT#16.)

OT#14: How Can the Scientific Account of Creation Be Reconciled with the Bible's Seven Days of Creation?

In OT#2 we discussed Robert Bellarmine's principle and Pope Pius XII's principle, which enable the rational reconciliation of the scientific and biblical accounts of creation. A brief review of these principles (as well as the principle of co-participative inspiration) should put the seeming contradictions between the Bible and science to rest:

- **St. Robert Bellarmine's principle:** If an interpretation of Scripture contradicts scientifically demonstrated fact, then the interpretation of Scripture should be modified to conform to this fact (or facts). See OT#2.
- **Pope Pius XII's principle of scriptural interpretation and inerrancy:** The purpose of Scripture is to give sacred truths needed for salvation. The purpose of natural science is to give a correct mathematical-empirical, demonstrable explanation of the physical universe. All Scripture is inspired by the Holy Spirit, but the Holy Spirit does not intend that Scripture inerrantly teach scientific truths (demonstrable explanations of the physical universe), because such truths are not needed for salvation. As such, when we encounter contradictions between science and Scripture (e.g., in the creation narrative), we should let science do its job (Bellarmine's principle) and look to Scripture for what is needed for salvation (Pope Pius XII's principle).
- **Two views of inspiration:** The Catholic Church subscribes to the co-participative view of inspiration — namely, that God works *with* the biblical author, who uses the conceptual frameworks and worldview of his time and culture. This is

distinct from the dictation view of inspiration, which holds that God dictates in His own words what the biblical author transcribes. This latter view almost forces biblical literalism and the de-emphasis of biblical hermeneutics. It also leads to irresolvable conflicts between the Bible and science.

- **Literary and cultural hermeneutics:** According to the co-participative view of biblical inspiration, the true meaning of the text requires knowledge of the biblical author's conceptual frameworks, religious viewpoint, worldview, and social-cultural situation, as well as his use of literary genre, metaphors, numeric designations, and other nonhistorical, nonliteral dimensions that may affect our twenty-first-century interpretation of the text.

Keeping these principles of interpretation in mind, there need be no contradictions between science and Scripture, and if we expand Bellarmine's principle to include *historically* demonstrated facts (as well as scientifically demonstrated facts), then there need be no contradictions between history and Scripture.

We have already examined the primeval narratives in Genesis 1–11 (see OT#4), in which we showed that the biblical authors (the Yahwist and the Priestly Author) were not concerned either with science or historicity as we conceive of them today. Rather, they were concerned with correcting the *theological* errors in origin myths (cosmogonies) of the countries surrounding Israel, which were filled with metaphor, symbol, and other nonhistorical, nonscientific ways of communicating meaning. If we recognize the biblical authors' theological intention in correcting these foreign cosmogonies, the irrelevance of science and historicity to the biblical author becomes readily apparent.

How does Scripture complement science? Though science can strongly imply the existence of a transcendent, intelligent Creator, it cannot get us beyond the "what" of that Creator (the transcendent, intelligent, causal power necessary for the existence of a life-permitting universe) to the "who" (the heart) of the Creator. As a consequence, science can only tell us about the "how" of the natural world, but not the "why" of the natural world, because the latter entails a knowledge of the Creator's mind and heart, which can only come from His self-Revelation. Catholics believe that this self-Revelation is found in the Old Testament and brought to fulfillment through Jesus (the incarnate Son of God) in the New Testament and the tradition of the Church.

As implied earlier, science can give significant probative evidence for an intelligent Creator of physical reality (regardless of whether physical reality is just our universe, a multiverse, a universe in the higher dimensional space of string theory, a bouncing universe, etc.). Similarly, philosophy (logical proofs) can demonstrate that a unique, uncaused, unrestricted Creator of everything else must exist, and we can also show that such an unrestricted reality must be an unrestricted act of intellection. Important as this is, science and philosophy cannot answer the hundreds of questions concerning God's subjective states and His relationship with us. For example, science and philosophy cannot answer the question of whether God is loving, indifferent, or disdainful. They cannot determine whether God is all good or only partly good; does He have two opposed sides in the way that human beings do? Furthermore, science and philosophy cannot answer the question of whether God hears our prayers, cares about us, inspires us, guides us, and protects us. They cannot answer whether God redeems suffering, whether there is a heaven or a hell, whether there is a resurrection from the dead, or whether a resurrection would entail the end of suffering and the fulfillment of our nature. Indeed, science and philosophy cannot tell us anything about God's mind, heart, or will — except that they must be unrestricted.

If science and philosophy cannot answer such questions, and God has created us with a transphysical soul capable of desiring perfect truth, love, goodness, beauty, and being, then we must conclude that if God did not intend to universally frustrate our nature, He must have created a way to fulfill the human nature He created. Hence, we must conclude that God intended from the creation of physical reality not simply to create human beings but to reveal himself to us in the fullest possible way. If so, then we would expect Him to reveal himself through prophetic figures (such as Moses, Elijah, Isaiah, and Jeremiah — see OT#24). We might also expect that He would want to go beyond what any human prophet could reveal and provide us with a *perfect* revelation in word, presence, action, and even complete, loving self-sacrifice. If this is something that a perfectly loving Creator would do, then Jesus, who carries out this precise mission, would seem to be the pure reflection of God's glory and the very stamp of His nature (Heb 1:3).

If God's intention was to reveal His interior mind, heart, and will to us as perfectly as possible, then would He not want to come in Person, where He would not only give us His word, but also His Presence and actions along with His complete gift of self? If so, then we might conclude in light of Jesus' message, miracles, glorious resurrection, complete self-sacrifice in His passion, and gift of the Holy Spirit, that He is the perfect "in Person" Presence of God among us.

If Jesus is "God with us" — the only-begotten Son of God — then we have a virtually perfect complementarity between faith, reason, and science. We not only have the "what" but also the "who" of God; not only the "how" but also the "why" of the physical universe. If we have all of this, we not only have the pathway to eternal salvation but also a practical knowledge of how to live this out in the world.

Correctly interpreted, Scripture, science, and history need not contradict one another. Rather, they form a remarkable complementarity that shows God's providential self-giving and unconditional love for each of us as individuals as well as in the communities we constitute. The complementarity and harmony of science, history, and Scripture is truly a revelation of the interrelated mind and heart of an unconditionally intelligent, loving, good, beautiful, and providential God. If we endeavor to learn about Him through faith, He will confirm this truth concretely, opening the way for us to freely and rationally choose Him and the way He has prescribed through His prophets, priests, and above all His Son.

If we are to achieve this complementarity and harmony between science, history, and Revelation, we will have to bear in mind the four principles of the Catholic Church set out at the beginning of this unit.

OT#15: What Is the Mainstream Catholic View of Evolution?

Evolution is a scientific theory that explains the development of species using evidence from genetic similarities among species, fossil delineation, and geographic distribution. Very basically, the theory of evolution states that biological species physically evolved to their present state over a long period of time. Evolution of species is driven by how small changes (mutations) in offspring make them more or less suited to survival than offspring that do not possess these changes; changes that are better suited to survival are more likely to be passed from one species' generation to the next. And so, a particular species evolves along the path of changes better suited to survival. Evolution is considered by the vast majority of scientists to explain biological (physical-organic) development within and among biological species.

1. The Insufficiency of Purely Materialistic, Neo-Darwinian Models of Evolution

There are three points at which materialistic, neo-Darwinian evolution is challenged to explain advances in physical-organic activities and processes:

1. The leap from nonliving to living beings
2. The leap from nonconscious (e.g., vegetative) beings to beings with sensate consciousness (e.g., self-moving animals)
3. The leap from sensate consciousness to rational, self-conscious beings

Scientists such as Michael Polanyi believe that each categorical leap requires a whole new system of organization that cannot be reduced to the lower one. In his seminal article, "Life's Irreducible Structure,"[14] Polanyi, a senior researcher in physical chemistry at the Universities of Manchester and Oxford, argued that living systems are "dual control," constituted by lower-level physical-chemical laws and activities as well as higher-level boundary conditions that harness these activities toward objectives that cannot be reduced to those lower-level laws and activities.[15] As Polanyi puts it:

A boundary condition is always extraneous to the process which it delimits ... their structure cannot be defined in terms of the laws which they harness. ... Therefore, if the structure of living things is a set of boundary conditions, this structure is extraneous to the laws of physics and chemistry which the organism is harnessing. Thus the morphology of living things transcends the laws of physics and chemistry.[16]

This irreducible hierarchy applies to all three "leaps" in the evolutionary development of human beings:

1. The higher-level boundary conditions of living things cannot be reduced to the lower-level physical-chemical activities being harnessed by them.[†]
2. The higher-level boundary conditions of sensate consciousness cannot be reduced to the lower-level physical-chemical-biological activities being harnessed by them.[17]
3. The higher-level boundary conditions of mind (rational self-consciousness) cannot be reduced to the lower-level physical-chemical-biological-sensate activities harnessed by them.[18]

Polanyi explains that the higher-level activities manifest "design" that cannot arise out of random assemblages of lower-level activities, which seems to put the three leaps leading to human development beyond merely materialistic evolution. He does not indicate what the explanation is for the occurrence of these seemingly designed higher organizational boundary conditions but strongly asserts that it is *not* attributable to the lower-level activities being harnessed by them.[19] In so doing, he implies that the rational self-consciousness of human beings cannot be fully explained by physical, chemical, biological, and sensate activities.

There is one further problem with a purely materialistic explanation of evolution. As we saw in OT#13, four billion years is not nearly

---

† The boundary conditions are not prescribed in the lower-level laws of physics and chemistry. Nevertheless, in living organisms, the boundary conditions are harnessing (controlling) these physical and chemical constituents toward higher-level activities of metabolism, replication, cell division, and survival.

enough time to allow for the billions of intricate transitional steps in the ongoing speciation between constituents of unicellular organisms and the emergence of the first hominid.[20] This is why atheists like Thomas Nagel admit that purely materialistic, neo-Darwinian evolution cannot explain the evolution of human life in our universe. One of his books is titled *Mind & Cosmos: Why the Materialist Neo-Darwinian Conception of Nature Is Almost Certainly False.*

So, where does that leave us? If materialism and physicalism are not enough, then what is the extra component leading to rapid successful complexification of living organisms? Nagel attempts to avoid the word *God* by calling this additional intelligent component *mind*. Inasmuch as mind transcends the merely physical cosmos, his position seems to resemble panpsychism. Perhaps Nagel's rejection of the materialistic, neo-Darwinian explanation of evolution is one of the reasons why so many scientists in recent times have declared themselves to be believers in God or a higher transcendent power (51 percent of the scientific community overall, and 66 percent of young scientists, according to the Pew survey[21] — see OT#5). If a transphysical, mentative component is integrated into evolutionary theory, then evolution in this broader sense provides an explanation for the development of continuously advancing speciation as well as the leaps from nonliving to living beings, non-conscious to conscious beings, and non-rationally self-conscious to rationally self-conscious beings. This is discussed in section 3 with respect to three conceptions of theistic evolution: nomogenesis, orthogenesis, and nomo-orthogenesis.

2. The Catholic Church's Teaching on Evolution

Before examining theistic evolution, we must first take account of the Catholic Church's position on it, which may be different from the views of other Christian denominations. In his well-known 1950 encyclical, *Humani Generis*, Pope Pius XII asserted that Catholics are not forbidden from adhering to an evolutionary explanation of human embodiment so long as it does not preclude the existence of a unique transphysical soul created by God in every human being:

For these reasons the Teaching Authority of the Church does not forbid that, in conformity with the present state of human sciences and sacred theology, research and discussions, on the part of men experienced in both fields, take place with regard to the doctrine of evolution, in as far as it inquires into the origin of the human body as coming from pre-existent and living matter — for the Catholic faith obliges us to hold that souls are immediately created by God.[22]

Pope St. John Paul II reinforced Pope Pius XII's teaching in a letter to the Papal Academy of Sciences in 1996, by declaring that the scientific validation of evolution moves it from the status of hypothesis to a well-grounded theory:

Today, more than a half-century after the appearance of [*Humani Generis*], some new findings lead us toward the recognition of evolution as more than a hypothesis. In fact it is remarkable that this theory has had progressively greater influence on the spirit of researchers, following a series of discoveries in different scholarly disciplines. The convergence in the results of these independent studies — which was neither planned nor sought — constitutes in itself a significant argument in favor of the theory.[23]

The above declaration clearly indicates that Catholics can believe in the theory of evolution so long as they do not deny the creation of a unique, transphysical soul by God in every human being. This means that Catholics cannot believe in a purely materialistic view of evolution, because evolution is a physical-biological process, which cannot explain a transphysical soul that is beyond such processes.[24] Thus Catholics can believe in any view of evolution that will accommodate a transphysical soul, which would have to be created by a transphysical cause — like God.

Can Catholics believe that the physical-biological dimension of human beings evolved from other species? Yes. Can they believe that even the cerebral cortex came from an evolutionary process — from great apes to Australopithecus, to Homo habilis to Homo erectus to Homo sapien? Yes. In fact, it is most reasonable to believe on the basis of all the evidence that the human frontal and cerebral cortices evolved in a remarkable way to meet all the conditions required to accommodate a transphysical soul capable of thinking activities completely beyond physical processes — for example, conceptual ideas, syntactically significant language, abstract mathematics, self-consciousness, and transcendental and religious thought.[25]

The transphysical soul outside of the physical body (during near-death experiences) manifests sensation, imagination, and memory, as well as its unique activities of conceptual ideas, syntactically significant language, mathematics, self-consciousness, and transcendental and religious consciousness.[26] Interestingly, the physical brain also has the capacity for sensation, imagination, and memory. Why the overlap between the powers of the soul and the brain/body? The Nobel Prize–winning physiologist Sir John Eccles believes that the overlap constitutes a point of contact that allows for quantum reduction mediation between soul (mind) and body.[27] In light of this, Eccles proposes a model for how the cerebral and frontal cortices might have developed to accommodate a soul/mind in the final stages of the evolutionary process.[28]

Our rational, self-conscious, transphysical soul is precisely what distinguishes us from all other animals (OT#12).[29] Our soul, which makes us capable of reason, morality, love, art, and free will, demonstrates that we are not just any kind of animal. We are animals capable of knowing and loving God. Only human beings are capable of religion. The fact that all of us equally possess spiritual souls is what gives us our equal human dignity and our special value as human beings — a special value that is at the basis of human rights.

3. Theistic Evolution

How do non-materialist philosophers and scientists view evolution? The most prevalent view is theistic evolution, which holds that there is a God, that God is the Creator of the material universe and all life within it, and that biological evolution is a natural process within that creation for which God is ultimately responsible.[30] As noted above, 51 percent of scientists (and 66 percent of young scientists) and the vast majority of physicians (76 percent) are theists — believers in God or a higher super-natural power (see OT#5). The vast majority of scientists also believe in evolution, so we may infer that the majority of scientists and physicians subscribe to some kind theistic evolution, which is the view of the Catholic Church as well as of mainline Protestant churches.[31]

There are several different theories of theistic evolution, but three major schools represent the majority:

1. **Nomogenesis:** Evolution according to finely tuned fixed laws and constants infused by God at the big bang (God acting as efficient cause). In this view, God "frontloads" His creation with fine-tuning of universal constants and initial conditions as well as physical, chemical, biological, and sensitive psychological laws and conditions (which come into play sometime after creation) so that the evolutionary process can proceed naturally without ongoing direction from Him. A large number of religious scientists and philosophers subscribe to this view, such as Francis Collins (the celebrated director of the Human Genome Project in the United States), who asserts that God "frontloads" all that's required for an autonomous, ongoing evolutionary process that can proceed naturally without intermittent influence from Him.[32]

2. **Orthogenesis:** Evolutionary processes directed by God acting as a goal (final cause). The most famous proponent of this view was the celebrated Jesuit priest and paleontologist Pierre Teilhard de Chardin, who viewed evolution as directed toward an ultimate goal — "an omega-point" — within the mind of God.[33]

3. **Nomo-Orthogenesis:** God acting as both efficient cause and final cause. In this view, God "frontloads" creation with the laws, constants, and initial conditions required for an ascending evolutionary process but also remains present to it (e.g., as a transcendent mind). The physical chemist Michael Polanyi (cited above) combines both positions, advocating

for a robust fine-tuning of initial constants and conditions at the creation of the universe with a transcendent mind that pervades and influences the ongoing physical evolutionary process.[34] This enables him to combine natural processes of evolution with his non-reductionistic, multilevel view of nature. Bernard Lonergan (a Jesuit priest, metaphysician, philosopher of science, and theologian) implicitly argues a similar position to explain human knowing as well as a non-reductionistic multilevel ontology.[35]

We might sum up by noting that the majority of scientists, physicians, Catholics, and mainline Protestants subscribe to some form of theistic evolution, allowing for a divine intelligence to influence physical processes toward higher and higher levels of activity and being. Though religious belief influences many theistic evolutionists, they are also influenced by the inadequacy of purely materialistic neo-Darwinian theories, which cannot explain the origin of transphysical activities in human intelligence (implying a soul) and the astronomically high improbability of the ascendency of species by physical reductionistic random processes over 4.6 billion years. In view of this, Catholics are justified in holding a theistic evolutionary position, which is not only consistent with their religious beliefs but also with sound evidence and scientific reasoning.

OT#16: Who Are Our First Ensouled Parents?

Who are Adam and Eve — whom we might call "our first ensouled parents"? How do they fit into the evolutionary development of hominids? The vast majority of scientists concur that Homo sapiens, the species of modern human beings, evolved from earlier hominids — Ardipithecus (5.8 million years ago), to Australopithecus (4 million to 3 million years ago), to Homo habilis (2.5 million years ago), to Homo erectus (2 million years ago), to Homo Neanderthalensis (430,000 years ago), to Homo sapiens (300,000 years ago).[36] Our first *genetic* ancestors sprang from early Homo sapiens between 200,000 and 150,000 years ago — Mitochondrial Eve and Y Chromosome Adam.[37] Mitochondrial Eve is the common woman genetic ancestor of every modern human being. Her mitochondrial DNA is integral to the genome of every human being around the world (without exception). Mitochondrial DNA is transmitted through mothers, but all human beings possess it.

Additionally, every modern man has a common male ancestor — named "Y Chromosome Adam" — who is the origin of the male "Y" chromosome. Mitochondrial Eve and Y Chromosome Adam lived about the same time (200,000 to 150,000 years ago[38]) and came from a similar region (southwestern coastal Africa — around the border between Angola and Namibia near the Atlantic Ocean). Though they may have had acquaintance with one another, it is by no means certain — and seems quite unlikely (given the large region and time spans involved).

Did Mitochondrial Eve and Y Chromosome Adam have souls? Were they distinct from all other animal species with the capacity for rational self-consciousness, syntactical language, and transcendental-religious consciousness? It seems very *unlikely* that they were. Rather, all anthropological and linguistic evidence points strongly to one individual (or couple),[39] who was the progeny of Mitochondrial Eve and Y Chromosome Adam, living around seventy thousand to fifty thousand years ago — the time of the "great leap forward." My book *Science at the Doorstep to God* (see chap. 5, sec. 1.B) gives an expanded discussion of the groundbreaking volume by Robert Berwick and Noam Chomsky, *Why Only Us*, showing the as-yet-inexplicable leap from animal communication to uniquely human conceptual and syntactically significant language that occurred between seventy thousand and fifty thousand years ago in a single member[40] of Homo sapiens:

> The atomic elements [of syntactical language] pose deep mysteries. The minimal meaning-bearing elements of human languages — word-like, but not words — are radically different from anything known in animal communication systems. Their origin is entirely obscure, posing a very serious problem for the evolution of human cognitive capacities, language in particular. There are insights about these topics tracing back to the pre-Socratics, developed further by prominent philosophers of the

early modern scientific revolution and the Enlightenment ... though they remain insufficiently explored.[41]

Berwick and Chomsky's insight into these atomic elements of meaning and language correlate with what philosophers call "the conceptual frameworks necessary to relate ideas to one another" (needed for abstraction of conceptual ideas). As shown there, these fundamental conceptual frameworks (giving rise to conceptual ideas) must be pre-experiential (innate). Moreover, their purely abstract nature implies that they are not producible solely by the physical processes of the brain, further implying origination through a transphysical agency, like a soul.[42]

If we suppose Berwick and Chomsky's insight is true, then we might infer that our first ensouled ancestors lived between 70,000 and 50,000 years ago (about 100,000–150,000 years after our genetic ancestors, Mitochondrial Eve and Y Chromosome Adam). This dating of our first ensouled ancestors corresponds with what anthropologists call "the great leap forward" in the development of Homo sapiens about 65,000 to 50,000 years ago. In the words of Longrich:

> For 200,000–300,000 years after *Homo sapiens* first appeared, tools and artefacts remained surprisingly simple, little better than Neanderthal technology, and simpler than those of modern hunter-gatherers such as certain indigenous Americans. Starting about 65,000 to 50,000 years ago, more advanced technology started appearing: complex projectile weapons such as bows and spear-throwers, fishhooks, ceramics, sewing needles.
>
> People made representational art — cave paintings of horses, ivory goddesses, lion-headed idols, showing artistic flair and imagination. A bird-bone flute hints at music. Meanwhile, arrival of humans in Australia 65,000 years ago shows we'd mastered seafaring.[43]

Thus the period between 65,000 and 50,000 years ago had multiple occurrences pointing to the existence of rational, religious, and aesthetic self-consciousness. Prior to this time, Homo sapiens showed little difference between themselves and Neanderthals, remaining sedentary, using simple tools, with no sign of aesthetic or religious consciousness. If we suppose that Berwick and Chomsky are correct about syntactically significant language developing in a single member[44] of Homo sapiens about seventy thousand to sixty-five thousand years ago, then we might conjecture that the above higher-level capabilities, which developed about the same time, also originated in the same single human ancestor. Closer examination of the origin of these other higher-level capabilities will help to bear this out, implying that sixty-five thousand to fifty thousand years ago was the approximate time at which our first ensouled ancestor appeared on the earth.

What are these higher-level capabilities and when did they develop in human history?

1. **The development of conceptual thought**, manifest in abstract language and reasoning, 70,000 to 60,000 years ago.[45]
2. **The discovery of abstract mathematics**, manifest in simple and complex counting and tallying sticks, 40,000 years ago, and the triple-column Ishango bone for complex operations, 25,000 years ago.[46] Prior to this time, there is no evidence of counting or tallying devices indicating mathematical abstraction by our genetic ancestors or any other Homo sapiens.
3. **Creative advancements in technology**, 50,000 years ago, including developments in weaponry (bows and arrows, hardened spears, knives with handles), seafaring and navigation technology, fishing technologies (e.g., fishhooks), sewing needles, and fire-making technology.[47]
4. **Awareness of deities, afterlife, and the spiritual world**, 40,000 years ago. Grave goods (for the afterlife), fertility figurines, and deities like the lion-man figurine from the Stadel Cave in Baden-Württemberg, Germany, originated between 40,000 and 35,000 thousand years ago.[48] This awareness of deities and the afterlife is not evidenced in Neanderthals or any Homo sapien ancestors prior to 50,000 to 40,000 years ago.

5. Awareness of demons, evil, and possibly taboos (morality),
    11,600 years ago. (Though religion and morality have been
    intrinsically connected throughout the last twelve millen-
    nia, we have no specific evidence of this before 11,600 years
    ago.) The Shigir Idol, carved from a log by hunter-gatherers
    and found near the Russian city of Yekaterinburg, depicts an
    idol with what appears to be demons and zigzag lines, which
    may indicate "keep out" ("taboo").[49] The late date may well
    be attributable to the difficulty of communicating moral ta-
    boos without a written language.‡

6. **The development of visual and auditory aesthetics (beau-
    ty)**, 40,000 years ago. Colorful, symbolic cave paintings
    from Sulawesi, Indonesia, date back to 35,000 thousand
    years ago.[50] The oldest known bone flute (40,000 years old,
    from the upper paleolithic period) was found in Hohle Fels
    site (Swabian Jura, Germany).[51] We have no evidence of vi-
    sual or auditory aesthetics in any other hominid species or
    in Homo sapiens prior to 50,000 to 40,000 years ago.

7. **The Great African Diaspora**, 60,000 years ago. For about
    140,000 years, our genetic ancestors (the line coming from
    Mitochondrial Eve and Y Chromosome Adam) stayed close
    to the border of Angola and Namibia and moved along the
    Atlantic coastline when climatic conditions required small
    migrations. Suddenly, about 60,000 years ago, our ances-
    tors became geographical explorers.[52] They moved up to
    the frontiers of northern Africa, invented technologies suf-
    ficient for crossing bodies of water, moved into the Middle
    East and Asia (and across the sea to Indonesia), and then
    migrated into Europe — moving to southern Europe and all
    the way to the uppermost parts of northern Europe/Siberia,
    and then crossing the arctic land bridge[53] to North Amer-
    ica. They then moved south from Alaska to the southern
    tip of North America, then to Central and South America,

---

‡ Written language first occurred when pictorial signs were converted into written symbols. This seems to have
first occurred with respect to the Sumerian language (Mesopotamia — near modern-day Iraq) in about 5500 BC.

finally ending at the southernmost tip of Argentina 14,000 to 13,000 years ago (the "Arroyo Seco 2" site).[54] This complete change in attitude and capability from 160,000 years of quasi-sedentary dwelling to sudden geographical expansionism (covering most of the globe in forty-five thousand years) needs an explanation, just as our sudden capacity for conceptual thought and language, mathematics, technology, religion, morality, and aesthetics.

When we look at these seven capabilities that lifted us out of a highly developed animal domain into what might be called the abstract-conceptual-transcendent-moral-aesthetic domain, we must ask whether these capabilities can be completely explained by physical processes alone. In OT#12, we referenced several scientific and philosophical studies showing why human intellection, self-consciousness, awareness of transcendence-religion, and awareness of morality and beauty cannot be explained by physical processes alone.[55] This implies that those activities be at least partially caused by a transphysical agent like a soul. If so, then about 60,000 years ago, human beings became categorically different from their genetic ancestors, manifesting capabilities apparently requiring a transphysical soul.

It is not unreasonable to conclude from this that our first ensouled ancestors — ensouled Adam and Eve — originated sixty thousand years ago in Africa, and that their progeny was also given a soul by the same transcendent cause/Creator — God. As noted in OT#12, section 2, human beings are unique in the above seven capabilities, and it does not seem that the animal kingdom would be able to develop them from a merely physical-organic evolutionary process.

If our first ensouled parents came into existence through a transphysical soul about 60,000 years ago, it agrees with two important biblical assertions: that human beings are the highest creation on earth and that God has made human beings in His own image and likeness (Gn 1:27). This insight is truly extraordinary, because the Judeo-Christian Bible is the only religious source to claim that a transcendent God created human beings in His own image and likeness,[56] elevating us from mere slaves and "playthings" of the gods to the very image of God himself — deserving of the respect, dignity, and justice of this divine image. This moves us to ask: How did the biblical author of Genesis 1:27 (the Priestly Author, writing around 587–530 BC) come to this unique conclusion about the special creation of human beings without the influence of Greek philosophical speculation on the soul? When we reflect on how this belief (when brought to full light by Christianity) influenced not only the development of religion, but also the development of philosophy, rights theory, and culture, it is hard to resist the idea that it was inspired by God himself.

OT#17: How Can Original Sin and Its Consequences Be Reconciled with the Scientific View of Creation?

Original sin is one of the key doctrines of Christianity, yet some anthropologists and theologians have suggested that it conflicts with the scientific view of the unfolding of creation and the evolution of species. What are some of these supposed points of conflict? The two most prominent are (1) monogenism versus polygenism and (2) the idea that original sin brought physical death and suffering into the world. We will first examine the scriptural background of these issues and then respond to the seeming conflicts between faith and science.

The Bible transformed the world's viewpoint on human beings by emphasizing human transcendence (being made in the image of God) and human freedom (the capability to choose between good and evil). These two doctrines freed the world from the fatalism of Greek and Roman philosophy, the degradation of belonging to the lower classes (particularly slaves), the heartlessness and cruelties associated with Stoic ethics, and the hedonism connected with Epicurean ethics. These two interrelated, liberating doctrines originated in the Bible — specifically in Genesis 1 and 2 (the creation of the world and man, written in the sixth and tenth centuries BC, respectively) and Genesis 3 (the Fall of man, written in the tenth century BC). Is this mere coincidence, or does it once again imply the inspiration of God? Coincidence alone seems highly unlikely. We now turn to the biblical accounts.

1. The Biblical Account of the Fall and Original Sin

Recall from OT#4 that in Genesis 3, the Yahwist author is reinterpreting a primeval myth called the Atrahasis for his Israelite audience. Recall also that the Atrahasis presents a very different picture of the initial relationship between God (or the gods) and humanity than the Yahwist view. The Atrahasis portrays a rebellion of primeval men against the gods because of the harsh conditions and natural rivalry into which they had been created, whereas the Yahwist portrays an initial condition of harmony and happiness between the one God and humanity's first parents. Both narratives are trying to explain why there is alienation between God (or the gods) and humans. In the Atrahasis the alienation is the fault of the gods, who have built harsh conditions and rivalry into creation. But in Genesis 3, the alienation is the fault of the first couple, who ruined the harmonious and happy relationship into which they were created by willfully disobeying a command from God in order to be like Him (self-idolatry).

Before considering the biblical narrative, recall Pope Pius XII's teaching that the biblical authors can use a multitude of literary genres (such as the mythopoetic genre) as well as metaphors (figurative language) to communicate truths needed for salvation.[57] So, what are the enduring messages of Genesis 2–3 that are necessary for salvation that remain valid today? The fundamental truth is that there is cosmic struggle between God (the good) and Satan (evil), in which human beings are caught up. This struggle has particular characteristics and consequences portrayed in Genesis 3:

- The serpent, representing the evil spirit,[§] appears on the scene and makes several suggestions that both tempt and deceive the couple.
- The tactics of the evil spirit focus on God withholding something from them — something that would be good for them and to which they are entitled. This is a lie — because God has made them in His very image and likeness and has

---

§ The evil spirit does not appear frequently in the Old Testament but is a key figure in the New Testament — particularly in the life and ministry of Jesus (in all four Gospels). In this remarkable narrative, the serpent plays a key role, which closely resembles the role that Jesus attributes to the evil spirit five hundred years later.

satisfied their desires for everything, except to be divine like Him.

- Satan begins by undermining Eve's trust in God, implying that God has lied to them. When Eve submits to the temptation, she immediately pulls her husband into it, which causes their "eyes [to be] opened" (Gn 3:7). The resultant alienation and loss of harmony and happiness with Yahweh incites them to hide from Him.

- Yahweh does not abandon the sinful couple. He comes into the garden looking for them, asking, "Where are you?" (Gn 3:9). When Adam admits to the sin, he immediately blames his wife, who in turn blames the serpent (Gn 3:12–13). The disingenuousness of blaming others without taking any personal responsibility shows the effects of being alienated from God. This evil (represented by disingenuousness) is now embedded in the couple's nature. They are weakened by their self-idolatry, giving rise to the enduring effect of concupiscence (explained in section 2). Serious as this is, it is not the only consequence of the couple's sin.

- Yahweh goes on to say that this sin will result in constant struggle with the powers of Satan (who will strike at the heels of their progeny), that they will experience suffering, that they will be separated from the tree of life (implying subjection to death), and that they will be banished from the garden (continued alienation from the original harmony and happiness with God before the sin).

The above list of the Fall's consequences should not be interpreted in a way that opposes a proven scientific account of the physical world. Recall St. Robert Bellarmine's principle (articulated in OT#2) that scientifically demonstrated fact takes precedence over scriptural interpretation to the contrary. Recall also that Pope Pius XII affirmed this by noting that the intention of God in Scripture is not to communicate science (an empirical-mathematical explanation of the physical universe) but rather sacred truths necessary for salvation.[58]

Since the Holy Spirit did not intend that Scripture explain the essential nature of the physical world, and since such truths are not necessary for salvation, we must not impose an interpretation of Scripture that is contrary to demonstrated scientific fact. Thus we should not say that the Holy Spirit intended to say that physical death came into the world at the Fall, because this directly contradicts scientifically validated evidence of 3.9 billion years of physical death prior to the time of our first ensouled ancestors (about 60,000 years ago). As will be explained, we must interpret the idea of "death" in some other way (see section 2). Furthermore, the term *suffering* should not be interpreted as physical pain because that would contradict a validated scientific fact of physical pain occurring throughout the 460-million-year history (since the occurrence of cartilaginous fish) prior to the time of our first ensouled ancestors.

So, what is the point of the biblical narrative? It is decidedly spiritual and *not* physical-biological. The spiritual interpretation indicates that God created humans in His own image in an initial harmonious and happy relationship with Him (precisely the opposite of the view of the Atrahasis and other rival myths). Furthermore, the first couple was aware of their creatureliness and the essential commandment of God against self-idolatry. They disobeyed that commandment by submitting to the temptation of Satan and subsequently became alienated from God, losing not only their initial harmony and happiness with Him but also becoming disingenuous in their intentionality. Thus they allowed darkness and evil into their nature. As a consequence, they were weakened in their capacity for good and resistance to evil, which burdened them with an ongoing battle with Satan and the depression and anguish of suffering and death. Inasmuch as they still had a transphysical soul, they longed for eternal life, but after the Fall, they were faced with the reality of death — the cessation of everything they had previously believed to be an ongoing and eternal condition — the worst possible consequence of their self-idolatrous desire to be like God.

Could our first parents — ensouled Adam and Eve — have committed such a sin 50,000 to 60,000 years ago? If we assume that God gave them souls similar to our own, then they would have received the transphysical power needed for self-consciousness, conceptual ideas, and abstract intelligence. Furthermore, God would have given them a numinous awareness of himself as well as a felt recognition of His commandments through conscience. With these powers of the soul, our first parents would have had the capacity for rational reflection and free choice and would have known the supremacy of the Creator and His commandments against self-idolatry, pride, and envy (see OT#12 and OT#16). Furthermore, their spiritual nature would have been able to apprehend the temptations and alienation of the evil spirit, who no doubt was present at the very creation of ensouled humans to undermine the loving plan of God. Thus, if our first ensouled ancestors had souls like ours, they were quite capable of committing the sin portrayed in Genesis 3, leading to a limitation of their capacity to apprehend the Presence of God to do good and resist evil.

Though this spiritual message is bleak, Christianity provides a horizon of hope, indicating that those who follow Christ in His Church and His sacraments will find the way back to eternal harmony and happiness with God — and ultimately, in the glory of Christ's resurrection.

2. Church Teaching on Original Sin

In addition to the biblical narrative on the Fall, Saint Paul, the Church Fathers (Saint Augustine in particular), and the Church's Magisterium gave further interpretation of original sin. Rather than review a lengthy history, it will be best to summarize by noting the *Catechism of the Catholic Church*'s teaching on original sin and concupiscence:

> By yielding to the tempter, Adam and Eve committed a *personal sin*, but this sin affected the *human nature* that they would then transmit *in a fallen state*. ... Original sin is called "sin" only in an analogical sense: it is a sin "contracted" and not "committed" — a state and not an act. (404)
>
> It is a deprivation of original holiness and justice, but human nature has not been totally corrupted: it is wounded in the natural powers proper to it; subject to ignorance, suffering and the dominion of death. (405)

The *Catechism* goes on to explain that the main effect of original sin is concupiscence, which it defines thus: "As a result of original sin, human nature is weakened in its powers, subject to ignorance, suffering and the domination of death, and inclined to sin" (418).

The Church's teaching is careful to distinguish between personal sin, for which we are responsible, and original sin, which negatively affects us in multiple ways, but for which we are not responsible (CCC 404). Concupiscence is the depreciated state of human beings following from the Fall of our first ensouled parents, which weakens us in our harmony with God, subjecting us to a more challenging struggle with evil.

Recall from above that our interpretation of the consequences of original sin should not contradict scientifically demonstrated fact. Thus we cannot interpret "death coming into the world" as the point at which the first organism died on the earth (3.9 billion years ago). Recall also, that God ensouled the first human being on the earth around 60,000 years ago, empowering human beings to survive physical death (see the medical evidence in OT#11). God gave our first parents the ability to experience eternal life as their natural condition (showing that He did not intend them to die — CCC 1008), but when they succumbed to self-idolatry and envy, separating themselves from their Creator, He took away this original condition, exposing them to the reality of impending physical death — the apparent end of everything that mattered. Inasmuch as they still had transphysical souls, they yearned for the eternal life, which was no longer within reach, causing great fear and dread of death.

Similarly, we cannot hold that suffering coming into the world means the first occurrence of physical pain in the natural world, as this took place 460 million years ago, with the occurrence of cartilaginous fish. Hence, we should interpret "suffering" to mean the self-conscious recognition of both physical and emotional pain coming from uncertainty about its efficacy and resolution. This uncertainty about death and suffering comes from our fallen state, which impedes our relationship with God and makes us more vulnerable to the temptations, doubts, and distortions of the evil spirit.

It is important to note that the Church teaches that we have not been completely corrupted through the Fall, meaning that we have not lost the whole of our harmony, awareness, and communion with God and His teaching in our consciences. We could say that even though we might be 49 percent corrupted, we are still 51 percent uncorrupted after the Fall. Furthermore, everyone can benefit from the redemption and reconciliation from sin wrought by Jesus Christ in His self-sacrificial passion, death, and resurrection.

Though non-Christians can also benefit from Jesus' redemptive act,[59] those who know Jesus Christ can more *directly* enter into the salvific path created by Jesus by following Him in His Church, sacraments, and moral teachings. This is the clearest and surest way to eternal salvation because it brings the truth and grace of Jesus Christ into the process of contending with concupiscence, resisting temptation, and being the light of God's truth and love in the world.

3. Monogenism and Polygenism: The Biblical Narrative and Science

In section 2, we answered two of the major problems concerned with science and the doctrine of original sin: the meaning of suffering and death coming into the world through the Fall. It now remains to address the problem of monogenism and polygenism.

Monogenism refers to the view that the first generation of human beings was *one* couple — a first man and a first woman. *Polygenism* refers to the view that the first generation of humans had more than one couple — which might be as many as thousands. In the same encyclical in which Pope Pius XII allowed Catholics to believe in evolution, he seems to have prohibited belief in polygenism with these words:

> When, however, there is a question of another conjectural opinion, namely, polygenism, then the children of the Church by no means enjoy such liberty. For the faithful cannot embrace that opinion which maintains that either after Adam there existed on this earth true men who did not take their origin through natural generation from him as from the first parent of all, or that Adam represents a certain number of first parents. Now it is in no way apparent how such an opinion can be reconciled with

that which the sources of revealed truth and the documents of the Teaching Authority of the Church propose with regard to original sin, which proceeds from a sin actually committed by an individual Adam and which, through generation, is passed on to all and is in everyone as his own.[60]

Pope Pius XII hedged the definitiveness of his declaration against polygenism by stating that "*it is in no way apparent* how such an opinion [polygenism] can *be reconciled* with ... the sources of revealed truth." Does this mean that if polygenism *can* be reconciled with the sources of revealed truth about original sin, then polygenism would be doctrinally acceptable?

Whatever the case, monogenism is compatible with the evolutionary picture of the emergence of the first ensouled human beings (capable of conceptual ideas, syntactical language, mathematics, self-consciousness, conscience, awareness of the sacred, aesthetics, etc. — see OT#16). These capabilities require a transphysical soul similar to that detected in peer-reviewed medical studies of near-death experiences (see OT#11 and OT#12, and SDG, chaps. 5 and 6). As noted earlier, our first ensouled parents were of the lineage of our first genetic parents — Mitochondrial Eve and Y Chromosome Adam. Recall that our first genetic parents probably lived about 200,000 years ago, but our first ensouled parents lived about 60,000 years ago, meaning that our first ensouled parents were progeny of our first genetic parents after about seven thousand generations (140,000 years). Recall also that Berwick and Chomsky believe that syntactically significant language occurred in a single member of the progeny of Mitochondrial Eve and Y Chromosome Adam.[61] If this is correct, and syntactically significant language requires a transphysical process of abstraction (entailing a soul), then our first ensouled parents (capable of syntactically significant language, mathematics, religion, etc.) could have occurred through divine intervention (a transphysical cause) in one member (or couple) of the progeny of Mitochondrial Eve and Y Chromosome Adam about sixty thousand years ago. Prior to that first ensouled human being, the seven thousand generations of our genetic ancestors did not have a soul given to them in a special creation by

God. Since a transphysical reality, like a soul, cannot evolve through a purely physical evolutionary process, it would have to be given to each individual member of the progeny of our first ensouled parents in a special creation by God.

In view of the above, it is not necessary to postulate the existence of more than two human beings with transphysical souls at this originative moment. All that is required is that God select one couple who could have propagated progeny to whom He would also give a transphysical soul. These ensouled progeny would have had the conceptual self-reflective intelligence needed for the great leap forward and the great African diaspora that occurred about ten thousand years after the creation of ensouled Adam and Eve — around fifty thousand years ago (see OT#16). Ten thousand years is about five hundred generations and, assuming large family sizes, would be more than enough progeny to explain the multiple migrations out of Africa that settled in almost every region of the world (with distinct languages and cultures) over forty thousand years.

According to Scripture and Church doctrine, our first ensouled parents committed the first sin, which weakened their nature. As a result, their capacity to resist sin was compromised, and they became subject to anguish from suffering and death (see above, section 2). This weakened nature was also transmitted to all the progeny of our first ensouled parents, which also subjected them to these negative effects.

Though these negative effects remain with us today, they can be mitigated by the redemptive act of Jesus, the participation in His Church and sacraments, and the help of the Holy Spirit in following His teachings.

CHAPTER 4
Questions Concerned with the Historicity of the Old Testament

OT#18: Are the Patriarchal Narratives Historical?

In OT#3, we discussed the formation and authorship of the Pentateuch (Torah) — the first five books of the Old Testament, and in OT#4, we discussed the origin, authorship, and purpose of the primeval narratives (see Gn 1–11). Though there are genealogies of the nations of the world in the primeval narratives, the origin (and genealogy) of *Israel* begins in Genesis 12 — the call of Abraham, which initiates the patriarchal narratives (Gn 12–50). Recall that the patriarchal narratives are grounded in historical traditions but are not, strictly speaking, history as we conceive of it today. In OT#3, it was recommended that those without substantial knowledge of biblical historiography consult a history of Israel (such as that of John Bright) and a modern biblical commentary (such as *The*

New Jerome Biblical Commentary). We have relied heavily on these two authoritative sources in this chapter so that readers seeking additional information can make recourse to these volumes for themselves. These sources have been supplemented by recent archaeological, historical, and exegetical sources.

This chapter will be divided into four parts, covering the period between the patriarchs and the initiation of the Israelite confederation — the period most challenged by modern historical criticism:

1. Patriarchal narratives (OT#18)
2. The exodus and desert wandering narrative (OT#19)
3. The uniqueness and significance of Mosaic Yahwism (OT#20)
4. The conquest and confederation narrative (OT#21)

We will not discuss the monarchy, the exile, and the post-exilic period in this book, because the historical facts are not as disputed as those in the earlier narratives. Preliminarily, we might say that though these earlier narratives are challenged by biblical skeptics, archaeological, historical, and exegetical studies indicate that they are grounded in history as it has been remembered in various oral traditions. It should be noted that these oral traditions are not formulated in the same fashion as modern history, so as we discuss them, we will try to show where the differences are likely to be.

It is difficult to confirm the historicity of *specific* incidents for which we have no archaeological or textual evidence beyond the Bible, but here we must invoke Bright's hermeneutical principle that those who challenge the historicity of extraordinary incidents simply because they are extraordinary go beyond the objective evidence.[1] Unless we have archaeological, historical, or scientific evidence showing the high unlikelihood of a specific incident or can demonstrate that it is midrash or theological interpretation (as distinct from history), we have no objective evidence to support a skeptical judgment about it.

Let us now consider the historicity of the patriarchal narratives. What can be confirmed as historical in the patriarchal narratives? The names of patriarchs and towns in the Genesis narrative are from second millennium Upper Mesopotamia (today, northwestern Iraq, northeastern Syria, and southeastern Turkey) and are best identified with the Amorites.[2] The Nuzi texts show that the customs and laws of the patriarchal narratives belong to Upper Mesopotamia in the early part of the second millennium (not later periods). The patriarchs and their people were, according to Bright "seminomadic breeders of sheep ... who confined their wanderings to the settled land and its fringes, where seasonal pasturage might be found."[3] They originally came from Aram and spoke Aramaic, giving credence to "a wandering Aramean was my father" (Dt 26:5).[4] Eventually, they came to roam in the central mountain range of Palestine from the area of Shechem south to the Negeb, in the Negeb, and east of the Jordan. The above congruences between the patriarchal narratives and texts of the early second millennium show that they "preserve an old and tenacious historical memory."[5]

Though the prophetic tradition in Israel is unique in its development, its early roots are found in the Mari texts, going back to upper Mesopotamia in the early second millennium. This is also the case with the patriarchs' view of law and covenant. Bright concludes: "[There is] evidence from all over northern Mesopotamia that a population akin to the Hebrews was actually present there in the first half of the second millennium; and ... various patriarchal customs have parallels among the population of approximately the same area at approximately the same time."[6]

We may now return to the patriarchs themselves. Bright brings together five historical points about the patriarchs that we can know with reasonable confidence. First, there is every reason to believe that Abraham, Isaac, and Jacob existed as historical figures. Though we cannot reconstruct their lives from the biblical narratives, we can know that they were influential leaders of sizable clans who were the predecessors to the people who ventured from Upper Mesopotamia to the region of Palestine[7] around 1500 BC or earlier and eventually constituted the people of the exodus.

Secondly, we must be careful about denying the historical basis of the patriarchal narratives simply because we lack external evidence of particular incidents related in them. As Bright puts it, "One may question the Bible's story or parts of it … but it must be remembered that in so doing one is moving beyond objective evidence."[8] Thus, at the very least, we must be respectful of the historicity of particular patriarchal stories, within the theological framework through which they are interpreted, until we have objective evidence to the contrary. Hence, stories such as Abraham's intended sacrifice of Isaac, Isaac's giving Jacob his blessing, and Joseph being sold into slavery by his brothers (within the framework of their theological interpretation) should be accorded historicity until objective evidence shows otherwise.

Thirdly, the people of Upper Mesopotamia with which the people of the Bible are associated are called *Hapiru*, which refers not to the Hebrew people specifically, but to a "class of people without citizenship who lived on the fringes of the existing social structure, without roots or a fixed place in it."[9] When need arose, these people hired themselves out as mercenary soldiers, servants of the elite class, and sometimes sold themselves as slaves.

Fourthly, records indicate that large numbers of the *Hapiru* people were pressed into labor on royal projects in Egypt and that some of them rose to high positions in the government (as the Bible portrays Joseph).[10] Records also indicate that the *Hapiru* were laborers on the construction projects of Ramesses II, who may well have been the Pharoah of the Exodus story.[11]

Fifthly, the god of the patriarchs is not the monotheistic god, Yahweh, whose name is used throughout the narrative. Yahweh comes from the Mosaic Revelation and the Sinai covenant, and the Yahwist author, who wove together many of the oral and written traditions of the patriarchal period,[12] retrojected the divine name from Moses into the narratives.[*] The God of the patriarchs is a predecessor to the God of the Mosaic Revelation, but as we shall see, Moses adds considerably to it. It should not be thought that the Yahwist retrojecting the divine name into the patriarchal traditions diminished the historicity of those narratives. In conformity with the ancient mode of writing history, he thought it appropriate to "update" the patriarchal traditions with the new, more

---

[*] Recall that the Mosaic covenant occurred around 1200 BC, and the Yahwist author wrote between 1000 and 950 BC.

profound Mosaic Revelation.

So who was the God of the patriarchs? He is conceived quite differently than what is found in the official polytheism of Upper Mesopotamia, the fertility cults of Canaan (Baal), and polydaemonism. The God of the patriarchs (*El*) is a personal God and a God of the clans governed by Abraham, Isaac, and Jacob — "the God of Abraham" (*'elohê 'abraham*: e.g., Gn 28:13; 31:42, 53), the "Fear" of Isaac (*pa ad yi aq*: Gn 31:42, 53), and the Champion (Mighty One) of Jacob (*'abir ya'qob*: Gn 49:24).[13]

This notion of God was not, strictly speaking, monotheistic, for the patriarchs were aware of other gods in surrounding clans and did not dispute their existence. Nevertheless, they believed that their God was superior to other gods, was associated with creation, and was active in the world as a whole (e.g., *El-Shaddai* — "the god of the cosmic mountain" whom they subsumed into their god, *El*).[14] This superior-Creator God was specially attached to the clans of Abraham, Isaac, and Jacob, and very specially attached to the clan leaders themselves. Abraham had a particularly significant spiritual experience, because he not only left the cult of his Aramean forefathers but replaced it with a new personal deity who apparently impelled him to leave everything he knew to follow His call.

As noted above, this personal, superior-Creator God of the patriarchal clans was the predecessor to the Mosaic Revelation, but that Revelation added so much more — the one God, His goodness, His gift of the Torah, and His merciful love. These attributes were added into the understanding of God who made the new covenant with Moses on Mount Sinai. We will discuss this in OT#20.

OT#19: Are the Exodus, Desert Wandering, and Sinai Covenant Historical?

The general historicity of the biblical accounts of Hebrews being state slaves in Egypt (during the Nineteenth Dynasty of Ramesses II), the exodus from Egypt, the wandering in the desert, and the Sinai covenant can scarcely be doubted. The evidence from archaeology, indirect written references, and Egyptian and Hebrew names is abundant.[15] The evidence for many individual stories in the biblical accounts is lacking, but as noted in OT#18, this does not mean they are historically false. As noted above, claiming such falsity goes beyond the objective evidence. As we shall see, there is considerable evidence for the exodus, desert wanderings, and Sinai covenant themselves. No doubt, the events in the Bible are telescoped into a briefer time period than occurred in history, and those events are seen through the eyes of interpreters of that time. Yet the events themselves seem to be the only plausible explanation for the radical transformation of the history of religions that occurred through them.

In light of this, we will examine the biblical narratives of the exodus, desert wandering, and Sinai covenant in two sections:

1. The historicity of slavery and exodus (section 1)
2. The historicity of the covenant at Mount Sinai (section 2)

1. The Historicity of Slavery in Egypt and Exodus

As noted in OT#18, *Hapiru* (Aramaean semi-nomadic people without citizenship living on the fringes of society) made their way from Northern Mesopotamia to Southern Mesopotamia and then to Palestine. Some of them went from Mesopotamia to Egypt and some from Palestine to Egypt. Though particular individuals who were educated and esteemed as leaders rose to high rank (perhaps Joseph), many of them hired themselves out as mercenary soldiers or servants of the elite class. In times of dire need, some sold themselves into state slavery.[16]

There is considerable archaeological and other indirect evidence of *Hapiru* (Hebrew) slaves in Egypt during the building campaigns of Ramesses II (Nineteenth Dynasty) in Egypt, such as the following:

- We should take the biblical account of Hebrew slavery at face value, because as Bright asserts, it is a culturally shameful foundation of the biblical people.[17] Why would Hebrew authors talk about this humble and disgraceful beginning unless it were true? (See NT#4, "The Criterion of Embarrassment.")
- There are many Israelite leaders who had Egyptian names, including Moses, Hophni, Phinehas, Merari, and probably Aaron.[18]

- Hundreds of Semitic words entered the Egyptian language at this time.[19]

There is significantly more evidence of the biblical accounts of slavery in Egypt if we assign the time of the exodus to the Nineteenth Dynasty of Ramesses II (thirteenth century BC) instead of the fifteenth century BC. Most scholars today believe that specific aspects of the biblical narrative favor the thirteenth century BC and that the disagreement is attributable to a problematic calculation of the number of years in a generation. 1 Kings 6:1 says that the number of years between the exodus and the fourth year of Solomon (about 958 BC) was 480. However, as Bright suggests, this was a round number probably used to signify twelve generations. If we calculate a generation as the time from the birth of the father to the time of the birth of his son, it is more realistically twenty-five years, not forty as the biblical author probably viewed it.[20] According to this more realistic calculation, the time of the Exodus would have been three hundred years before 958 BC, which would place it at 1258 BC (in the middle of the thirteenth century BC). This calculation corresponds precisely with the archaeological evidence. What is this evidence?

- Three place names in the exodus account correspond to Egyptian place names that exist only during the reign of Ramesses II — Pithom (see Ex 1:11) corresponding to Pi-Atum in Egyptian; Ramses (Ex 1:11)[†] corresponding to Pi-Ramesse in Egyptian; and the word for the Reed Sea, Yam Suph (Ex 10:19; 13:18; 15:22; 23:31), corresponding to Pa-Tjuf in Egyptian.[21] Why would the biblical accounts preserve Egyptian place names that were used only during the reign of Ramesses II (the thirteenth century BC) unless these were the names preserved in Israel's oral traditions?
- The Egyptian list of names and categories, *Onomasticon Amenope*, from Egypt's Third Intermediate Period (starting in 1069 BC), uses the Semitic name "b-r-k-t" (which refers to the

---

† Pi-Ramesses is the former Hyksos capital (Avaris), which was rebuilt by Ramesses II and then called the "House of Ramesses." The name was later changed to Tanis. Nevertheless, the reference to the capital as "House of Ramesses" is particular to the thirteenth century.

Lakes of Pithom) instead of the Egyptian name used in the pre-Ramesses II period. It seems that the Hebrews were in the region of the Lakes of Pithom for so long (during the reign of Ramesses II) that their name for the region replaced the Egyptian name as the standard reference.[22]

- A worker's four-room house discovered near the construction site of a Thebes temple corresponds architecturally to the four-room house very common to Hebrew settlements in Canaan, indicating that Hebrews were the workers (slaves) doing construction work for the pharaohs.

When we examine the six kinds of evidence from the above two lists (from the shameful background of slavery to the Bible's use of Egyptian place names and other archaeological evidence), it is reasonable to conclude that a moderately large group of Hebrews (around several thousand) under the leadership of Moses fled servitude from the cities of Pithom and Ramesses in about 1250 BC. The circumstances surrounding the event were so extraordinary that it became the foundation (along with the covenant of Mount Sinai) of the Israelite people, which was etched into their collective memory and self-identity for 3,200 years. As Bright puts it: "A belief so ancient and so entrenched will admit of no explanation save that Israel actually escaped from Egypt to the accompaniment of events so stupendous that they were impressed forever on her memory."[23] This is why Bright contends, "Almost no one today would question [the exodus event]."[24]

So, what probable route did the people of the exodus take from Pithom and Ramesses, under the leadership of Moses, to Mount Sinai? Since the biblical authors do not provide us with precise geographical locations using modern places and names, we have to answer two questions using a cross section of biblical evidence, archaeological evidence, and non-biblical texts:

1. What is meant by *Yam Suph* — the Reed Sea or the Red Sea?
2. What did the Israelites mean by "Mount Sinai" — the current Mount Sinai or somewhere else?

With respect to the first question, the name *Yam Suph* literally means "sea" (*yam*) "of reeds" (*suph*). Though the Septuagint (the official Greek translation of the Hebrew Bible) translated this as "Red Sea," which seems to have misled many for a long time, it is unlikely that this is the right location for *Yam Suph*, because there are no reeds in or near the Red Sea, and more importantly, it is too distant from Pithom and Ramesses to have allowed the Hebrews to escape from the Egyptians. As Bright puts it:

> It is unlikely that Israel crossed the tip of the Red Sea (Gulf of Suez) itself. This is so far to the south that the Egyptian cavalry would surely have caught them long before they reached it. We cannot suppose that the Red Sea then extended north of its present shoreline to connect with the Bitter Lakes, for there is now evidence that it did not.[25]

Under the circumstances, the Reed Sea would seem to be a more likely place. So, what did the biblical author mean by the Reed Sea? Richard Clifford, after analyzing the archaeological and textual data, notes the following:

> For the Hebrews escaping from Ramesses, there was virtually only one route that avoided the Egyptian observation posts South of Lake Balah and the important fortress at Zilu astride the Way of the Philistines; that route led through the swampy regions of Lake Balah. This shallow lake has the best claim to the *Yam Suph* — literally, "Sea of Reeds."[26]

It seems that the Israelites tricked the Egyptian detachment into following them into the swampy, shallow Lake Balah, which bogged down their chariots and horses as well as the equipped Egyptian soldiers. The very ancient victory songs recorded in biblical literature suggest that the Egyptian detachment gave up the pursuit of the Israelites, and they were able to proceed on the next phase of their journey toward which Moses would receive direction from God.

The Israelites proceeded to what was called "Mount Sinai," at which point Moses received the extraordinary revelation that gave birth to

Yahwism (see section 2). Though there is disagreement among scholars about the location of Mount Sinai (at the northern or southern part of the Sinai Peninsula), John Bright believes the traditional site (on the southern tip of the Sinai Peninsula — the site of the Monastery of Saint Catherines) is preferable for multiple reasons.[27] Whatever the case, the location of Mount Sinai is not crucial to the faith of Israel or Christianity. For the moment, suffice it to say that the people of the exodus were the people of the covenant, which multiple biblical references from different periods universally attest happened at Mount Sinai. As we shall see (OT#20), this covenant transformed the history of world religions and created such a strong identity of the exodus people that it enabled them to eventually confederate the entire region of Canaan.

2. The Historicity of the Covenant at Mount Sinai

Was there really a covenant made at Mount Sinai among Yahweh, Moses, and the people of the exodus? This seems virtually undeniable *prima facie* because there was nothing like Mosaic Yahwism[28] (integrating election, covenant, and the commandments of the law into the worship of Yahweh) before the Canaanite conquest. But after the Canaanite conquest, it is everywhere to be found in biblical literature.[29] What could possibly explain this except a profound historical event connected to Moses at what was called Mount Sinai around 1200 BC? Some scholars have suggested that the election, covenant, and Ten Commandments occurred after the conquest when Israel was settled, but this is highly unlikely for several reasons:

- For two hundred years (between 1220 and 1020 BC),[30] Israel maintained unity and incorporated multiple *Hapiru* residents of Palestine into herself without any central government or machinery of state, in the midst of multiple challenges. How could this have occurred without a strong theological-social-historical identity? Biblical literature identifies only one such theological-social event as the historical ground of her identity: the exodus culminating in the covenant at Mount Sinai. Why would we doubt this? All other reasons for this strong unity and identity pale in comparison with

Israel's own explanation.

- Israel's earliest poems (e.g., Ex 15:1–18) do not refer to her as "Israel" but rather to "Yahweh's people," or "the people whom thou hast redeemed" (Ex 15:13), or "your people, O LORD," or "the people you created."[31] These clear references to the people as "Yahweh's creation," "Yahweh's possession," and "the people redeemed by Yahweh" are all references to the covenant on Sinai, which shows that it is a much stronger force of identity-unity than a geographical-social-political association (such as "Israel"). Why would this be unless the covenant identity-unity was stronger than the geographical-social-political one before Israel was settled as a political confederation?

- There can be no doubt that the Decalogue (see Ex 20:1–17) is part of the covenant of Yahweh with Israel and predates even the earliest strata of Israelite legal codes given in Exodus 21–23 (from the time of the judges), because those primitive legal strands presume the Decalogue and the covenant as the foundation for the Israelite community and legal system. So Bright concludes that the Decalogue and covenant are of "Mosaic origin" — prior to the conquest.[32]

In view of the above, it is very likely that the covenant at Mount Sinai between Yahweh and His people occurred prior to the beginning of the Canaanite conquest around 1200 BC and became the foundation for the people of the Exodus to become the people of Yahweh and ultimately to become the nation of Israel.

OT#20: Is Mosaic Yahwism Unique and Inspired?

What happened at Mount Sinai? It was the place of the second most significant event in the history of religions (surpassed only by the Incarnation, passion, resurrection, and Revelation of Jesus Christ). Why is this event so extraordinary? It is nothing less than a revelation of God to Moses that transformed the idea of God, the morality of God, the historical oversight of God, and the personal relationship between God and His people — both individually and collectively. It was the unique font of Revelation, which continued to develop throughout Israel's history by priests, prophets, experts on the law, and wisdom writers, and ultimately found its fulfillment in Jesus Christ.[33]

What is so amazing is that this multifaceted transformation of the nature of God and religion happened in what appears to be one fell swoop. Such a transformation had not occurred anywhere in history — not even by small increments — prior to Moses' gathering of several thousand newly freed slaves at Mount Sinai around 1200 BC. Though the name *Yahweh* preceded the Sinai Covenant and perhaps even Moses, Mosaic Yahwism was quite unique. Some scholars believe that the Midianites (Kenites) worshiped "Yahweh" and that Moses learned of Yahweh from his father-in-law, Jethro, a priest of Midian.[34] Be that as it may, Mosaic Yahwism after the covenant of Mount Sinai was categorically different from Midianite Yahwism.[35] As we shall see, Yahwism underwent one of the most significant religious transformations in history shortly after the covenant of Sinai under the prophetic leadership of Moses. To appreciate the staggering nature of this transformation, we need to shed light on the various dimensions of Mosaic Yahwism compared with other religions, specifically:

- The centrality of election and covenant
- The monotheism of Mosaic Yahwism
- The morality of Yahweh
- Yahweh's personal and providential relationship with His people

These features are all unique to Mosaic Yahwism, and all are significant transformations in the history of religions.

1. The Centrality of Election and Covenant
The transformation of Yahwism did not occur through abstract theological reflection but rather through two historical events in which Moses claimed to receive the Revelation from Yahweh himself: the Exodus and the covenant of Mount Sinai. We have already seen that some kind of

spectacular event, apparently miraculous, enabled the Hebrew slaves to escape from the Egyptian cities of Pithom and Ramesses to flee into the desert. They were eventually pursued into the desert and managed to cross the Sea of Reeds, while the Egyptian detachment pursuing them became bogged down. This remarkable event allowed the Israelites to finalize their escape to make their way to Mount Sinai (about four hundred miles to the south). During that journey, Moses began to call the people of the exodus "the People of Yahweh," which was apparently confirmed during Moses' encounter with Yahweh on Mount Sinai.

Sometime after the revelation on Mount Sinai, the terms *election* and *covenant* began to be used to describe the great Mosaic revelation. *Election* was used to describe Yahweh's action in adopting the people of exodus for himself — as *His* special people. The proof of this adoption was the miraculous event of the exodus, which could have happened only through the powerful intervention of Yahweh.

During the revelation to Moses, Yahweh gave him the Ten Commandments. This was intended to seal the bond between Yahweh and His people, for if the people obeyed these commandments (which were the terms of the covenant), Yahweh would protect them, inspire them, and bless them with prosperity — just as He had done during the exodus and at the Sea of Reeds. The covenant not only formed "Yahweh's people" but also transformed the idea and identity of God in the history of religions. The identity of God ("El") moves from a local god (the God of Abraham, Isaac, and Jacob) to the God above all gods and pantheons — the God who created *everything*, who is righteous, just, and merciful. This implicitly monotheistic, moral, and providential Creator-God is categorically beyond anything the middle eastern, pagan, Abrahamic religions, or other world religions *ever* conceived. It is the foundation from which world religion would be transcendently and immanently transformed. We may say, then, that Israel's religion is based on experience rather than intellectual reflection. It is first and foremost a historical experience, a miraculous experience, and an unmistakable sign of Yahweh's love and choice — Yahweh's election.

2. The Monotheism of Mosaic Yahwism

The monotheism of Mosaic Yahwism is practical — not theoretical. It is not derived from an abstract proof (as in Aristotle's physics or metaphysics) nor from Egyptian Atenism (the worship of the one sun god). Though Atenism admitted only one deity, that deity was but a dimension of Ra — the sun god. Early Israel was careful never to associate Yahweh with a mere creation like the sun and strictly prohibited any images of Yahweh (disallowing the circular symbolism of Aten). Furthermore, Mosaic monotheism asserted that Yahweh was Creator and that all power and authority came from Him.

All this being said, Israel did not explicitly deny the existence of other gods but rather rejected their efficacy and authority. From a functional or practical point of view, Yahweh is far more than the top of a pantheon; He completely transcends pantheons altogether, because next to Him all gods are as nothing. As Bright notes: "The other gods, allowed neither part in creation, nor function in the cosmos, nor power over events, nor cult, were robbed of all that made them gods and rendered nonentities, in short, were 'undeified.'"[36]

Early Mosaic Yahwism prohibited making images of Yahweh (see second commandment, Ex 20:4–6). This prevented associations of Yahweh with pagan gods, images of nature associated with Yahweh, and sensualist images associated with pagan cults. Since Yahweh was above all gods, pantheons, and natural forces, and since making an image of Him would put Him on the same level with them, images had to be strictly prohibited. Indeed, the prohibition of images is second only in importance to the commandment not to worship any other god but Yahweh.[37] This explains why no image of Yahweh has ever been found in an excavation of early or later Israel in three thousand years.[38] No doubt Israel had a very personal and relational conception of God, which was often portrayed in prayer, poetry, and prophecy in anthropomorphic terms, but these terms were meant metaphorically, since intending them literally would have at least implicitly associated Him with the image of a human being.

Though Israel would go on to refine this notion of monotheism, and in the first century BC interpret it in light of Greek abstract monotheism (as in the case of Jewish philosophers such as Aristobulus and Philo of Alexandria), she maintained the primacy of experience and Revelation over abstract thought and proof. As the centuries progressed, Mosaic Yahwism ruled out polytheism altogether, and by the time the Priestly Author wrote the first creation narrative in the Book of Genesis (500 BC), Yahweh was thought to have created everything in reality — from the sun to the stars to the earth to the moon, and everything else that was deemed in previous generations to have been divine.

As noted above, Mosaic Yahwism was the first religion to insist upon monotheism in this predominant and pervasive way, which provokes the question of how Moses and his group of relatively uneducated slaves came to this revolutionary transformation of the history of religions on a desert mountain in about 1200 BC. Was this merely creative speculation by Moses? This seems very unlikely, making Moses' explanation appear much more likely — namely, that Yahweh himself revealed it to him.

3. The Morality of Yahweh

Mosaic Yahwism breaks with the pagan myths, epics, and portrayals of gods in another unique and transformative way in the history of religions. Yahweh is portrayed not as capricious, arbitrary, and indifferent to justice but quite the contrary. He is thoroughly just, good, and righteous — and His holiness (sacredness) consists precisely in this justice, goodness, and righteousness. Pagan gods sought constantly to control, use, enslave, and toy with human beings, and their "justice" was filled with capriciousness, arbitrariness, and outright injustice.

When Yahweh required the people to obey the Decalogue as part of His election of and covenant with them, He did not do so as an arbitrary assertion of power but rather to call His people to be *like Him* in His righteousness, justice, and goodness. Thus they would truly be *His* people, and He would be their God (see Ex 6:7). Though Yahweh *chose* the people of the Exodus to be His people, they had to adhere to the conditions of the covenant (the Decalogue) *to be* His people.

Yahweh has yet another distinctive attribute. He is not only righteous and just but goes beyond the confines of justice to offer mercy and forgiveness, even when His people have egregiously failed. This notion of mercy is closely linked with His personal love for His people (e.g., Dt 7:7–9; Is 54:10; Jer 31:3) — a love that is compared to that of a mother for her children (e.g., Is 66:13; Is 49:15; Ps 131:2). This brings out the distinctive personal and intimate character of God's love, kindness, mercy, and compassion — the foundation for Jesus' revelation of the unconditional love of His Father (see NT#7).

4. Yahweh's Personal and Providential Relationship with His People

Mosaic Yahwism has yet another distinctive feature: Yahweh is not aloof from His people and the direction of their history. On the contrary, He is interested in every detail of it, interacting with Moses, Aaron, Joshua, and other prophets and leaders throughout Israel's history. Yahweh's interaction has to be continuous because He guides His people amidst incorrect choices, infidelity of kings and leaders, and disobedience. He is constantly watching, guiding, correcting, and admonishing through His prophets. When His people are obedient, he blesses them with progeny and abundance, but when they disobey, He allows them to suffer the consequences of their actions, the hostility of outsiders, and the harmful effects of nature. Though Israel's prophets and leaders are not always sure where He is leading, they are assured He is leading them toward a destiny that will fulfill His plan, not only for His people but also for "the nations" and the world.

Conclusion

Was Mosaic Yahwism a miracle (a divine intervention) in the history of religions? There are certainly reasonable grounds for believing so. How could Moses and his formerly enslaved people so radically change the history of religion without the help of Yahweh? How could they have developed such an overriding and distinctive kind of monotheism without His Revelation? How could they be so sure about the righteousness, justice, and goodness of Yahweh in the midst of every other religion surrounding them emphasizing the capriciousness and arbitrariness of the gods? How could Israel be so sure that Yahweh had chosen them in their helplessness rather than the other, more powerful nations surrounding them? How did the Chosen People develop such a strong Yahwistic identity that they could dispense with the machinery of state for two hundred years while they conquered other nations, convinced other nations to join them, and confederated the many city states throughout the Canaanite region? I would submit that this can be explained only by extraordinary (miraculous) events:

1. Several extraordinary (seemingly miraculous) occurrences leading to the exodus event that were attributed to Yahweh and His desire to make the *Hapiru* slaves His people. Some of these extraordinary occurrences include:

   - The plagues (which are discussed in OT#23) and Moses' role in them
   - The seemingly insurmountable hurdles that would have to have been overcome for several thousand slaves to leave the treasure cities of Pithom and Ramesses (important cities that would have had military detachments and surrounding outposts)
   - The seemingly insurmountable hurdles that would have to have been overcome for the Israelite slaves to outrun Egyptian military detachments to get to the Sea of Reeds and to cross it without further Egyptian pursuit

2. An extraordinary revelatory event on Mount Sinai that enabled Moses to break with every religion and culture around him and reveal that Yahweh was categorically different from them monotheistically, morally, providentially, and personally

This radical self-Revelation of Yahweh ultimately transformed the history of religions from the domain of superstition, sensualism, anthropomorphism, and capriciousness to belief in one God who is perfect righteousness, goodness, and justice. This radically new foundation was destined to be completed by the Revelation of Jesus Christ.

OT#21: Is Israel's Conquest of Canaan Historical?

From OT#19 and OT#20, we might adduce that when the people of the covenant left Mount Sinai, they were only several thousand in number but with a very strong and distinctive theological-spiritual identity. Yes — this early nucleus of the Israelite people had the bond of blood kinship and a *Hapiru* background (of northwest Semitic stock — see OT#18), but her real unity was produced by the historical events initiated by Yahweh (the exodus) and the theological-spiritual identity that came from His covenant with them at Mount Sinai. Though this early nucleus of the Israelite people was only several thousand slaves (including women and children) and lacked a geographical-political unity, she was stronger in her covenant identity and religious faith than the peoples of the Canaanite city-states to which she was led. This strong identity, unity, and faith made her attractive to many of the *Hapiru*/Semitic people who lived in Canaan;[39] however, it had the opposite effect on the Canaanite people living in those regions, who looked upon the Israelites as intimidating and relentless. This was probably a correct perception, because the Israelite community's strong unity and faith gave them a fervor, sense of purpose, and drive that the people of Canaan had rarely, if ever, witnessed.[40]

What was the situation like in Canaan before Israel made her first incursion? In brief, some city-states predominantly constituted by *Hapiru*/Semitic peoples would have been predisposed to joining Israel. Other city-states with a predominance of Canaanite people and a strong military would have fought mightily, and city-states with a mixed population and a less organized military would have put up weak resistance. This resembles what archaeologists have found in the various excavations around the ancient land of Canaan (today, this would be Israel, Palestine, northwestern Jordan, western Lebanon, and western Syria).

Some of the ancient city-states have almost no sign of fighting (suggesting that they were inclined to peacefully incorporate into Israel); some show evidence of almost total annihilation — from the walls to the inner city, indicating terrific battles; and some show signs of resistance, but not all-out battle.[41] Recall that the Old Testament biblical narratives had to telescope events to fit into relatively short historical books (in this case, mostly Judges and Joshua), and so what might appear to be a few decades in the narrative is really almost two hundred years in history (between 1200 BC and about 1000 BC — the time of Iron Age 1). It so happens that the transition between the Late Bronze Age and the Early Iron Age occurred around the time of the Israelite conquest, which is manifest in more sophisticated Bronze Age structures (of Canaanite communities) being replaced by the less sophisticated Iron Age communities of Israel.[42]

Dr. Eero Junkkaala (professor at the Finnish Bible Institute and author of fifty-one books on biblical archaeology) notes that the archeological evidence in most cases corresponds well with the biblical accounts:

> There are cities where archaeological information confirms or at least does not contradict the biblical tradition, for instance Beth-shemesh, Timnah, Tell Beit Mirsim, Tel Halif, Hazor, Dan, Bethel, Shechem, Lachish and the list of the so-called unconquered cities in Judges 1:27–35 and Joshua 13:2–6. Furthermore, there emerged hundreds of new small sites in the Central Hill Country.[43]

However, there are a few sites that do not seem to correspond to the biblical account: Kadesh-Barnea, Arad, Yarmuth, Jericho, and Ai. Given the accuracy of so much of the biblical account, biblical scholars and archaeologists are puzzled over the seeming discontinuities of dates between the Bible and these latter sites — particularly Jericho and Ai. Might not these discontinuities be attributable to telescoping of the narrative, theological interpretation of the narrative, and/or undiscovered archaeological evidence? For these and other reasons, Junkkaala asserts that there are good explanations of the dating discrepancies in the above cases.[44] In view of the above, the biblical accounts are, in general, quite consistent with the archaeological evidence obtained in recent excavations, and so we may be confident that they accurately portray the events that led to the eventual conquest of the region of Canaan by Israel.

The biblical narrative (in Deuteronomy, Joshua, Numbers, and Judges) supported by archaeological evidence gives the following as a likely sequence of events:

- After the Sinai covenant, the nucleus of the Israelite community went to Kadesh (near the southern border of Israel
  today) and settled there for about forty years (see Dt 1:46;
  Nm 20:1; Jos 15:13). This is the place where Moses made
  water come from the rock (Nm 20:1–13). It is also the burial place of Miriam and Aaron (Nm 20:22–29).
- While Israel was settled in Kadesh, her strong Yahwistic
  faith and covenant identity were no doubt attractive to
  many people of Semitic background in the region (mostly escaped slaves from Egypt and rootless *Hapiru*).[45] As
  Bright notes: "[Israel] not only offered [these escaped
  slaves and *Hapiru*] community and identity such as they
  had never had before; it proclaimed Yahweh as the God
  who had delivered them in order that he might lead them
  into the land which he had promised to their ancestors. We
  may suppose that numerous conversions to the new faith
  took place."[46] As a result of this assimilation, Israel grew in
  numbers sufficient to consider incursion into Canaan.
- The Israelites made their first incursion into south Canaan
  from Kadesh but were repelled (see Nm 13:35–49). This
  led to additional desert wanderings, where Bright believes
  that Israel brought in additional numbers, became tougher,
  and moved out of its semi-nomadic form to something like
  an irregular military form.[47]
- Israel then went to the Eastern side of Canaan, careful to
  avoid Edom and Moab (the king of Edom denied them access — Nm 20:14–21). With their increased numbers they
  pushed their way into Heshbon, which initiated their long
  road to conquest (see Nm 21:21–32).[48] Bright suggests that
  Heshbon was a predominantly Semitic/*Hapiru* land, which
  was taken over by the Amorites (King Sihon), and that the
  incursion of the Israelite army gave the Semitic residents
  the opportunity to join ranks with the Israelites to over-

throw Sihon and the Amorites.[49]

- The Israelites then moved northward toward Bashan (King Og) and conquered that territory in much the same way (see Nm 21:33–35).[50] The Israelites soon incorporated the Semitic population of these city-states into their growing population, further strengthening their overall numbers and their military.

- At the beginning of the twelfth century BC, Israel was strong enough to make a westward push and began to take over the city-states of western Canaan. Some campaigns were bloody military conquests, while others were relatively peaceful overthrows of Canaanite kings followed by incorporation of the Semitic population into the people of Israel and its army.[51] Joshua was instrumental in these conquests, uprisings, and incorporations of Canaanite people into the ranks of Israel (see Jos 1–24). There is considerable archaeological evidence to support this sequence of Israel's conquests.[52] As Bright implies, this was a long process that went on over five decades (until about 1150 BC), during which coalitions were formed by Canaanite kings to hold off the Israelites.[53] After much back-and-forth, Joshua and the Israelites solidified the conquered territory that would become the nation of Israel for centuries to come (around 1150 BC).[54]

- At the end of the conquest, Joshua brought together all the constituents of the new Israel — both those from the desert and the incorporated residents of the Canaanite city-states — into a solemn covenant at Shechem around 1150 BC (see Jos 24).[55] The new people of Yahweh solemnly promised to worship Yahweh alone and so to become part of His people.[56]

After the covenant at Shechem, Israel entered the period of the Judges (from 1150 BC to 1000 BC). Bright indicates that this is very difficult to correlate with external records from the period because of ambiguities in both the biblical narrative and these external records. Nevertheless, Bright contends that the events in the Book of Judges correlate well with the customs and archaeological evidence of the period.[57]

During the period of the judges, Israel had time to consolidate and stabilize the confederation of city-states she took over (or conquered) from Canaan. Most of her holdings were in the highlands of Palestine to the south and Galilee to the north, but these two large areas were split in two by continued Canaanite possession of the Plain of Esdraelon. This time of needed consolidation and stabilization was handed over to the confederation because of Egypt's defeat by multiple powers, which rendered her ineffective in interfering with Israel's Canaanite conquests and confederation.[58] Fortunate as this was, less threatening powers — for example, the Philistines, who occupied the coastal region, and unconquered Canaanites, who occupied the Plain of Esdraelon, began to make incursions into Israel's loose confederation of city-states, which had taken on tribal designations.[59]

As noted above, the principal reason that Israel maintained its unity without a strong central government amidst geographical separation and diverse populations was Yahwism. Israel's sense of election and covenant and her Yahwistic religious identity provided the unity needed to rally forces from among different tribes to resist the incursion of peoples surrounding her and even in her midst (e.g., the Plain of Esdraelon). During this period Israel had no desire to consolidate more strongly in a state/monarchy. The tribes appreciated their local autonomy, and when enemies had to be confronted, they rallied troops to quell the crisis.[60]

The crisis of the Philistines was much greater than a local rallying of troops. As Bright indicates, this crisis forced Israel out of its preference for a tribal confederation that placed its trust exclusively in Yahweh and maintained its unity through His covenant and Revelation.[61] Israel now had to seriously consider a unified central government through a united monarchy (traditionally dated between 1047 BC and 930 BC). This led to the anointing of Saul and, later, David, and finally, Solomon. After the time of the united monarchy (around 930 BC), the kingdom was divided between Israel (the Northern Kingdom) and Judah (the Southern Kingdom) until Israel was conquered by the Assyrians (732 BC) and Judah was conquered by the Babylonians (597 BC) and led into exile.

The facts surrounding the monarchical period, the division of the kingdom, the conquest of Israel and Judah, the exile, and the post-exilic period are much better established than the period from the patriarchs through the conquest of Canaan, so it is much less necessary to provide extended historical validation of the major events of that period. Hence, we will conclude our examination of historicity at this point.[‡]

---

‡ Readers seeking an extended explanation of these later periods may want to consult John Bright's *History of Israel* (4th ed.), cited extensively in this chapter.

CHAPTER 5

Questions Concerned with the Development of Morality, the Historicity of Miracles, and the Inspiration of Prophecy in the Old Testament

OT#22: Is There Development in the Moral Teaching of the Old Testament?

In OT#2, we discussed Joseph Ratzinger's writings on the conditions of biblical inerrancy, including religious and moral matters. In sum, Ratzinger holds that there are two components to scriptural expression: the essential core of the message, which is divinely revealed and inerrant, and the outward form of the expression, which is human and therefore subject to the transitoriness of time and culture — not inerrant.[1] Ratzinger notes that as thought frameworks (which include religious and moral frameworks) develop over the course of time, they become more comprehensive and precise, and when Divine Revelation is brought to fulfillment in Jesus Christ, previous Revelation finds its fullest interpretative context.

This gives rise to questions: Who is competent to judge the distinction between the central core of the message (divinely revealed and inerrant) and the merely human outward expression of the message (not inerrant)? And who is competent to give definitive interpretation to Jesus' Revelation and how previous Revelation is to be seen in light of it? As Ratzinger shows, no human scholar or scholarly method can possibly do this, because God alone, in the Person of Jesus who is the fullness of Revelation, can be the definitive interpreter of what is divinely revealed (and what is not). Ratzinger then concludes that the Catholic Church alone can be the definitive interpreter of what is divinely revealed (inerrant) and what is merely human outward expression (not inerrant), because the Catholic Church was established by Jesus Christ precisely for that purpose (see OT#2 and NT#18) — "I will give you the keys of the kingdom of heaven, and whatever you bind on earth shall be bound in heaven, and whatever you loose on earth shall be loosed in heaven" (Mt 16:19).

With Ratzinger's general framework in mind, we turn to the Pontifical Biblical Commission's document *The Bible and Morality: Biblical Roots of Christian Conduct*.[2] The commission sets out two basic principles:

1. That religious and moral doctrine in the Bible develop progressively and in dialogue between God and His people[3]
2. That all gradually developing Revelation prior to Christ must be interpreted in light of the Revelation of Christ (its fullness)[4]

The underlying assumption is that the Church (the living Presence of Christ) is the competent authority to declare what is the central message (inerrant) and what is merely human outward expression of the message (not inerrant).

The commission applies these principles to three religious/moral issues presented in the Sermon on the Mount's antitheses.[*] We will take

---

[*] An "antithesis" refers to Jesus' superseding previous Old Testament Revelation in the contrasted statement, "You have heard it said … but I say to you …"

up two of them:

1. Conflict with neighbors (Matthew 5:38–42)
2. The morals of matrimony (Matthew 5:31–32)

We will examine each in turn and then consider three other areas of concern in Old Testament morality: human sacrifice (see Jgs 11:30–39), the divine command to kill everything that breathes (Dt 20:16–18), and the imprecatory psalms in which enemies are cursed.[5]

Let us begin with conflict with neighbors. The Pontifical Biblical Commission sees this progressive development of moral requirements in three stages:

- **The patriarchal period**, in which an excess of vengeance for crimes committed is allowed by God, who asserts that He will avenge Cain seven times against anyone who kills him (see Gn 4:15), from which Lamech (a descendent of Cain) justifies his right to be avenged seventy-seven times (Gn 4:23–24).
- **The Mosaic law**, which restricts the right of vengeance to parity or equality — "eye for eye, tooth for tooth" — no more (see Ex 21:24; Lv 24:20; Dt 19:21). This is a significant development, from an excess of vengeance to equal vengeance, in which the latter teaching replaces the former.
- **Jesus' teaching**, which surpasses the right to vengeance and replaces it with turning the other cheek: "You have heard that it was said, 'An eye for an eye and a tooth for a tooth.' But I say to you, do not resist one who is evil. But if any one strikes you on [your] right cheek, turn to him the other also" (Mt 5:38–39).

Jesus does not stop there. He commands Peter to forgive his brother not only seven times but seventy-seven times, directly controverting God's assertion to Cain that He will avenge him seven times and undermining Lamech's claim to be avenged seventy-seven times.

Does this mean that God is changing His mind throughout history? Of course not. The best way of understanding this development is to start with Jesus' teaching (which is God's complete and eternal will) and move backward. Recall that God's full and eternal will inspired the biblical author, who was inextricably bound up in the thought framework of his day. As noted in OT#2, if God did not work with and through the biblical author and his thought framework, He would not have been able to effectively communicate with the people of the author's time and culture. Imagine what the scientific picture of creation would have sounded like to a barely educated Israelite in the sixth century BC. It would be as if a mathematician who recognizes that calculus is a much fuller expression of the truth of mathematics than arithmetic should say to himself, "I want first and second graders to have the full expression of mathematics rather than a little slice of the truth — they should be taught calculus!"

The same holds true for moral truths. Certain moral truths can fit easily into certain thought frameworks, but not others. For example, Jesus' moral proclamation to refrain from vengeance and forgive seventy-seven times was hard enough for people within the New Testament thought framework to understand and accept — people who had been prepared by the prophets and wisdom literature (see Prv 25:21–22). But can you imagine having Moses or Joshua preach "turning the other cheek" to a warrior society? They would have been, to say the least, scorned and rejected. Society was not ready for it yet. The best that Moses could do to approach the fullness of Revelation was to limit vengeance to equality with the harm committed to the avenger. This was a hard enough step to take in a culture that believed it had the right of excessive vengeance. It was a stretch, but the thought framework of that warrior society could accept it.

Now let's apply Ratzinger's distinction to this. We know the fullness of God's Revelation given by Jesus. This gives us an idea of what the Church will say is the merely human outward expression of the thought framework of the Old Testament writers into which God's inspiration was inserted in order to make it intelligible. The fullness of Revelation is to avoid vengeance and to forgive without limit, but the merely human (non-inerrant) thought framework into which it is inserted allows for retaliation to achieve "justice"[6] and discourage enemies. When Jesus makes the fullness of Revelation known, He simply supersedes the old, merely human thought framework (non-inerrant) and allows His full Revelation to shine forth. Hence, He proclaims the avoidance of vengeance and limitless forgiveness.

Let's now proceed to the second example given by the Biblical Pontifical Commission: the morals of matrimony. Once again, we see gradual development. In the patriarchal period through much of the monarchical period (David and Solomon), we see an acceptance of polygamy as consistent with God's law. However, in the period of the later prophets, we see monogamy being compared to God's exclusive relationship with Israel and polygamy being compared to polytheism (see Hos 1–2; Is 54; Jer 3; Ez 16). This gave preference to monogamy as an ideal (Mal 2:14–16). In post-exilic Israel monogamy had become the norm, and polygamy was a rare exception (e.g., Tb 1:10).[7] Thus the norm was monogamy, but with the possibility of divorce.

In Matthew 19:8, Jesus reveals God's complete and eternal will, saying, "For your hardness of heart Moses allowed you to divorce your wives, but from the beginning it was not so." Here, Jesus explicitly states that God's eternal will ("from the beginning") is not to allow divorce. He adds that *Moses* allowed divorce because of the hardness of their hearts. We might also add that permanent and inseparable monogamy was not part of the thought framework in which Moses and later prophets were preaching. There was no preparation for it, so it would have seemed unintelligible. However, after centuries of prophetic proclamation of the preference for monogamy and the recommendation of monogamy and wisdom literature, Jesus is able to reveal the fullness of God's Revelation about marriage as a permanent, exclusive commitment between one man and one woman (disallowing divorce). God's eternal will throughout the course of human history was a permanent, exclusive, monogamous commitment, but this could not have been understood (let alone accepted) in the patriarchal and Mosaic periods. Its intelligibility only gained acceptance with the prophetic preaching of the ideal of monogamy intrinsic to God's relationship with Israel. At the time of Jesus, the eternal will of God was ready to be revealed in its fullness.

We now proceed to three other issues in the Bible difficult to understand: human sacrifice, the command to kill everything that breathes, and the imprecatory psalms. We begin with human sacrifice. Though there are several condemnations of human sacrifice as practiced by Canaanites and other foreigners in the Old Testament,[8] there are only two instances of uncondemned human sacrifices occurring in Israel. One is during the patriarchal period — Abraham's willingness to sacrifice his son Isaac (see Gn 22) — and one during the period of the judges (early post-Mosaic period) — Jephthah's sacrifice of his daughter (Jgs 11:30–39). We begin with the observation that Jesus did not have to condemn human sacrifice, because it was strongly condemned by the Mosaic law (Lv 18:21; 20:1–5; Dt 12:31; 18:10; cf. Gn 22:2, 12–13), which led to it being declared an "abomination" associated with the Canaanite religion (Dt 12:31; 18:9–14; see 2 Kgs 17:31; Is 66:3). Though the practice was strictly condemned in the early period of the Canaanite conquest, some people who allowed themselves to be influenced by the Canaanites practiced it and were condemned for it.

So why were the above two instances of human sacrifice included in the Old Testament? Certainly, it was not in any way to approve the practice, because it was strongly condemned at the time when the Deuteronomic books (Deuteronomy, Joshua, Judges, 1 and 2 Samuel, and 1 and 2 Kings) were consolidated, around 600 BC. Thus its inclusion seems to be explicable because it actually happened, and the historical instance serves as an example of the negativity of the practice.

Jephthah's sacrifice of his daughter (see Jgs 11:30–39) illustrates what happens when Israelites take on the forbidden Canaanite practice of human sacrifice. Jephthah has broken faith with Mosaic Yahwism and has sunken back into Canaanite practices. In his corruption, he vows that if "God" delivers the Ammonites into his power, he will sacrifice whoever comes out of the door of his house to meet him to celebrate the victory. When Jephthah conquers the Ammonites, he is so steeped in his Canaanite practice that he feels compelled to carry out the vow even when his daughter is the one who comes to meet him — his only child. The moral of the story is clear: If you follow the way of the Canaanites, you will lose everything that matters to you. To the audience of the time, this is hardly a resounding approval of the practice of human sacrifice. It illustrates why Yahweh has condemned it.

The story of Abraham's attempted sacrifice of Isaac was written by the Yahwist (about 950 BC). No doubt, the Yahwist was aware of a strong historical tradition about Abraham's attempted sacrifice of Isaac, and even though it was contrary to the Mosaic law at the time (see Dt 12:29–31),[9] he includes it as an integral part of his patriarchal history. Why did he risk causing confusion about this practice in the minds of his readers?

There are two likely reasons for so doing. First, the story of Abraham and Isaac was a long and strong oral tradition, which was integral to God's covenant with Abraham. Secondly, when Abraham's intention to kill his son becomes clear, God does not allow Abraham to do any harm to Isaac (see Gn 22:12). Yet we must query, why does the narrative say that *God* asked Abraham to sacrifice his son (Gn 22:1–2)? Though Abraham certainly believed that God asked him to sacrifice his son (perhaps because it was an accepted practice of proving one's fidelity during the patriarchal period), it is impossible that God would have asked Abraham to do something that explicitly violates His moral codes throughout the rest of Israelite history. Again, Ratzinger's distinction between the central core of the message (inerrant) and the outward expression of the message (not inerrant) is helpful. The central core of the message is Abraham's absolute fidelity to God, which stands at the foundation of God's covenant with him. The outward expression of this message is Abraham's interpretation (within the patriarchal religious understanding) of how God wished him to prove his absolute fidelity — the sacrifice of his most precious son. Evidently, this patriarchal religious understanding is not part of the core message of the passage, because it is explicitly condemned by Moses and most other religious authorities through the time of Jesus.

We now move to the prescription of Moses to the Israelites to kill everything that breathes in the Canaanite nations conquered by Israel:

> But in the cities of these peoples that the LORD your God gives you for an inheritance, you shall save alive nothing that breathes, but you shall utterly destroy them, the Hittites and the Amorites, the Canaanites and the Perizzites, the Hivites and the Jebusites, as the LORD your God has commanded; that they may not teach

you to do according to all their abominable practices which they have done in the service of their gods, and so to sin against the LORD your God. (Deuteronomy 20:16–18)

How can God be commanding genocide when clearly all killing of innocent people is condemned in both the Old Testament[10] and New Testament?[11] Again, Ratzinger's distinction proves helpful because God's condemnation of killing the innocent means that He cannot be commanding Israel to do genocide. So, what is the central core of the message in the above passage from Deuteronomy? First and foremost, Israel should not accept any religious teaching or practice from the nations it has conquered. The maintenance and faithful practice of God's Revelation to Israel on Mount Sinai is the most important moral priority for the people of Yahweh. The outward expression of this message (not inerrant) is Moses' decision about *how* to maintain and faithfully practice this Revelation — "killing the competition."

Recall the threefold development of Israel's relationship with neighbors articulated by the Pontifical Biblical Commission's document on the Bible and morality: (1) excess vengeance is allowed (patriarchal period); (2) retaliation is restricted to equal vengeance alone (Mosaic period); and (3) forgiveness and turning the other cheek surpasses vengeance (Jesus). We can see something similar occurring with respect to eliminating the threat of heterodoxy: (1) the killing of heterodox peoples (patriarchal, Mosaic, and confederation periods); (2) the prophets do not require killing of the heterodox but warn of punishment of Israel for following heterodox practices (monarchical through post-exilic period); (3) loving your enemies and doing good (and praying) for those who hate you — including evangelizing them (see Mt 5:44; Lk 6:27).

As noted above, the eternal will of God is manifest in Jesus' fullness of Revelation: to love your enemies and do good to those who hate you. Recognizing God's true and eternal will in Jesus reveals the non-inerrancy of Moses' command to kill everything that breathes. The central core of the message is to maintain and faithfully practice Yahweh's Revelation as the highest moral priority. However, the outward expression of that core message (non-inerrant) is *how* to do this — killing the competition. In light of Jesus' Revelation, the command in Deuteronomy comes partially from God (to maintain and faithfully practice Yahweh's Revelation) and partly from man — Moses' interpretation of how to do this.

We now encounter the final interpretative challenge: the imprecatory psalms — psalms that curse or wish evil upon enemies.[12] Psalm 109 is a good example:

> May his children be fatherless,
>   and his wife a widow!
> May his children wander about and beg;
>   may they be driven out of the ruins they inhabit!
> May the creditor seize all that he has;
>   may strangers plunder the fruits of his toil! (vv. 9–11)

We are once again faced with a seeming conflict between the Old Testament, in which the psalmist is calling down vengeance and curses from God, and Jesus' proclamation to avoid vengeance (see Mt 5:38–39), forgive others indefinitely (Mt 18:21–22), and pray for those who hate you (Mt 5:44). The conflict is even more stark when we consider Jesus' Revelation that the perfection of His Father consists precisely in loving His enemies (Mt 5:44–48 and Lk 6:35–36). Evidently, Jesus has superseded imprecatory prayers, teaching us instead to pray compassionately and forgivingly for those who have trespassed against us (see the Our Father, Mt 6:12).

The Pontifical Biblical Commission's delineation of the three stages of development of treatment of neighbors again proves helpful. The vast majority of the imprecatory psalms were written in the Mosaic through monarchical periods, in which the prescription "an eye for an eye and a tooth for a tooth" was experienced as a restriction of the patriarchal period's allowance of an excess of vengeance. In this context, calling down a curse on one's enemy would not have been viewed as contrary to proper religious practice. However, in light of Jesus' commandment to imitate His Father's perfection in forgiving others and loving enemies, imprecatory psalms are superseded by Jesus' "fulfillment of the law" in the same way that strict justice is superseded by mercy and forgiveness. As noted above, the eternal will of the Father to forgive and love enemies would have been exceedingly difficult to understand and accept in a warrior society in which excess vengeance had to be modified by equal vengeance. In Ratzinger's words, these outward expressions of the message were a concession to the undeveloped thought frameworks[13] of the patriarchal, Mosaic, and monarchical periods.

In conclusion, how can we interpret passages of Scripture that seem to be superseded by Jesus' teaching? Two principles are most helpful:

1. The Pontifical Biblical Commission's three stages of moral development in the Old and New Testaments: (i) Patriarchal-Mosaic-Confederation, (ii) Monarchical–Post-Exilic, and (iii) Jesus himself

2. Joseph Ratzinger's distinction between the central core of the message (inerrant) and the outward form of the message that is subject to undeveloped thought frameworks (which is not inerrant)

OT#23: Are the Old Testament Miracles Historical?

Miracles, which we will broadly define as "events that are scientifically and naturalistically inexplicable," cover a wide range in the Old Testament. For example, they include extraordinarily late childbirth; plagues on Egypt; "a pillar of cloud by day and fire by night"; the parting of the Reed Sea; the sun standing still after Joshua's conquest; Elijah going up to heaven in a chariot of fire; a dead man brought back to life by Elisha; Jonah swallowed by a whale; and Shadrach, Meshach, and Abednego kept alive in a burning furnace.

How are we to interpret these miracles? Should we simply take them at face value? Four interpretative principles may prove helpful in reconciling Scripture, science, and history:

1. **Bright's principle:** Denying the historicity of certain events *a priori* because they are miraculous goes beyond the objective evidence.

2. **Bellarmine's principle:** Scientifically demonstrated fact must take precedence over scriptural interpretation to the contrary. This means that a particular scriptural interpretation cannot contradict scientifically demonstrated fact.
3. **The canon of scientific explanation:** We should first look for all possible naturalistic explanations before classifying a particular event as a miracle, "naturalistically and scientifically inexplicable."
4. **Metaphor, literary genre, and different cultural thought frameworks must be taken into consideration** alongside scientific explanation and the literal interpretation of the text to properly interpret Scripture.

We will use six Old Testament miracle stories to show how these four principles can be applied to obtain a proper interpretation of the text:

1. The ten plagues of Egypt (Exodus 7–12)
2. Israel's crossing of the Red Sea/Reed Sea (Exodus 14:22)
3. The sun and moon standing still (Joshua 10:12–14)
4. Shadrach, Meshach, and Abednego kept alive in a burning furnace (Daniel 3:19–30)
5. Jonah remaining alive in the belly of a whale (Jonah 1–2)
6. Elijah raising a boy from the dead (1 Kings 17:17–24)

We must remember that the *a priori* denial of miracles and providential action in history (the deistic enterprise) is neither scientific nor Catholic. As we shall see in NT#6 and NT#12, there are many contemporary, scientifically investigated miracles that can be reasonably and responsibly shown to be beyond current scientific explanation. If this is accepted, then we should judge a miracle to be a miracle unless we find one of the following:

- A scientific or naturalistic explanation
- A contradiction of scientifically demonstrated fact
- A highly probable use of metaphor to reinterpret a previous mythical explanation from another religion or culture (as we

saw multiple times in the primeval narratives in Genesis 1–11 — see OT#4)

- The clear use of mythopoetic literary genre or other genre not intended to communicate fact or history, but rather an illustrative fictional story or midrash

1. Were the Ten Plagues Historical and Providential?

We now turn to the plagues in Exodus 7–12. As recent scholarship has revealed, many of these plagues can be explained naturalistically, such as:

- The water that turned into "blood" (see 7:14–24) can be explained by a fast-growing red algae that can proliferate in the Nile, causing not only red coloration, but stench and even toxicity. The research of J. S. Marr and C. D. Malloy asserts: "We conclude that a freshwater dinoflagellate biomass bloom … was responsible for the change in the color of the Nile [and] the death of fish."[14]

- Frogs, gnats, flies, locusts, and pestilence of livestock are all naturalistically explicable and have occurred multiple times in documented scientific history. As we shall see, the combination of these events in spatial and temporal proximity is highly unusual and might be explained as hypernaturalistic (difficult to explain naturalistically), as distinct from supernaturalistic or "miraculous" (currently scientifically inexplicable). Even if the combination of events occurs over two years or so, it would still be hypernaturalistic — exceedingly unusual.

- Boils can be attributed to contagious skin infections. Furthermore, powerful hail and lightning storms occur in various places around the world annually, and darkness for three days can be explained in terms of naturalistic atmospheric phenomena of several kinds. Though these things should not be explained supernaturalistically, their combination in spatial and temporal proximity is exceedingly unusual and hypernaturalistic.

- The death of the Egyptian firstborn can also be explained naturalistically as coming from airborne mycotoxins resulting from moldy grain produced by the dwindling food supply in Egypt (perhaps as a result of the other plagues).[15] The fact that the disease seems to have been restricted mostly to Egyptians (rather than Hebrews) can also be explained by genetic susceptibility or circumstantial susceptibility (e.g., the Egyptians having more access to grain than the Hebrews) and the like.

Did the plagues happen? If we do not doubt the veracity of the biblical accounts simply because they are unusual, then it is not unreasonable to assert that they probably did occur, perhaps over two to three years. The coincidence of these "plagues" could reasonably be said to have affected the Egyptian grain supply, leading to the production of mycotoxins to which Egyptian infants and young children were particularly susceptible. Were these "plagues" supernatural or miraculous? Inasmuch as they can be naturalistically explained, it would not be reasonable to assert this. Nevertheless, as noted above, the spatial and temporal proximity of these unusual events makes the collection of them exceedingly unusual — what we have called *hypernaturalistic.*

Could this hypernaturalistic concurrence of unusual events have caused the Egyptian leadership to be fearful of the Hebrews? This is not out of the question, because several thousand Hebrew slaves took flight from their Egyptian captors, and made a successful journey to the Reed Sea ahead of the Egyptian military forces who pursued them. Why did the Egyptians allow this to happen — and how did the Hebrew slaves get such a considerable head start on the Egyptian military? As noted in OT#19, something truly remarkable must have stymied the Egyptian guards and military. Why wouldn't the plagues be that "remarkable something"? Why wouldn't the biblical explanation be the correct explanation? Why wouldn't Yahweh (who was about to reveal himself in a most remarkable way to Moses on Mount Sinai) be the providential power orchestrating this hypernaturalistic occurrence?

2. Was Israel's Crossing of the Red Sea/
Reed Sea Historical and Providential?

As explained in OT#19, it is highly unlikely that the Israelites crossed the Red Sea, because it is so far to the south of Pithom and Ramesses that the Egyptian detachment would have caught up to them long before they reached it. Furthermore, the Bible uses the term *Yam suph* (which is derived from an Egyptian place name), meaning "Sea of Reeds." The Septuagint translated this as "Red Sea," but this is clearly mistaken because there are no reeds near, in, or around the Red Sea. As historians look over the possibilities of crossing points for the Israelites to move from Egypt into the wilderness of Shur and the desert, the only one that appears to be close enough to avoid an Egyptian detachment while permitting an achievable, though challenging, crossing for the Israelites on foot is the marshy area between Lake Menzaleh and Lake Balah. As noted by Professor Olaf Alfred Toffteen:

> The place where Lake Menzaleh connects with Lake Balah. Between these two lakes there is now dry land. ... Formerly they were connected by shallow water, as geologists have been able to determine. ... An examination of the map will show that the only place the Hebrews could hope to penetrate ... and so pass out into the desert was across the shallow waters between Lake Balah and Lake Menzaleh. And it is not at all unlikely that a strong eastern wind could so have driven back the waters from this narrow strip of land that the place would have become passable. The two lakes, Balah and Menzaleh, would then have been the two metaphorical "walls of water on either side," of the biblical account. ... Finally that this was the route of the P [Priestly Author's] account is made more plain by the statement that after leaving "the Sea" they came into the wilderness of Shur, which is, as we have seen, to be found in this locality and nowhere else.[16]

If Toffteen is correct, then the most likely route the Israelites could have taken to avoid the Egyptian observation posts[17] while finding a passable area into the desert would have been this place. If we suppose that the

Israelites arrived a few days ahead of the Egyptian pursuers and that they were aided by a strong east wind that helped to make this marshy area more passable, then it would not be unreasonable to conjecture that the Egyptian detachment, which would have had chariots loaded with heavy armament, followed the Israelites into this marshy area, at which point they would have become bogged down, allowing the Israelites to cross safely over to the wilderness of Shur and out of the detachment's reach.[18]

Was this a miracle — a scientifically inexplicable supernatural event? Inasmuch as it can be naturalistically explained, it would not be reasonable to infer this. However, it is hypernaturalistic in the combination of so many "fortunate coincidences." How did the Israelites manage to find this best possible crossing, which avoided the Egyptian observation posts, quickly enough to avoid Egyptian capture before the crossing? Did they have scouts who were familiar with the area? Did they simply follow the route that avoided the Egyptian observation posts, which ultimately led to this crossing, which the Egyptian army with its chariots and armaments could not traverse? Was there some kind of providential inspiration as well (as the biblical text asserts)? It seems very coincidental that all the puzzle pieces needed for the escape just happened to come together before the Egyptian detachment caught up with them.

Whatever the case, the historicity of an Israelite crossing into the desert, which was not followed up by an Egyptian detachment, cannot be doubted unless one is willing to doubt the exodus itself. However, if we deny the exodus, how are we to explain how several thousand cohesively united slaves arrived at Mount Sinai to receive the Revelation of Yahweh, which formed the basis for the Israelite military detachments that initiated the Canaanite conquest? If denying the exodus is unreasonable, then the Israelites' escape into the desert is virtually certain. Did it happen between Lake Menzaleh and Lake Balah? If it did not happen there, then where? What would be more reasonable than this "perfect" spot — perfect for the Israelite crossing, perfect to prevent the Egyptians from pursuing them, perfect in its avoidance of Egyptian outposts along the way, and perfect in its proximity to achieve an Israelite crossing before the Egyptian detachment could arrive? This may not be, strictly speaking, a "miracle," but it strongly suggests a providential guiding hand to explain the perfect coincidences. Why wouldn't such a providential guiding hand be that of Yahweh himself guiding His people to one of the most extraordinary revelations at Mount Sinai that would change the course of the history of religions forever (see OT#20)?

3. Is the Sun and Moon Standing Still Historical and Providential?
In Joshua 10:12–14, we read:

> Then spoke Joshua to the LORD in the day when the LORD gave the Amorites over to the men of Israel; and he said in the sight of Israel,
>
> > "Sun, stand thou still at Gibeon,
> > and thou Moon in the valley of Aijalon."
> > And the sun stood still, and the moon stayed,
> > until the nation took vengeance on their enemies.
>
> Is this not written in the Book of Jashar? The sun stayed in the midst of heaven, and did not hasten to go down for about a whole day. There has been no day like it before or since, when the LORD hearkened to the voice of a man; for the LORD fought for Israel.

From a scientific perspective, a literal interpretation of this text cannot have been factual. For if the sun and moon were to stand still, it would require the earth to cease rotating on its own axis. We can be sure that this did not happen, because it would mean total geological disaster, basically putting an end to civilization and life on earth as we know it.[19]

So, is there another way of interpreting this passage that might allow it to be factual or historical? There is if we allow the Hebrew terms ordinarily translated as "stand still" to mean, "the sun and moon to stop doing what they ordinarily do." Sir Colin Humphreys believes that this is a plausible translation of the Hebrew: "Going back to the original Hebrew text, we determined that an alternative meaning could be that the sun and moon just stopped doing what they normally do: they stopped shining."[20]

The Hebrew translated as "stand still" is דֹם (do·vm). According to *Strong's Concordance*, this phrase means to be or grow dumb, silent, or still.[21] Sir Colin Humphreys' interpretation of דֹם (do·vm) as the sun and moon stopping doing what they ordinarily do — shining — is quite reasonable and, as we shall see, more plausible than the translation "stand still."

Is there a plausible scientific explanation for why the sun and moon would stop shining throughout the better course of a day when Joshua is fighting the Amorites? The most obvious answer would be an atmospheric phenomenon, which blocked solar and lunar radiation — such as a thick cloud of dust, desert sand, volcanic ash, an extra-heavy hailstorm, or another natural obstruction that is more opaque than a thick cluster of clouds.[22] If such an atmospheric obstruction occurred between 1200 and 1150 BC, it would be very difficult to validate today because these kinds of phenomena dissipate with the wind, rain, and other natural clearing forces. Such natural phenomena are well within plausible scientific explanation, and so the passage translated as "the sun and moon not doing what they ordinarily do" is not a violation of observable fact.

Humphreys and his colleague in astrophysics, Dr. Graeme Waddington, believe that the explanation may lie in a solar/lunar phenomenon rather than an atmospheric one. Though this explanation need not be entertained to maintain the scientific defensibility of the biblical passage, it offers another interesting naturalistic alternative explanation. Thanks to new computerized calculations that can factor in slight variations in the earth's rotation, Humphreys and Waddington show that there could well have been an annular eclipse (where the moon passes between the sun and the earth) causing significant darkening (though not total darkening) for a few hours. According to their calculations, it would have occurred October 30, 1207 BC, starting in the afternoon. If Joshua was fighting the Amorites on that day (which is consistent with the timeline established by most modern scholars), then this might also be a plausible scientific explanation for the reported phenomenon in the Book of Joshua.

Was this a *super*natural (miraculous) event (scientifically inexplicable)? Once again, it cannot be considered to be *super*natural because it can be naturalistically explained. However, it appears to be *hyper*natural, because if this highly unusual atmospheric or solar/lunar event actually coincided with Joshua's victory over the Amorites, the timing coincidence would be very remarkable. What are the odds?

So, was there a darkening of the sun and moon during Joshua's fight against the Amorites? It is certainly within the realm of scientific and historical plausibility. Was it a miracle? Strictly speaking, it was not, but once again we are faced with a truly remarkable coincidence whose probability is so low that the event appears to be hypernatural.

4. Is the Story of the Fiery Furnace of Shadrack, Meshach, and Abednego Historical and Providential?

The previous three miracle stories resemble one another insofar as they are historically and scientifically plausible, and hypernaturalistic in their exceedingly low probability but are not miraculous *per se* (scientifically inexplicable). This miracle story and the next one (concerning Jonah) were selected to contrast with the previous three stories to illustrate other criteria of analysis, particularly that of literary genre. In Daniel 3, we read:

> Then these men were bound in their mantles, their tunics, their hats, and their other garments, and they were cast into the burning fiery furnace. Because the king's order was strict and the furnace very hot, the flame of the fire slew those men who took up Shadrach, Meshach, and Abednego. And these three men, Shadrach, Meshach, and Abednego, fell bound into the burning fiery furnace. *But the angel of the Lord came down into the furnace to be with Azariah and his companions, and drove the fiery flame out of the furnace, and made the midst of the furnace like a moist whistling wind, so that the fire did not touch them at all or hurt or trouble them.* (vv. 21–23, 26–27)

Is this miracle scientifically plausible? Though no non-contradictory event is impossible for God, the event described in Daniel 3 would be naturalistically impossible, scientifically inexplicable, and miraculous if it really did occur as described in the above passage. Since miracles are possible for God, science (which is restricted to the naturalistic domain) cannot rule them out.

However, it is quite likely that the event as described was not meant to be historical but rather a haggadic story used to illustrate a moral theme — that God will protect and reward those who keep His law, even in times of persecution. The vast majority of Scripture scholars today would view Daniel 1–6 as either haggada or haggadic.[23] *Haggada* is a story that has no basis in history; haggadic midrash is a story that is based to some limited extent on history and is a fictional elaboration of it. The purpose of both kinds of stories is a moral lesson — not history. According to Fr. Louis Hartman (chairman of the board of editors of the New Catholic Bible in English) and Fr. Alexander Di Lella, OFM (professor of semitic languages at the Catholic University of America):

> Stories about Daniel are clearly haggadic; in their entirety, they cannot be taken as strict history. Inasmuch as their author does not intend them as historical, he cannot be accused of error if he makes inaccurate statements about history. We have no way of knowing whether the Daniel of these stories was really a historical character, about whom popular legends gradually clustered, or whether he was simply a creation of Jewish folklore.[24]

As can be seen, the literary genre of a particular text reveals the intention of its author. Insofar as Daniel 1–6 is either haggada (a story unrelated to history) or haggadic midrash (a story grounded in a historical event but a free, fictional elaboration of it), the intention of its author is decidedly *not* historical but rather moral (and possibly prophetic).[25]

So, what might we glean from our analysis of the story of the fiery furnace? Inasmuch as it was not intended to be historical, we cannot suppose that the miracle occurred as described; rather, it is a fictional story (possibly based on historical characters) meant to elaborate the moral lesson of remaining faithful to God's law in the midst of persecution. Can this be viewed as deceptive intent on the part of the author of Daniel? Of course not. The Jewish audience would be able to recognize haggada and haggadic midrash (which were common to Jewish biblical expression in the Old Testament and intertestamental periods) and would have searched for the moral lesson — not a historical fact. This was the point that Pope Pius XII made in his encyclical *Divino Afflante Spiritu* when he said:

> Let the interpreter then, with all care and without neglecting any
> light derived from recent research, endeavor to determine the pe-
> culiar character and circumstances of the sacred writer, the age
> in which he lived, the sources written or oral to which he had re-
> course and the forms of expression [literary genre] he employed.[26]

In view of the haggadic literary genre intended by the author, it is highly
probable that the fiery-furnace incident related in Daniel was not historical, and therefore, we need not consider whether or not it was a miracle.
It is meant only to illustrate a moral lesson.

5. Jonah Remaining Alive in the Belly of a Whale

Many people wonder whether the story about Jonah being in the belly
of the whale for three days is historical. Evidently, if it were historical,
it would be indisputably miraculous. However, the vast majority of the
scholarly community do not consider it to be historical for the same reason as the Daniel story of the fiery furnace: literary genre. Fr. Anthony
Ceresko, DBS (former professor of biblical studies at the University of St.
Michael's in Toronto) indicates that the entire Book of Jonah, including
the story about Jonah in the belly of the whale, was not meant to be historical, but rather a prophetic story or legend with a moral theme:

> The author [of Jonah] is clearly not intent on presenting us with
> an historical account. The issues with which he deals — primar-
> ily the mercy and justice of God — as well as the obvious exag-
> gerations the book contains indicate that he has another purpose
> in mind. Thus critical scholarship has rightly abandoned the at-
> tempt to treat the book as history. ... It thus may accurately be
> described as a *masal* or parable: a "comparison" in brilliant story
> form that seeks to illuminate an issue ... it is found among "the
> Prophets," and rightly so. Its story form is reminiscent of the so-
> called prophetic legends.[27]

Thus the Jonah story should not be considered historical.

6. Elijah Raises a Boy from the Dead

This miracle story contrasts with the previous two in that the intention of the author is to report history. It does not contradict any known historical facts, and if it really did occur, it would be miraculous (scientifically inexplicable). In 1 Kings 17:17–22, we read:

> After this the son of the woman, the mistress of the house, became ill; and his illness was so severe that there was no breath left in him. And she said to Elijah, "What have you against me, O man of God? You have come to me to bring my sin to remembrance, and to cause the death of my son!" And he said to her, "Give me your son." And he took him from her bosom, and carried him up into the upper chamber, where he lodged, and laid him upon his own bed. And he cried to the LORD, "O LORD my God, hast thou brought calamity even upon the widow with whom I sojourn, by slaying her son?" Then he stretched himself upon the child three times, and cried to the LORD, "O LORD my God, let this child's soul come into him again." And the LORD hearkened to the voice of Elijah; and the soul of the child came into him again, and he revived.

So what is the literary genre of 1 and 2 Kings? Though they are intended as historical, they are not history as we would conceive of it today, with reportorial accuracy, verifiability, and exhaustiveness.[28] Neither are they social or political history but rather, theological history — a set of traditions and narratives (stories) assembled in a generally chronologically accurate way for a primarily theological purpose: to explain why Israel failed in its covenant with Yahweh requiring purification through exile into Babylon.[29] Thus there can be errors in the chronicling of events, inaccuracies in traditions and stories, and the subordination of historical accuracy to the requirements for illustrating the main theological point.[30] Notwithstanding these departures from modern historical objectives and method, 1 and 2 Kings have considerable historical value, and as Bright implies, should be assumed to be historically accurate unless they disagree with historical records, observable naturalistic facts, or suffer from internal inconsistencies.

What about the specific narrative of Elijah raising a dead boy to life (see 1 Kgs 17:17–24)? First, we may be fairly certain that Elijah was a miracle worker — not only because of the number of miracle stories associated with him (in contrast to other prophets) but also because of the number of different sources that mention or allude to this in both the Old and New Testaments.[†] Within this general context, this narrative of Elijah stretching himself over the boy three times (and other details) seems to be referring to a specific set of historical circumstances in a specific narrative tradition, with which the author of 1 Kings — the Deuteronomist — was familiar.

What might science say about such a historical narrative? If we assume the details mentioned in the story are accurate, and the boy in question was truly dead (not in a profound comatose or vegetative state), then following Bright's principle of according historicity unless proven otherwise, we conclude that Elijah performed a miracle of similar magnitude to Jesus' and Saint Paul's raisings of the dead. Elijah performs the miracle by being an intercessor of *God's* power, but Jesus raises the dead by His own power, and Paul raises the dead through the power of the *Holy Spirit* in the name of *Jesus*.

Conclusion

So how should we interpret miracles in the Old Testament? The following five-step process is a systematic way of applying the principles about which we have spoken:

1. We must first check the literary genre of the narrative to determine whether the author's intention is to be historical or something else. If something else, then it is not a real miracle.
2. If there is good reason to believe in the historicity of the narrative, we must ascertain whether or not there is a contradiction of some verified *natural* facts in the narrative. If so, then

---

† There are multiple references in 1 and 2 Kings, as well as 2 Chronicles 21:12–17, and the three Synoptic Gospels, particularly in Elijah's appearance at Jesus' Transfiguration, and also in the epistles of James and Hebrews. His mention at the Transfiguration reveals his high stature, similar to that of Moses, in the Old Testament. His miracle working, along with his prophetic importance, is integral to this high stature.

the event in question is neither historical nor a miracle.

3. If there are no contradictions of natural fact, we must try to explain the extraordinary phenomenon by means of natural causation.

4. If there are possible natural causes, then we may infer that the event is either purely natural or, if highly improbable, *hyper-natural*, implying some form of providential action to explain its occurrence amidst high improbability.

5. If there is no natural explanation, and the event is scientifically inexplicable, then it can be reasonably viewed as a likely miracle.

OT#24: Are Old Testament Prophecies Inspired by God?

About 25 percent of the Old Testament is concerned with prophecy — not simply in the eighteen prophetic books but also in the historical books, particularly on the lips of Moses, Samuel, Elijah, and Elisha. Most Christians and Jews hold that most of the fulfilled prophecies were inspired by God, for which there is considerable evidence, not only in the fulfilled prophecies themselves but also in the unique objectives of Jewish prophecy. Though some skeptics believe that fulfilled prophecies are mere coincidences or the result of later generations reading later events into the writings of earlier prophets, deeper analysis shows that this is far too simplistic and that Old Testament prophecy is uncannily predictive and quite mysterious. When all the facts are considered, particularly the historical Jesus as the fulfillment of Messianic prophecies, the best explanation for this unique historical phenomenon is the inspiration of God. We will examine this phenomenon in three sections:

1. The unique high development of Jewish prophecy (section 1)
2. Prophecies fulfilled in the Old Testament (section 2)
3. Messianic prophecies fulfilled in Jesus Christ (section 3)

1. The Unique and High Development of Israelite Prophecy

Israel's view of prophecy was so unique in its personal morality, social morality, eschatology, and independence from governmental authority that it cannot be derived from any other religion or culture in the Near East. Israelite prophecy originated in large part from within the Yahwistic community. This unique form of prophecy is highly developed in five areas, which affected not only the religion of Israel but also her culture and society. When this is combined with the Messianic prophecies fulfilled in Jesus, we see a huge development in the history of religion and culture: a God who not only cares about His people but makes religious, moral, and social demands of them.

As Judeo-Christian thought spread into the world of Asia Minor and Rome, it began to transform law, government, society, and culture — not only in Europe but to every point on the globe. As such, Yahwistic monotheism and Israelite prophecy fulfilled by Jesus Christ became the most powerful transformative forces in world history.

Like in other nations, several individuals in Israel found themselves "called" to be seers or interpreters of the divine will. The inspiration of these seers and diviners often included ecstasies, visions, and spiritual experiences that bore the qualities of awe, mystery, spirit, and sacredness. Though Israelite prophets shared with other prophets the call to be interpreters of the divine will, the will of Israel's singular divinity was quite different from that of the many divinities of Israel's neighbors. Yahweh demanded personal integrity and justice because He created human beings in His own image. However, the deities of Israel's neighbors were frequently capricious, unjust, needlessly destructive, and subjugators of humanity. In addition to the demand for personal and social justice, Yahweh also required compassion for widows, orphans, aliens, and the poor. These unique advances of Israelite prophecy eventually found their way into the social and legal system, became embedded in the culture, and when combined with the message and practice of Jesus, transformed the history of religions as well as the evolution of justice, natural law, natural rights, the common good, social welfare, and the intrinsic dignity of individuals throughout the world.

So what are the five unique, advanced characteristics of Israelite prophets?

1. Israelite prophets were not primarily diviners or seers of the future but interpreters of the *moral* will of Yahweh. They predicted the future only in relation to how Israel obeyed or disobeyed His moral will. The prophets of surrounding countries attempted to forecast the future to give their *kings* advantage in war, trade, and politics, while Israelite prophets' primary responsibility was to manifest the moral will of *Yahweh*, which if obeyed would allow Israel to prosper but if disobeyed, would lead to Israel's disadvantage and downfall.[31]

2. Israelite prophets acted as the conscience of Israel. They judged not only individuals but the highest social authorities, including the king. The court prophets of other nations existed to serve the king — not to judge, speak against, or oppose him. However, Israel's prophets served Yahweh, having the responsibility to judge the king as Yahweh's representatives.[32]

3. Israelite prophets considered themselves the spokesmen for widows, orphans, the poor, and above all, the oppressed, who were close to the heart of Yahweh. They spoke out frequently to oppose the unjust actions of kings against the powerless and the poor — for example, Nathan's judgment of David for taking Bathsheba and killing Uriah her husband (see 2 Sm 12:1–12), and Elijah's judgment of Ahab and Jezebel (1 Kgs 21:17–28).[33]

4. Israelite prophets forecasted the future only in terms of Israel's fidelity or infidelity to Yahweh; they did not view the future as cast in stone, but rather as malleable — in Yahweh's hands to determine as He chose according to the conduct of Israel and her leaders. Thus Israel's prophets did not adhere to "an eternal return" or fatalistic view of history and the future but rather to a linear, malleable view of history and the future. This view of prophecy, history, and the future was distinctive to Israel.[34]

5. Israelite prophecy was not viewed as merely "for Israel" but affected Yahweh's plan for the entire world throughout the course of history. This universalistic eschatological view of Israel's significance for the world and human history is again quite distinctive, not only in the prophetic realm but also in the history of religions itself. How could such a small nation (and the itinerant prophets of this small nation) be so confident about Israel's (and their own) universal, historical, and eschatological significance?[35]

From the time of Moses through the times of Samuel, Nathan, Gad, Elijah, Elisha, Isaiah, Jeremiah, Ezekiel, Daniel, Zechariah, and all the other remarkable Israelite prophets, Israel was distinctive in its practice of prophecy, reflecting a most distinctive, if not unique, conception of herself. The five areas in which Israel's prophets showed their distinctiveness had world-transforming effects with respect to: the moral conception of God; the moral requirements of individuals and political authorities; the moral requirement for compassion and justice toward the poor and oppressed; divine interaction with human history; the non-fatalistic view of history in the future; and the universal and eschatological significance of the Chosen People and their Messiah for world history.

The significance of this view of prophecy (and messiahship) — for the development of morality, social justice, compassion for the poor, and the conception of God and divine providence in world history — cannot be underestimated. Without it, we would have a completely different world, and not for the better. Israelite prophecy alone would not bring about this transformation. It needed and anticipated the fulfillment of Israel's Messiah, who would be more than a prophet; He would be Yahweh's own anointed (Messiah), destined to bring the law and prophets to their fulfillment in Israel and beyond (for example, see Ps 22; Is 7:14, 9:6, 52:13–53:12; Dn 7:13–14).

We are again confronted with the question stated above: How did little Israel (and its comparatively small band of distinctive prophets) come up with this world-transforming view of prophecy and messiahship? No doubt, this goes back to Moses' revelation of what we have called Yahwistic monotheism, with its distinctive view of God (Yahweh), Yahweh's moral intention, and Israel's distinctive role in human history (see OT#20). Yet, this still leaves us with the question of how Moses came to this distinctive view of Yahweh's moral intention and how the Israelite prophets came to their unique practice of prophecy to reveal Yahweh's continued moral interaction with Israel in her ongoing history. To believe that this incredibly transformative revelation happened through the creativity of Moses and some of his successor prophets alone is beyond the realm of reason. Moses and the prophets' own explanation is much more likely: Yahweh inspired them so that the Revelation of Israel could inspire the world.

Is there any other way of validating the inspiration of Yahweh in Israel's prophets besides the remarkable occurrence of Israelite prophecy itself? Yes — by the fulfillment of their prophecies. This is the subject of our next section.

2. Prophecies Fulfilled in the Old Testament

The following table shows several prophecies that were fulfilled in the Old Testament itself. The first column shows the prophecy and its source; the second column, the approximate date of the prophecy; the third column, the fulfillment of the prophecy; and the fourth column, the approximate date of the fulfillment.

Prophecy and Source	Approximate Date of Prophecy	Event Fulfilling the Prophecy	Approximate Date of Fulfillment
Yahweh's promise to Moses of the promised land (see Ex 3:8)	Approximately 1200 BC. This is a Mosaic prophecy — not Yahwist author.[‡]	The conquest of the many lands of Canaan	Approximately 1000 BC — conquest completed (see OT#21)

[‡] Moses needed inspiration and promise from Yahweh both for himself and the Israelite people he was to congregate and galvanize for the exodus. Without such a promise, it is highly unlikely that Moses or the people would have dared to leave their Egyptian captors.

Proto-Isaiah's prophecy of the fall of the Northern Kingdom (Israel) to Assyria (Is 28:1–4)§	Approximately 742–730 BC	The fall of the Northern Kingdom to Assyria — documented in 2 Kings 17. Also documented in Assyrian records.	Approximately 723–722 BC
Amos's prophecy of the fall of the Northern Kingdom (Israel) to Assyria (Am 2:13–16)	Approximately 750 BC	The fall of the Northern Kingdom to Assyria — documented in 2 Kings 17. Also documented in Assyrian records.	Approximately 723–722 BC
Jeremiah prophecies not only the fall of the Southern Kingdom (Judah) but also seventy years of exile and ultimate restoration of Judah, the temple, and Israelite court (Jer 25:9–12; 28:3–4, 11; 29:10)	Approximately 605 BC[36]	First and second deportation of Judah to Babylon, sixty years of exile, and ultimate restoration of Judah by Cyrus the Great of Persia	First deportation — approximately 598/597 BC. Second deportation — approximately 587 BC. Exile ends — approximately 538 BC. Restoration of temple completed — approximately 516–515 BC.

3. Messianic Prophecies Fulfilled in Jesus Christ

The topic of Messianic prophecies requires some special preparation, but once done, allows us to enter into a world of the Lord's plan for salvation and His preannouncement of it through Israel's prophets. To do this, we will divide this section into three parts:

---

§ The Book of Isaiah has three authors: Proto-Isaiah, a pre-exilic prophet who wrote chapters 1 through 39; Deutero-Isaiah, an exilic prophet living in Babylon during the time of exile, who wrote chapters 40 through 55; and Trito-Isaiah, a post-exilic prophet who wrote chapters 56 through 66.

3.A. Three Senses of Scripture

There are three major senses of Scripture addressed in the Pontifical Biblical Commission's document *On the Interpretation of the Bible in the Church*[37]: the literal sense, the spiritual sense, and the fuller sense. The literal sense of Scripture has two elements: the literal meaning of the words and how those words were intended by the biblical author within his time and culture. In the exegetical process, one first establishes the text to be investigated (examining the manuscript evidence), then pieces together the writer's outlook and intention, and then applies exegetical methods to interpret the way it was likely intended by the biblical author. The spiritual sense is the reading of the literal text through the inspiration of the Holy Spirit to derive spiritual benefit, growth, and conversion.[38]

The fuller sense (*sensus plenior*) is the deeper meaning of a scriptural text, which is intended by God but not clearly expressed by the biblical author. The fuller sense can be identified when a particular passage (say, an Old Testament prophecy) is seen in the light of a later Scripture passage that gives it a new meaning or application beyond the one directly intended by the biblical author. So, for example, if we take the text of Isaiah 7:14 ("Therefore the Lord himself will give you a sign. Behold, a young woman shall conceive and bear a son, and shall call his name Immanuel") and see it through the interpretive lens of a later Scripture text like Matthew 1:22–23 ("All this took place to fulfil what the Lord had spoken by the prophet: 'Behold, a virgin shall conceive and bear a son, and his name shall be called Emmanuel'"), we may infer that God intended the Isaiah text to refer to His Son, Jesus, even though the biblical author seemingly did not intend this.[39] The Pontifical Biblical Commission also added that if a Scripture text is given subsequent interpretation by an official Church doctrine, this too would indicate that the Holy Spirit intended this fuller meaning (given in the Church doctrine), even though the biblical author did not intend or express it.[40]

How does this apply to Messianic prophecies? It shows that God's intention is sufficient for the biblical author's prophecy to have a fuller (Messianic) meaning even though the biblical author did not intend it. Furthermore, God's intention can be discerned in the text's interpretation in a later passage of Scripture or an official Church document. In view of this, the Emmanuel prophecy (in Isaiah 7:14) can be legitimately interpreted as God's intended reference to His Son, Jesus Christ, even though the biblical author seems to have been referring to a non-Messianic future event — that a wife of Ahaz would bear a son, which would enable the dynasty to continue ensuring that "God" would "remain with us."[41]

3.B. The Relevance of Jewish Targums

The Targums are an expanded Aramaic translation of the Hebrew Bible, which weaves interpretive comments and alternative expressions into the original text.[42] In the first century AD, Aramaic was the common language, while Hebrew was little understood among the majority of the Jewish community. As a result, Jewish Scripture scholars translated the Hebrew text into Aramaic while interweaving explanatory words or phrases. By looking at early Targums such as Targum Jonathan (written around the first or second century AD), we can discover how non-Christian Jewish Scripture scholars interpreted the scriptural text. This is particularly important for determining whether Jewish scholars and interpreters believed that a particular prophetic text was intended Messianically, independent of any knowledge or recognition of Jesus Christ as the fulfillment of those prophecies.

Due to space limitations, we will focus on Targum Jonathan,[43] because it was an early Targum in Palestine before it was moved to Babylon, becoming a well-known Aramaic translation of the prophets in that area.[44] If Targum Jonathan holds that a particular prophecy was intended to be Messianic from a non-Christian point of view, it helps to eliminate the accusation that Christians are reading a Messianic interpretation of these prophecies back into a text that was not intended in that way. Combining the likelihood of the prophet's Messianic intention (according to Jewish interpreters) with the remarkable fulfillment of those prophecies in Jesus Christ provides significant insight into the Lord's providential plan to save us through His incarnate Son, not only as it unfolded in history but also as

He foretold it through His appointed prophets.

3.C. Table of Fulfilled Old Testament Messianic Prophecies in Jesus Christ

The Prophet and Prophecy	Approximate Date of Prophecy	Jewish/Targum Reference	Fulfillment of Prophecy in Jesus Christ and Scripture Source
Proto-Isaiah — "A young woman shall conceive and bear a son, and shall call his name Immanuel." (Is 7:14)	Approximately 742–730 BC	No Targum, but pre-Christian Jewish translators of Septuagint translated *almah* as "virgin"	Matthew believes this to be fulfilled in Jesus Christ (see Mt 1:22–23)
Proto-Isaiah prophecies that a child will be called "Wonderful Counselor, Mighty God, Everlasting Father, Prince of Peace," and His reign will have no end (Is 9:6–7)	Approximately 742–730 BC	Targum Jonathan identifies as Messianic (probably because of divine characteristics and endless reign)[45]	Implicitly fulfilled in all four Gospel references to the divinity and endless reign of Jesus
Deutero-Isaiah's First Servant Song, indicating that the servant will have Yahweh's own Spirit, will bring justice to the whole world — not just Israel — and will be gentle and humble of heart (Is 42:1–4)	Approximately 538 BC	Targum Jonathan calls it Messianic (probably because of the mention of God's Spirit and having authority to bring universal justice)	Matthew explicitly indicates that this prophecy is fulfilled in Jesus (Mt 12:18–21)

Deutero-Isaiah's Fourth Servant Song (Suffering Servant), indicating that God's chosen, high, exalted, and innocent servant will suffer greatly to redeem the sins of many (Is 52:13–53:12)	Approximately 538 BC	Most pre-Christian Jewish commentators indicated that this prophecy was Messianic.[46] Targum Jonathan also indicates it is Messianic (probably because the servant is innocent and has the authority to redeem the sins of people throughout the world on behalf of Yahweh).	Jesus explicitly declares this prophecy fulfilled in himself in His Eucharistic words, "This is my blood of the covenant, which is poured out for many for the forgiveness of sins" (Mt 26:28 — see Is 53:12).
Trito-Isaiah's prophecy that the Lord will bring good tidings to the afflicted, brokenhearted, and prisoners (Is 61:1)	Approximately 537 to 534 BC	No Targums or Jewish Messianic references	Jesus himself states that this prophecy finds its true fulfillment in Him, because it is freedom from death, sin, and the evil spirit — not simply freedom from Babylon. (See Luke 4:18. This is an example of the fuller sense.)

| Psalm 22 — "My God, my God, why have you forsaken me?," which is not a psalm of abandonment but one of trust and victory through suffering, leading to universal redemption — for Israel and the Gentiles — past, present, and future (Ps 22:27–31) | Before 600 BC (the Babylonian Exile) | Non-Christian Jewish midrash of the eighth century indicates that this psalm refers not just to David's suffering but future events[47] | By quoting this psalm on the cross (Mt 27:46), Jesus claims it to be fulfilled in himself. Therefore, He gives the last verses about universal salvation for all places and times (Ps 22:27–31) fulfillment in His self-sacrificial death. There are also four dimensions of the psalm fulfilled in Jesus' historical crucifixion: 1) Being despised by the people/onlookers who mock and deride Him (Mt 27:39–43); 2) "my tongue cleaves to my jaws" (Ps 22:15) and "I thirst" (Jn 19:28); 3) "pierced my hands and my feet" (Ps 22:16) and piercing wounds of crucifixion (Lk 24:39; Jn 20:20, 25–27)[48]; 4) "they divide my garments … and cast lots" (Ps 22:18) — fulfilled in Mt 27:35. |

There are other Messianic prophecies in the Book of Zechariah (see Zec 9:9; 11:12–13, and especially 12:10–12), but the above prophecies are sufficient to show that these prophecies (identified as Messianic by pre-Christian and non-Christian Jewish scholars) are fulfilled in an amazingly accurate way in Jesus Christ. When we consider that these prophecies were attributed Messianically to a future Redeemer of the whole world many hundreds of years before Jesus, it strongly suggests divine intention and inspiration far beyond human capacity. A summary of some of the prophetic oracles given in the above table are as follows:

- There will be one designated as Emmanuel ("God with us") who will reign over the nations (see Is 7:14).
- There will be one called Mighty God, Wonder Counselor, and Prince of Peace whose reign will not end (Is 9:6–7).
- There will be a Servant with the Spirit of Yahweh to bring justice to the world with true gentleness and humbleness of heart (Is 42:1–4).
- There will be an exalted and high servant of Yahweh who will suffer greatly and self-sacrificially to intercede for the sins of many throughout the world (Is 52:13–53:12).
- There will be one who is persecuted, mocked, derided, pierced, and tortured, who will through His sacrifice win redemption for Israel and the world in the past, present, and future (Ps 22).

These prophecies differ from the mainstream expectations of the Messiah, who was conceived of as very powerful, soldierly, and heroic in the classical sense. The one who emerged showed himself to be Emmanuel, the mighty God, through His compassion, gentleness, and humbleness of heart, and above all, His self-sacrificial suffering unto death that demonstrated conclusively that God is unconditional love. How could these Messianic prophecies have anticipated this without the inspiration of God himself?

Conclusion to Part One — The Old Testament

The Old Testament is constituted by traditions, stories, prophecies, prayers, and poetry developed throughout hundreds of years. It contains Revelation about the creation of the world, the specialness of human beings, the election of Israel, and the unique Yahwistic religious tradition arising out of the Mosaic covenant at Sinai and the prophetic tradition following from it. This means that it must be interpreted in the light of its literary genre, as well as the facts of history and science understood through their proper methods — a procedure approved by the Catholic Church (see OT#2). Furthermore, the Old Testament Revelation must be seen in the light of the fullness of Revelation — Jesus Christ. This means, as Joseph Ratzinger notes, a definitive interpretation of the Old Testament lies beyond any individual or group of Scripture scholars and historians who might have biases and lacunae in their interpretation. Therefore, definitive interpretation must reside in the Church given the supreme authority to do so by Jesus himself — the Catholic Church (see OT#2 and NT#18).[49]

In the twenty-four units of part 1, we have set out several sets of rules to allow the light of science, reason, history, and other rational disciplines to help discover the historicity, meaning, and importance of the Revelation that Yahweh gave His covenant people over many centuries:

- Rules for interpreting the creation of the world and natural events (OT#2 and OT#4)
- Rules for determining biblical inerrancy (OT #2)
- Rules for interpreting historical events (OT#3 and OT#18–OT#19)
- Rules for interpreting Old Testament miracles (OT#23)
- Rules for interpreting Old Testament prophecies (OT#24)

We have seen that there is considerable complementarity among Old Testament Revelation, science, history, and New Testament Revelation, particularly in the following areas:

- Science provides the "what" and "how" of creation and the natural world, while Scripture provides the "why" of creation. Furthermore, science and philosophy can corroborate the "whether" and the "what" of God (a unique, uncaused, unrestricted, intelligent Creator of everything else), and Scripture can reveal the "who" (heart) of God.
- The scientific view of creation and evolution can be reconciled with the biblical account of creation if we do not force the Bible to do science or force science to give the revelation of the "why" and "who" of God (see OT#2 and OT#13–OT#17).
- The Old Testament revelation of the soul, transcendence, and the specialness of human beings is now confirmed by science (peer-reviewed medical studies of near-death experiences and terminal lucidity), current philosophy of mind /consciousness, and contemporary anthropological and linguistic studies. The human soul is not only likely to survive bodily death but is the source for intellectual and linguistic activities, self-consciousness, and transcendental awareness that cannot be explained by physical processes alone (see OT#11–OT#12).
- If we follow the norms of contemporary biblical exegesis and history, we can confirm the historicity of many parts of the narratives concerned with the patriarchs, the descent into Egypt, the exodus and desert wandering, the covenant at Sinai, the Israelite conquest of the promised land, and the establishment of the monarchy (see OT#18–OT#21).
- Yahwism is unique in its importance for the development of religion, personal morality, social morality, and culture (see OT#20).
- We can determine the validity of both hypernatural and supernatural phenomena in the Old Testament by using the rules to make such a determination (see OT#23).
- The Old Testament prophecies are unique and valid — both those fulfilled in the Old Testament and the Messianic prophecies fulfilled in Jesus in the New Testament (see OT#24).

When these fundamental truths of the Old Testament are seen in light of the fullness of Revelation — Jesus Christ — we can see the providential hand of God, establishing the many layers of foundation for the coming of His Son to redeem humanity from the power of darkness and to reveal His unconditional love and the path to salvation. This is the subject of part 2 — the New Testament.

Part Two

Questions about the New Testament

The purpose of this part is to answer the "great questions" of science, reason, and faith arising out of the New Testament. In part 1, we discussed topics concerned with science and the existence of God and a transphysical soul, science and the Old Testament, the historicity of the Old Testament, and miracles and prophecies in the Old Testament. We now turn to four areas of reason and faith arising out of the New Testament:

1. The historicity of Jesus Christ and the events recounted in the New Testament
2. Recent scientifically testable evidence for Jesus' miracles,

crucifixion, and resurrection
3. Contemporary scientifically investigated miracles associated with Jesus, the holy Eucharist, and Mary (the mother of Jesus)
4. The historicity of Jesus' commission of Peter and founding of the Catholic Church

As we have already seen in part 1, scientific, historiographical, and exegetical research do not run contrary to the existence of God, the soul, and the Old Testament but rather support them probatively, allowing each pursuit — reason and faith — to complement and elucidate the other. This is demonstrated even more probatively in the historiographical and scientific investigation of the New Testament.

Part 2 has four chapters:

- **Chapter 6**: **NT#1–NT#4** — The Historicity of the Gospels
- **Chapter 7**: **NT#5–NT#8** — The Life and Miracles of Jesus: History and Science
- **Chapter 8**: **NT#9–NT#12** — The Passion of Jesus and the Eucharist: History and Science
- **Chapter 9**: **NT#13–NT#18** — The Resurrection, Holy Spirit, and Catholic Church: History and Science

CHAPTER 6
The Historicity of the Gospels

NT#1: What Is the Extratestamental Evidence for the Historical Jesus?

There are three extratestamental testimonies of the existence and crucifixion of Jesus that were written by hostile sources close to the time of Jesus:

1. The Roman historian Cornelius Tacitus (section 1)
2. The Jewish historian Flavius Josephus (section 2)
3. The Sanhedrin 43a text of the Babylonian Talmud (section 3)

1. The Roman Historian Cornelius Tacitus

The Roman historian Cornelius Tacitus, writing between AD 98 and 117, makes explicit reference to the crucifixion of Jesus in the *Annals* (15.44) when speaking about Nero's blaming the Christians for the burning of Rome:

> Consequently, to get rid of the report, Nero fastened the guilt

and inflicted the most exquisite tortures on a class hated for their abominations, called Christians by the populace. Christus, from whom the name had its origin, suffered the extreme penalty [crucifixion] during the reign of Tiberius at the hands of one of our procurators, Pontius Pilatus, and a most mischievous superstition, thus checked for the moment, again broke out not only in Judaea, the first source of the evil, but even in Rome, where all things hideous and shameful from every part of the world find their centre and become popular.[1]

There has been considerable discussion about the authenticity of this passage, but many mainstream scholars concur with Peter Kirby (editor of the website Early Christian Writings) that:

> The most persuasive case is made by those who maintain that Tacitus made use of a first century [*sic*] Roman document concerning the nature and status of the Christian religion. As to the reliability of that source, following normal historical practice, it is prudently assumed to be accurate until demonstrated otherwise. The reference from Tacitus constitutes *prima facie* evidence for the historicity of Jesus.[2]

2. The Jewish Historian Flavius Josephus

Flavius Josephus (a Jewish historian writing a history of the Jewish people for a Roman audience in approximately AD 93) provides the most impressive and detailed evidence for the historical Jesus outside Christian Scripture. Many historians and exegetes have written extensively on Josephus's testimony about Jesus because there were obvious Christian edits and interpolations of this text. Luke Timothy Johnson,[3] Raymond Brown,[4] and John P. Meier[5] have a very balanced (and somewhat minimalistic) approach to the critical passage. All three scholars believe that the beginning of the passage from Josephus's *Antiquities* has not been significantly changed or edited, though later parts clearly were. When the interpolations are removed, the passage reads as follows:

> Now there was about this time Jesus, a wise man, for he was a doer of wonderful works [miracles], a teacher of such men as receive the truth with pleasure. He drew over to him both many of the Jews and many of the Gentiles. And when Pilate, at the suggestion of the principal men amongst us, had condemned him to the cross. ... And the tribe of Christians, so named from him, are not extinct at this day.[6]

The reference to "doer of wonderful works" refers to miracles and is significant because Josephus rarely refers to such phenomena. According to John P. Meier:

> Thus Jesus of Nazareth stands out as a relative exception in *The Antiquities* [*of Josephus*] in that he is a named figure in first-century Jewish Palestine to whom Josephus is willing to attribute a number of miraculous deeds (*Ant.* 18.3.3, sec. 63: *paradoxōn ergōn poiētēs*). That Josephus did not transform first-century religious figures into miracles-workers in an irresponsible fashion is shown not only by his presentation of the "sign prophets" but also by the intriguing contrast between Jesus and the Baptist in book 18 of *The Antiquities*. The Baptist receives the longer and more laudatory notice (*Ant.* 18.5.2, secs. 16–19), but without benefit of miracles, while Jesus is presented as both miracle-worker and teacher. The distinction implied in Josephus is mirrored perfectly in the four Gospels.[7]

In view of this, we have contemporary non-Christian testimony not only for the existence of Jesus but also for His reputation of being wise, His miraculous deeds, and His crucifixion under the procurator Pontius Pilate.

3. Babylonian Talmud (Source: Sanhedrin 43a)

The Sanhedrin text (43a) from the Babylonian Talmud (written between AD 73 and 250), according to Peter Schäfer, is indisputably speaking about Jesus (*Yeshu*). The polemical tone indicates its Jewish origin (without Christian interpolation).[8] This text concerns the trial and execution of Jesus, calling Jesus a sorcerer who led Jews into apostasy. Since no witnesses speak on His behalf, He is stoned and hanged on the eve of the Passover.[9]

Though this text may have been written a century (or more) after Jesus, it is clearly referring to Jesus as a real Person, who had something like miraculous power (interpreted as sorcery) and who was hanged on the eve of the Passover. If there had not been a strong tradition in the Jewish community of Jesus (*Yeshu*) as a real historical individual, there would have been no reason to interpret His special powers as sorcery and His being hanged (crucified) on the eve of Passover as an act of apostasy.

Conclusion

We have reasonable, probative, contemporary, non-Christian testimonies of the existence of Jesus, which specify the following historical facts:

- Jesus was considered a wise man by contemporaries (Josephus)
- Jesus was a miracle worker (Josephus and Talmud, which calls Him "sorcerer")
- Jesus was crucified (Tacitus, Josephus, and Talmud)
- Jesus was crucified under the procurator Pontius Pilate (Tacitus and Josephus)

NT#2: Who Were the Eyewitnesses to the Gospel Traditions?

Dr. Richard Bauckham (senior scholar at Cambridge University), in collaboration with other contemporary scholars, has altered the course of historical biblical studies in a significant and radical way, moving away from the dominant view of form criticism[10] toward the restoration of direct eyewitness testimony, which lies at the source not only of the oral traditions preceding the Gospels but also the Gospels themselves. Some of Bauckham's contemporary collaborators are Samuel Byrskog,[11] Birger Gerhardsson,[12] Martin Hengel,[13] Kenneth Bailey,[14] James Dunn,[15] Jan Vansina,[16] Gerd Theissen,[17] and Grant Stanton,[18] who individually and collectively corrected the substantial misinterpretation of oral tradition and transmission of form criticism (described immediately below), as well as E. P. Sanders,[19] N. T. Wright,[20] John P. Meier,[21] and other contributors to the Third Quest for the historical Jesus.

So, what were the misleading conclusions of form criticism in New Testament exegesis? Form criticism was developed by Hermann Gunkel, Martin Noth, and Gerhard von Rad to assess the oral traditions behind the Old Testament narratives to supplement the Documentary Hypothesis (see OT#3). It identified several "forms" that could be assessed to determine the oral stages by which a particular narrative was formed. Rudolph Bultmann applied this technique to the New Testament, which gave the impression that the oral traditions soon became decoupled from their eyewitnesses and underwent a free-floating development, which was only loosely controlled by the apostles and the early Church.

The difference between Old Testament and New Testament oral traditions is that the former had a very long period of formation, while the latter had about thirty to forty years (between AD 33 and 70) for their formation. Since many of the apostles were living during that formative time, it cannot be supposed that those oral traditions were divorced from the apostolic eyewitnesses of those events. The critique of Bauckham and his collaborators of form-critical assumptions puts a whole new light on eyewitness testimony to Jesus and historical exegesis. This is discussed in detail throughout NT#2 and NT#3.

Bauckham provides the most comprehensive description and explanation of the eyewitnesses of the Gospels along with these other scholars in his book *Jesus and the Eyewitnesses: The Gospels as Eyewitness Testimonies.* He and his collaborators have made three important contributions that reconnect eyewitness testimonies to the Gospels themselves:

1. **A reexamination of eyewitness testimony to Jesus,** particularly from Papias (on Peter as the eyewitness source of Mark); the apostles in the Jerusalem church (as eyewitnesses, formulators, and overseers of the traditions in the Q Source and other sources); the *inclusio* of eyewitness in the Gospel of John; and the many eyewitnesses whose names are men-

tioned in Gospel narratives. Bauckham and his collaborators show that the testimony of these eyewitnesses, formerly marginalized by many Gospel scholars, can be validated by internal evidence from the Gospels, using techniques such as the *inclusio* of eyewitness; the shifts from the first person plural ("we") to the third person plural ("they") in the Gospel narratives; and the dominant point of view from which the Gospel is written (i.e., Peter's point of view in Mark).

2. **A heightened recognition of the role the Twelve Apostles must have played in the formulation, transmission, and authoritative oversight of the oral traditions through the mother church in Jerusalem.** The great exegete Vincent Taylor long ago criticized form criticism's view that the apostles, most of whom were still alive, had almost no role in the development, oversight, and transmission of the Jesus tradition. As he humorously noted, "If the Form Critics are right, the disciples must have been translated to heaven immediately after the resurrection."[22] Bauckham, Gerhardsson, and Byrskog make this case quite strongly (see section 2).

3. **A radical critique of form criticism's "informal and uncontrolled" view of the transmission of oral traditions.** Bauckham, Gerhardsson, Byrskog, and others who have studied oral transmission of Judaism in the first century and in contemporary Middle East culture show the strong likelihood that oral transmission was both formal, with specifically qualified formulators and teachers, and controlled, having core content that could not be changed and had to be committed to memory or something close to it (see NT#3).

The case made by Bauckham and his collaborators is so strong that it is difficult to imagine returning to the days of form-critical domination of historical-exegetical assumptions and method. As such, we can no longer view the forty years between Jesus' resurrection and the formulation of the Gospels as a period of free-floating development of oral tradition that became detached from the eyewitnesses of Jesus' ministry. Today, the best historical and exegetical scholarship shows strongly that the eyewitnesses to Jesus' work and deeds were accurate and careful in their formulation and transmission and that this transmission was controlled and formal, particularly by the Twelve and other eyewitnesses ("disciples") living in the Jerusalem church. As such, there is a strong and direct link between the eyewitnesses to the ministry of Jesus and the Gospel narratives themselves.

It is important to note that "testimony" in first-century Palestinian and Hellenistic historiography was not viewed as a mere record of the facts. As Bauckham defines it, "In testimony there is no gap between the events described and the interpretation given: 'there is an inextricable coinherence of observable event and perceptible meaning.'"[23]

Thus "testimony" included historical facts about Jesus' exorcisms, healings, raisings of the dead, controversies, alliances, parables, moral teaching, passion, and resurrection but it also included theological interpretation of the significance and meaning of those events and sayings. This interpretation could include redactions that might cause a contemporary reader to ask why there are different versions of the same tradition. However, these redactions were not viewed by the apostolic Church to be "unchangeable" parts of the eyewitness tradition. As will be seen below, certain parts of tradition were thought to be variable, while the core event and sayings were thought to be "unchangeable," making them stable from Gospel to Gospel.

Bauckham's study of early Church Fathers (specifically Papias, writing between AD 85 and 130) shows they believed that "priority in writing history should be given to the testimony of eyewitnesses, preferably *living eyewitnesses.*"[24] He shows through extensive analysis that the Gospels are a collection of eyewitness testimonies in which the memory of events by living witnesses is fused together with theological interpretation of those events. The eyewitnesses were frequently the fashioners of the initial oral traditions, which were later committed to writing and included in the Gospels.

Before discussing the identity of the eyewitnesses and Gospel writers, it might prove helpful to explain the criteria for canonicity in the Catholic Church. *Canonicity* indicates the formal acceptance of a book of Scripture into the collection that the Catholic Church declares to be inspired by the Holy Spirit — the collection that constitutes what we call "the Holy Bible." Four criteria were used to include (or exclude) books of Scripture into the canon of the New Testament. Fr. Felix Just, Ph.D. (professor of biblical studies and an editor for the revision of the New Testament of the New American Bible), summarizes those criteria as follows:

> (1) *Apostolic Origin* — attributed to and/or based on the preaching/teaching of the first-generation apostles (or their closest companions); (2) *Universal Acceptance* — acknowledged by all major Christian communities in the Mediterranean world (by the end of the fourth century); (3) *Liturgical Use* — read publicly along with the OT when early Christians gathered for the Lord's Supper (their weekly worship services); and (4) *Consistent Message* — containing theological ideas compatible with other accepted Christian writings (including the divinity and humanity of Jesus).[25]

The criterion of apostolic origin cannot be interpreted as "authorship by an apostle," because in the first four centuries of the Church it was well known that Mark and Luke were *not* apostles. As Just states, "apostolic origin" means "attributed to and/or based on the preaching/teaching of the first-generation apostles (or their closest companions)."[26] As will be shown in this unit, this criterion (as well as the other three criteria) of canonicity is certainly met by all four Gospel writers, because each of them had direct contact with apostolic witnesses (explained in secs. 1–7). The traditions they utilized were regulated in content and transmission by the apostolic "mother" church in Jerusalem (explained in NT#3), and their Gospels were also overseen by the apostolic Church in Jerusalem (explained in section 2).

The author of the Gospel of John calls himself "the beloved disciple," but his actual identity is (perhaps intentionally) obscured. Most in the scholarly community believe that he is not John, the son of Zebedee,[27] while others continue to maintain that he is. Whatever the case, the author of John's Gospel was himself an eyewitness to all the events he recounts, and he is part of Jesus' most intimate circle (along with the Twelve) in many of the events in Jerusalem as well as all the events of the passion, burial, and Resurrection (see below, section 4). This clearly qualifies him as meeting the criterion of apostolic origin in the broader sense used by the Church in Her designation of his Gospel as inspired. So, who were the eyewitnesses of the Gospel accounts?

- Saint Peter, the main source of Mark's Gospel (section 1)
- The Twelve Apostles (substituting Matthias for Judas Iscariot), who "from the beginning were eyewitnesses" (Lk 1:2) of the events and sayings of Jesus (section 2)
- Non-apostolic named sources in various Gospel traditions (section 3)
- The eyewitness source of John's Gospel — the beloved disciple (section 4)

1. Saint Peter as the Eyewitness Source of Mark's Gospel

Bauckham holds that Saint Peter is the eyewitness source of most of the pericopes in the Gospel of Mark.[28] He has several reasons for this, but the primary five are:

1. Papias (writing at the end of the first century or beginning of the second) stated the following about Mark hearing, recounting, and writing Peter's eyewitness accounts according to statements he heard from John the Elder (a disciple of Jesus but not one of the Twelve):[*]

> And the elder used to say this, Mark became Peter's interpreter [recorder and Greek translator] and wrote accurately all that he remembered, not, indeed, in order, of the things said and done by the Lord. For he had not heard the Lord, nor had followed him, but later on, followed Peter, who used to give teaching as ne-

---

[*] For a description of John the Elder, see below, sec. 4.

cessity demanded but not making, as it were, an arrangement of the Lord's oracles, so that Mark did nothing wrong in thus writing down single points as he remembered them. For to one thing he gave attention, to leave out nothing of what he had heard and to make no false statements in them.[29]

Several other early Church Fathers also assert that Mark heard and preserved the eyewitness accounts of Peter, such as Justin Martyr (writing about AD 150),[30] Irenaeus (writing about 180),[31] Clement of Alexandria (writing about 190),[32] and several others.

2. Mark uses a literary device called *inclusio* of eyewitness, which references Peter at the beginning of Mark's Gospel (the first to be called by Jesus, Mk 1:16, and the last to be named by Jesus, Mk 16:7). This literary technique was used by many ancient writers and historians (e.g., Lucian and Porphyry in their historical biographies) to indicate that the events mentioned between the beginning and end were witnessed by the first and last person named in the book. In Mark's Gospel, that person is Peter. The *inclusio* of eyewitness is also found in Luke's Gospel with respect to Peter as the main witness (borrowing from Mark) and a lesser *inclusio* of the women who followed Jesus (Mary Magdalene, Susanna, and particularly Joanna). The beloved disciple (the eyewitness and author of the fourth Gospel) also uses the *inclusio* of eyewitness for himself (see Jn 1:35–37 and Jn 21:23–24).

3. Additionally, John has a slightly smaller *inclusio* (within the slightly larger *inclusio* of the beloved disciple) for Peter — see below, section 4. The fact that Mark, Luke, and the beloved disciple all use the *inclusio* of eyewitness in their Gospel texts in the fashion of other ancient writers shows

that it was a well-recognized historiographical technique for identifying the main source of their narratives. These main sources of tradition are eyewitnesses but not necessarily authors of the Gospel. The beloved disciple alone is primary eyewitness as well as author of his Gospel. Mark and Luke used the *inclusio* to point to main eyewitness sources other than themselves. (See the discussion below in sections 4 and 6.)

4. Papias says that "the elder" is the source of his passage on Peter as the primary eyewitness of Mark, and as will be shown below (section 4), this probably refers to John the Elder, who was a disciple of Jesus but not one of the Twelve. If Papias is correct in attributing this passage to John the Elder, it would be a very credible source.

5. Papias does not use 1 Peter 5:13 ("my son Mark") as his source for Peter being the eyewitness of the accounts in Mark. Rather, he uses the elder (probably referring to John the Elder) as his primary source and refers to 1 Peter 5:13 only as corroboration of that fact. The reason that Papias preferred John the Elder to written Scripture (e.g., the First Letter of Peter) is his belief that living witnesses, who could be cross-examined and checked through other witnesses, were more credible and validatable sources than written Scripture to obtain historical facts. As Papias notes:

> If by chance anyone who had been in attendance on the elders should come my way, I inquired about the words of the elders — [that is,] what [according to the elders] Andrew or Peter said, or Philip, or Thomas or James, or John or Matthew or any other of the Lord's disciples, and whatever Aristion and the elder John, the Lord's disciples, were saying. For I did not think that information from books would profit me as much as information from a living and sur-

viving voice.[33]

6. Bauckham agrees with C. H. Turner that the awkwardness of Mark's use of the third person plural ("they") in his narratives reveals an underlying "we." When we retranslate Mark's "they" into a first person plural ("we"), the narratives run much more smoothly. This likely indicates that Mark took Peter's "we" narratives (which he delivered to groups of catechumens and others) and put them into the third person (an objective observer standing outside the narrative) to integrate into the rest of the Gospel narratives.[34] If so, we can actually hear the voice of Peter in most of Mark's narratives.

The above five points show that Peter is the likely eyewitness formulator and transmitter of most of the traditions in Mark's Gospel. This coincidence of internal evidence and Papias's preference for living eyewitnesses (or those who were in direct contact with living eyewitnesses), as well as other clues from Scripture (e.g., 1 Pt 5:13) gives credibility to Papias's assertion that he had heard John the Elder (or a colleague of John the Elder) testify that Peter was the eyewitness source of the Marcan narratives.

So, who was Mark, the author of the Gospel? He was probably John Mark,[35] who is mentioned by Peter as "my son" in 1 Peter 5:13. He is also the disciple journeying with Barnabas and Paul in Acts 12:25; 13:5; 13:13; and 15:37–40. His mother had a large home outside Jerusalem to which Peter fled after being miraculously released from prison (see Acts 12:11–16). Bauckham believes John Mark came from a diaspora family and was educated in Jerusalem, making him well qualified to record and translate Peter's Aramaic into Greek.[36] He was present at many of Peter's exhortations and catechetical and apologetical presentations and very probably worked with Peter individually to transcribe his eyewitness testimony and to do his Greek translations. The Gospel was probably finished around AD 66, a little before the Jewish War of 66–70.[37]

2. The Twelve Apostles as Eyewitnesses

Bauckham, following the lead of Birger Gerhardsson[38] and his mentor

Harald Riesenfeld,[39] holds that the Twelve Apostles (with Matthias[40] replacing Judas Iscariot) were eyewitnesses, who memorized and recounted the core events in Jesus' ministry, passion, and resurrection, both individually and collectively. Collectively, they constituted an authoritative collegium in Jerusalem:

> If they were close companions of Jesus throughout his ministry, as the Gospels claim they were, and if they were also, as most scholars agree, the first leaders of the mother church in Jerusalem and of its initial outreach elsewhere, we should certainly expect them to have been authoritative transmitters of the traditions of Jesus and to have had something like an official status for their formulations of those traditions.[41]

There are many pericopes in which individual apostles are named (e.g., Peter, Matthew, James, John, Nathaniel, Phillip, Thomas, and Andrew), and they were likely the eyewitness originators of the stories in which they are named. Bauckham and Gerhardsson believe that the Twelve Apostles were not only individual witnesses to specific traditions but also exercised their collective authority over the formulation of Gospel traditions while in Jerusalem.[42] This process continued throughout their lives, during which time they acted as eyewitness guarantors of the truth of those traditions.[43] This is important because it differs from the contention of form criticism, which holds that the interpretive theological content was added many years after the eyewitness accounts, almost independently of them.

For Bauckham, Gerhardsson, and their followers, the Twelve Apostles were more than able to give theological interpretation along with their eyewitness accounts when they were first formulated, meaning that the gap between the eyewitness accounts and the oral traditions that gave theological meaning to those accounts was mostly nonexistent.[44] If so, then the apostolic witnesses were contributors to the formulation of the oral traditions, making those traditions generally historically accurate.[45]

Bauckham believes that the lists of the apostles in all three Synoptic Gospels (see Mt 10:2–4; Mk 3:16–19; Lk 6:13–16) are more than a mere historical record. They act as a kind of *imprimatur* (seal of approval), because it was well known that many of the apostles were present in Jerusalem as the Gospel traditions were being formulated, and it would have been assumed that the collective apostles were an authoritative collegium overseeing and guaranteeing the truth of those traditions.[46]

This contention has been challenged because there is a discrepancy in one of the names on the lists. Thaddeus (given in the Mark and Matthew lists) is called "Judas son of James" in the lists in Luke and Acts. Some critics suggest that this deviation in one of the Twelve shows that the lists were not very authoritative when the Gospels were being written. Bauckham, relying on the work of previous scholars, shows that these two names refer to the same person: Thaddeus (shortened to Theudas) was the Greek name, and Judas (Yehudan) was the Hebrew name, which may have been interchangeable to fit a Greek or Palestinian context.[47]

In sum, it seems highly probable that the Twelve Apostles individually and collectively formulated many Gospel traditions, combining eyewitness accounts and theological interpretation. They also acted as an authoritative collegium, which oversaw and guaranteed the authenticity of *oral* traditions before and during the process of being committed to writing. The lists of the Twelve (in Matthew, Mark, Luke, and Acts) serve as a seal of approval by the apostles of the traditions in those Gospels. This is explained in detail in NT#3.

3. Other Eyewitnesses in the Synoptic Gospels

From statements of Papias and other ancient historians, Bauckham asserts that the source of historical events is often named in the account of that event:

> I want to suggest now the possibility that many of these named characters were eyewitnesses who not only originated the traditions to which their names are attached but also continued to tell these stories as authoritative guarantors of their traditions. In some cases, the Evangelists may well have known them.[48]

Bauckham emphasizes, in this regard, the importance of Cleopas (likely an uncle of Jesus) in Luke's resurrection appearance narrative. There is no need to mention a relative of Jesus who was well known in the Christian community in the narrative (while the other disciple remained anonymous) unless he was an eyewitness whose testimony could be checked.[49] This likely means that Cleopas was the source of the tradition in which he figures.

Bauckham also turns to the narratives in which the women are present at the passion, burial, and empty tomb. In all the Synoptic narratives, the verb phrase "they saw" is used six times, indicating that they were visual eyewitnesses (the strongest kind of eyewitness testimony in the ancient world).[50] Mary Magdalene is mentioned in all four Gospels, and Mary the mother of James in all three Synoptic Gospels, with the implication that several other women were present (explaining the variation in the name of the third woman).[51] Bauckham concludes from this, "It could hardly be clearer that the Gospels are appealing to [the women's] role as eyewitnesses."[52]

Following Martin Dibelius, Bauckham holds that Simon the Cyrenian is clearly the witness of his part of the Way of the Cross, but that Alexander and Rufus (Simon's two sons) may have been the conveyers of the tradition after Simon's passing (or disappearance from the community).[53]

Applying Bauckham and Gerhardsson's technique to narratives in the four Gospels, we can see a set of additional eyewitnesses beyond Peter, the Twelve Apostles, Cleopas, the women at the passion, burial, and empty tomb, and Simon the Cyrenian, who not only recounted the stories in which they were involved but also guaranteed the truth of these stories until they passed away. Some of these eyewitnesses are: Bartimaeus, Simon the Pharisee, Jairus, Joses, Joseph of Arimathea, Zacchaeus, Martha, and Mary (the sister of Martha). The Gospel of John also gives several names within its pericopes, such as Lazarus and Nicodemus.

4. Who Witnessed the Events in the Gospel of John?

The author of the Gospel of John identifies himself as "the beloved disciple." Over the last seven decades, there has been considerable debate among scholars (both Catholic and non-Catholic) about the precise identity of the beloved disciple. Was it John, the son of Zebedee, or another highly regarded and close disciple of Jesus? The debate continues to this day, with most scholars holding that the beloved disciple is not the son of Zebedee.[54] As noted above, this does not affect the canonicity (declaration by the Catholic Church of a book of Scripture being inspired by the Holy Spirit), because the Gospel writer clearly falls within the criterion of "apostolic origin" as understood by the Church: the book is "attributed to and/or based on the preaching/teaching of the first-generation apostles (or their closest companions)."[55] The author of the Gospel of John was the eyewitness of all the events in his Gospel, was a very close companion of Jesus and the apostles, and was also a member of the apostles after Jesus' resurrection (explained below). Inasmuch as John's Gospel meets this and the other three criteria of canonicity, it is clearly and always will be a canonical Gospel declared by the Catholic Church to be inspired by the Holy Spirit.

Bauckham has made a strong case that the Gospel of John, including the epilogue (see Jn 21), was written by a single eyewitness author who calls himself the beloved disciple.[56] This only becomes clear in the second to the last verse of the Gospel (Jn 21:24). Bauckham has several reasons for holding this position, the first being the phrasing of the conclusion to the Gospel:

> The saying spread abroad among the brethren that this disciple [earlier revealed to be the beloved disciple (21:7, 20)] was not to die; yet Jesus did not say to him that he was not to die, but, "If it is my will that he remain until I come, what is that to you?"
>
> This is the disciple who is bearing witness to these things, and who has written these things; and we know that his testimony is true. (John 21:23–24)

As Bauckham shows, John 21:24 identifies the writer of the Gospel as the disciple who was present at the seashore with Jesus and Peter. This disciple, as revealed in John 21:7 and 20, is the beloved disciple. Verse 20 also indicates that the beloved disciple was the one sitting next to Jesus at the Last Supper. If we are to take the Gospel conclusion (21:24) literally, and Bauckham believes there is no reason not to do so, then the beloved disciple who portrays himself as present at the Last Supper (13:23), the foot of the cross (19:26), the empty tomb (20:2, 8), and the Resurrection appearances (21:7, 20) is both the author and the main eyewitness of the events in his Gospel. Note that the beloved disciple is *both* the eyewitness of all the events ("the disciple who is *bearing witness* to these things," 21:24) *and* the single author ("the disciple who ... has *written* these things," 21:24).

There is a second reason for believing that the narratives of the events of Jesus' ministry, passion, and resurrection were authored by a single eyewitness who has identified himself as the beloved disciple: the *inclusio* of eyewitness. Recall that the *inclusio* of eyewitness identifies the main eyewitness with the first and last person mentioned in a particular collection of narratives (see section 1). Bauckham shows that the beloved disciple makes himself the main eyewitness (the largest *inclusio*),[57] and Peter the second eyewitness (an *inclusio* within the Johannine *inclusio*).[58] As Bauckham notes:

> John's Gospel thus uses the *inclusio* of eyewitness testimony in order to privilege the witness of the beloved disciple, which this Gospel embodies. It does so, however, not simply by ignoring the Petrine *inclusio* of Mark's Gospel, but by enclosing a Petrine *inclusio* within its *inclusio* of the beloved disciple.[59]

These two *inclusios* and the beloved disciple's claim to be both primary eyewitness and author meet the highest standards of ancient historiography,[60] which should be accepted as true unless there is evidence of willful deceit, which there certainly is not.

If Bauckham and his collaborators are correct, then we should not think, like some modern critics, that the narrated events in the Johannine Gospel were written by authors other than the one mentioned in the *inclusio* (the beloved disciple). So, the question is, who is the beloved disciple?

As noted above, the majority of scholars agree that the beloved disciple is a non-apostolic eyewitness of the events in the narratives in the fourth Gospel.[61] One major reason is that Mark 10:39 ("And Jesus said to them, 'The cup that I drink you will drink; and with the baptism with which I am baptized, you will be baptized'") implies that both sons of Zebedee would suffer martyrdom, but John 21:20–23 implies that the beloved disciple would not die a martyr's death and would live long enough to generate the rumor that he would not die.[62]

A second reason why most scholars believe that the beloved disciple is not Zebedee's son (a slightly educated Galilean fisherman) is the considerable evidence that the beloved disciple was from Jerusalem, was well educated, and may have been highly connected with the Sanhedrin, and later as a disciple of Jesus, with the mother church in Jerusalem.[63] In brief, there are several reasons for believing this:

- The eloquence with which the fourth Gospel is written reveals a source who is not only well educated, but very familiar with both Hellenistic philosophy and Jewish theology.
- Most of the events that he narrates are within the environs of Jerusalem: the Pool of Siloam, the Pool of Bethesda, Bethany (the home of Martha, Mary, and Lazarus), the Jerusalem temple (and precincts), and the like. Though there are events in Cana, other parts of Galilee, and the area where John was baptizing, the "main event" is centered in Jerusalem.
- Perhaps the most telling evidence is found in John 18:15–16:

> "Simon Peter followed Jesus, as did another disciple. As this disciple *was known to the high priest*, he entered the court of the high priest along with Jesus, while Peter stood outside at the door. So the other disciple, *who was known to the high priest*, went out and spoke to the maid who kept the door, and brought Peter in."

There are several indications that this "other disciple" is the beloved disciple. First, the author of the Gospel uses "other disciple" to refer to the beloved disciple on other occasions (i.e., Jn 20:2–3 and Jn 21:2, 7). Secondly, the description of the fire and those gathered around it in the

High Priest's courtyard in John 18:18 is much more detailed than what is found in Mark 14:66, suggesting that the author (the beloved disciple) was present near the fire in the High Priest's courtyard.

If "the other disciple" in John 18:15–18 is the beloved disciple, then he is evidently connected to the Sanhedrin, being known by the High Priest. If the beloved disciple was a friend of the High Priest, we would expect him to be from a family of high position, be from the area of Jerusalem, and have a fine education. This is precisely what the style and content of his Gospel indicates about him. Furthermore, it would explain how he apparently knows a ranking member of the Sanhedrin—Nicodemus — featured prominently in his Gospel.

Though some in the scholarly community continue to believe that the beloved disciple is John the apostle and son of Zebedee,[64] most scholars lean toward the view that he is a well-educated disciple of Jesus who was familiar with Jewish theology and Hellenistic philosophy and was connected with the Chief Priest and ranking members of the Sanhedrin. Who might this disciple be? Richard Bauckham has made an excellent case that it was John the Elder, a well-educated disciple whom Papias believed ranked among the apostles in the early Church and was the man who identified himself as "the Elder" and author of the Second and Third Letters of John.[65] The jury is out and may remain so. However, even if evidence is found for John the Elder or another well-educated and connected disciple of Jesus being the author of the fourth Gospel, it would not affect its canonicity for the reasons mentioned at the beginning of this section.

Bauckham believes that the beloved disciple was also responsible for the distinctive theological emphases and discourses in his Gospel.[66] Three major emphases, among many more, are as follows:

First, the Johannine community, which had probably relocated from Palestine to somewhere in Asia (seemingly Ephesus), had to struggle against two groups who threatened their identity and beliefs:[67]

- The disciples of John the Baptist (while the community was still in Palestine). This challenge explains the repeated emphasis that Jesus is the Messiah — not John the Baptist.
- The Jews who had expelled the Christians from the syna-

gogue in AD 80 (which may have compelled the community to relocate from Palestine to Ephesus). This challenge explains the repeated polemic against "the Jews" and the Jewish authorities.

Secondly, the fourth Gospel has an overarching Christological purpose to which virtually all other themes are subordinated. Put simply, the message is that Jesus is the Son of God and belief in Him will lead to eternal life. The divinity of Jesus is significant because the beloved disciple believed that this is what Jesus wanted to communicate to the world through His self-revelation, words, miracles, glorious resurrection, gift of the Holy Spirit, and above all, His self-sacrificial death on the cross, showing His unconditional love — "no greater love ..."

Thirdly, the Gospel manifests the centrality of the great love of Jesus and the Father. The beloved disciple makes a concerted attempt to reveal the heart of Jesus in His concrete relationships with His mother, the Twelve, disciples such as Mary Magdalene, Martha, Mary (the sister of Martha), and Lazarus, as well as the people He heals. By recognizing Jesus' love for these individuals, the author intends that the readers will recognize His same love for them and be inspired to follow His final commandment: "Love one another as I have loved you."

5. The Q Source and Its Eyewitnesses

The Q Source was a collection of Jesus' sayings from which Luke and Matthew borrowed extensively. It contains material that is not in the Gospel of Mark, making it the second foundation, along with Mark, of the Gospels of Luke and Matthew. According to Dunn, the Q Source was probably constructed from early oral traditions circulating in the Jerusalem church and perhaps Asia.[68] It is highly unlikely that such early oral traditions would not have come in great part from Peter and the Twelve Apostles through the mother church in Jerusalem (see section 2). There may be other eyewitness sources for the Q sayings, but they are unknown.

Scholars believe that the Q Source was written in Greek; otherwise the large number of similarities in the Greek wording of Matthew and Luke would be inexplicable. The Q Source probably originated sometime between the late thirties and late forties (perhaps early forties), but no longer exists as a separate written document. It was probably not copied, because its contents were almost completely present in Matthew and Luke, in which the Q sayings of Jesus were set within a narrative that gave them additional meaning and context. Since Matthew and Luke were frequently copied, the Q collection of sayings itself seems to have become superfluous.

6. The Author and Eyewitnesses of the Gospel of Luke

The author of the Gospel of Luke and the Acts of the Apostles was probably a Jew from Syrian Antioch,[69] who was brought into the Christian faith before his missionary travels with Saint Paul (described in Acts). No name is associated with either the Gospel of Luke or Acts (both written by the same author), but the Bodmer Papyrus (dating to about AD 200) indicates that it was Luke. Why would the early Church have invented such a relatively obscure figure to be the author of one of the three Gospels if it were not true?[70] Assuming this, Paul mentions him in his letters and identifies him as a physician. It is evident that he is a well-educated man in both Scripture and secular philosophy and literature. He is an accurate historian, who observed the requirements of ancient historiography. He died at the age of eighty-four between 85 and 100 in Thebes.

Luke probably composed his Gospel and the Acts of the Apostles between AD 80 and 85 (he was aware of the destruction of the Jerusalem temple in 70 but seems to have been unaware of the bitter persecutions under Domitian and the rift between the Christian Church and the Synagogue after the Pharisaic reconstruction of Judaism between 85 and 90).[71] Like Matthew, he makes extensive use of Mark's Gospel (and his Petrine eyewitness accounts) as well as the Q Source, whose sayings of Jesus were probably taken from oral traditions developed by the Twelve Apostles in the mother church of Jerusalem (see section 5). Though Luke was not a direct eyewitness to the events narrated in his Gospel, he claims in Luke 1:2 that the traditions on which he relied were those of eyewitnesses from the beginning — throughout the whole ministry of Jesus — whose transmission was controlled by those eyewitnesses: "just as they were delivered to us." As explained below, these eyewitnesses include Peter, the Twelve Apostles (in the Jerusalem church), the women who traveled with Jesus, and multiple eyewitnesses who are named in the Lukan narratives.

He provides an infancy narrative between his prologue on the eyewitness testimony of the Gospel (see Lk 1:1–4) and his narratives on the ministry, passion, and resurrection of Jesus (3:1–24:53). Bauckham believes that the infancy narrative of Luke (1:5–2:52) is not part of "those who from the beginning were eyewitnesses" to which Luke refers in his prologue (1:2),[72] because the *inclusio* of eyewitness begins with the Galilean ministry (4:14), with the specific mention of Simon (Peter in 4:38).

Luke is careful to preserve the accuracy of the events about which he has heard from eyewitnesses (or those who heard the eyewitnesses), but he also makes theological interpretations (redactions) of those events. He emphasizes several thematic areas, including the mercy/forgiveness of God the Father, the compassion of Jesus, the Holy Spirit, the important role of women, service to the poor, and the presence of the demonic.[73]

He was an eyewitness to many of the narrated events in the Acts of the Apostles where he was present with Saint Paul (in the so-called "we narratives"). His concern for accuracy and the requirements of ancient historiography moved him to reveal many names of the eyewitnesses of the oral traditions he received and used in his Gospel. So, who were these eyewitnesses to whom Luke refers? Bauckham has identified four sets of eyewitnesses, as follows.

First, Luke initiates his *inclusio* of Jesus' public ministry by naming Simon in 4:38 (the healing of Simon's mother-in-law). Simon is the first person in the Gospel who could have been an eyewitness of the entire ministry, passion, and resurrection of Jesus. The last person named in Luke's Gospel is again Simon Peter, in Luke 24:34 ("The Lord has risen indeed, and has appeared to Simon!"). Did Luke intend this as an *inclusio* of eyewitness, indicating that Peter was the primary eyewitness to the narratives in the Gospels? There can be little doubt of this, because Luke was well aware of the requirements of ancient historiography.[74] Indeed, Luke uses the technical terminology of ancient historiography in his prologue in a similar way to Papias (in his prologue).

For example, in Luke 1:1–4, he uses the technical terms *eyewitness-*

es from the beginning, ministers of the word, handed on (*paredosan*), and *orderly account.* Though Bauckham discusses these technical concepts in ancient historiography throughout his book,[75] one example here will suffice. The term *paredosan* ("handed on" or "delivered") is not meant in a casual way. In ancient historiography, it entails a process of study with the eyewitness (or someone connected with the eyewitness) and proficiency in memorizing (or close to memorizing) the tradition handed on according to the standards of the eyewitness or a teacher. When the process was successfully completed, the tradition was officially "received" (mastered).[76]

This is what Saint Paul meant in his declaration of the *kerygma* in 1 Corinthians 15:3, "For I delivered [*paredosan*] to you as of first importance what I also received, that Christ died for our sins in accordance with the scriptures." Most scholars assume that Paul underwent this process of officially receiving the eyewitness tradition handed on to him when he went to Jerusalem to study with Peter for fifteen days (Gal 1:18). We might conclude from this that Luke not only knowingly intended to make Peter the primary eyewitness to his Gospel by using the *inclusio* of eyewitness but also had checked the traditions he received from those who were eyewitnesses from the beginning (the Twelve) and those who were in direct contact with the Twelve. Luke believed himself to be qualified to have officially received (remembered through a process of study) what was handed on to him by an official teacher.

Secondly, Luke gives the list of the Twelve Apostles in Luke 6:12–16 immediately before his summary about Jesus' miracles and the Sermon on the Plain. Recall from section 2 above that these lists are like official seals of approval by the Twelve Apostles in the mother church at Jerusalem of the oral traditions in the Gospel. When this "imprimatur" is combined with Luke's Petrine *inclusio* and his awareness of ancient historiography (disclosed in Lk 1:2–4), we must conclude that Luke is asserting that the Twelve were not only eyewitnesses (along with Peter) of what was written in his Gospel but had approved the narratives in the form in which he used them. It also indicates that the apostles, particularly the mother church in Jerusalem, had oversight of the transmission of those traditions. (For the nature of this oversight, see NT#3.)

Thirdly, Luke has a smaller *inclusio* of eyewitness within the Petrine *inclusio* — the women who accompanied Jesus in His ministry and were the only ones who did not abandon Him during His passion and burial. The *inclusio* begins in Luke 8:1–3, where he notes: "And the twelve were with him, and also some women who had been healed of evil spirits and infirmities: Mary, called Magdalene, from whom seven demons had gone out, and Joanna, the wife of Chuza, Herod's steward, and Susanna, and many others, who provided for them out of their means."

The *inclusio* concludes when Jesus appears to the women after His resurrection in Luke 24:10, "Now it was Mary Magdalene and Joanna and Mary the mother of James and the other women with them who told this to the apostles." Mary Magdalene and Joanna are mentioned both at the beginning and end of the *inclusio*, but Susanna (at the beginning) and Mary the mother of James (at the end) do not overlap. Since Luke mentions at the beginning and end of the *inclusio* that there were many other women, these non-overlapping witnesses do not present a problem.

Though women did not have the same witness value as men in the Semitic world, Luke is not deterred, because women were the only official eyewitnesses to Jesus' crucifixion (except for the beloved disciple in the fourth Gospel). If Luke did not include the women as major eyewitnesses, he would not have been able to strictly follow the requirements of ancient historiography — that all the major narratives have an eyewitness or eyewitnesses who were with Jesus from the beginning of His ministry. Beyond being the only official eyewitnesses of the passion, burial, and initial recognition of the empty tomb, many women function as prime actors in Jesus' ministry as well as recipients of His forgiveness and healing. See, for example, Luke 7:36–38 (a sinful woman washes Jesus' feet with her tears), Luke 8:2–3 (women took care of the needs of Jesus and the apostles), and Luke 10:38–42 (Martha and Mary disagree about priorities).

Fourthly, Luke mentions several eyewitnesses who were very probably sources of the narratives in which they appear: Mary the mother of Jesus, the widow of Nain, the woman who bathed Jesus' feet with her tears, Martha and Mary, Zacchaeus, Simon the Pharisee, and Cleopas.

In sum, Luke is one of the best-attested and fullest Gospels we have.

Given his appreciation and application of ancient historiography, we must assume that he attempted to validate all of the oral traditions in his Gospel by consulting eyewitness sources or those who knew those eyewitness sources.

7. The Author and Eyewitnesses of the Gospel of Matthew

The Gospel of Matthew is the only one that does not use the *inclusio* of eyewitness, and so it is difficult to determine much beyond what we already know about his two primary sources, Mark and Q. Since Peter is the primary eyewitness of his Marcan material, and the Twelve (in the apostolic Church) are the primary eyewitnesses of his Q material, we know many, if not most, of his eyewitnesses. As in Mark and Luke, Matthew puts a list of the names of the Twelve near the beginning of his Gospel, indicating their "imprimatur" (Mt 10:2–4).

Not much is known about the author of Matthew's Gospel, other than the fact that he wrote in Greek, had a loyalty to and deep knowledge of the Jewish law and traditions, and seems to have substituted "Matthew" (Mt 9:9–10) for the tax collector Levi, son of Alphaeus (in Mk 2:14–15). Matthew alone uses the designation "Matthew the tax collector" in his list of apostles (Mt 10:3). According to Bauckham:

> [This] has one significant implication: that the author of Matthew's Gospel intended to associate the Gospel with the apostle Matthew but was not himself the apostle Matthew. Matthew himself could have described his own call without having to take over the way Mark described Levi's call.[77]

Bauckham concludes by noting, "Since it is not likely that the apostle Matthew wrote the Gospel as we have it … the attribution … could reflect a role that the apostle Matthew actually played in the genesis of the Gospel, while not being its final author."[78]

If Bauckham is correct, then it seems that the apostle Matthew may have had a role in the initial formulation of this Gospel. Perhaps this connects with Papias's reference to Matthew, "Therefore Matthew put the *logia* in an ordered arrangement in the Hebrew language, but each person interpreted them as best he could."[79] Bauckham believes that "the Matthew" to which Papias (and presumably John the Elder) referred was an eyewitness, and as such, was able to order his Gospel properly (while Mark was not an eyewitness and did not know how to properly order the traditions he received from Peter).[80] Matthew (the eyewitness) wrote in Hebrew/Aramaic, but as Papias suggests, the Greek translations of this Gospel (one of which is our canonical Gospel of Matthew) were not particularly sensitive to the order in which the eyewitness Matthew had placed the narratives.[81] We might conclude from the above that our canonical Gospel of Matthew is built mostly on the foundations of the Gospel of Mark (Peter being the primary eyewitness) and the Q Source (the apostles in the Jerusalem Church being the primary eyewitnesses). Additionally, the apostle Matthew (who seems to have written in Hebrew/Aramaic) made some contributions, but much of his ordering of the Gospel was changed by the Greek translators/editors. The ordering in our canonical Matthew is partially taken from the Gospel of Mark, but divergences from it may be related to an earlier version of Matthew (by the eyewitness to whom Papias refers).

One further problem: We do not know who the final Greek editor was, and so we must piece together a hypothetical description of him on the basis of his mature Gospel. Benedict Viviano, professor of New Testament at the University of Fribourg, suggests that our canonical Gospel was likely written by a Jewish-Christian (former Jewish scribe) who was open to the Gentile mission.[82] He was still closely tied to Jewish tradition and wrote for mostly a Jewish-Christian community.[83] However, his community was placed outside the official confines of Judaism by the rabbis (at Jamnia in AD 80), and so the community felt itself to be both inside and outside Judaism.[84] The probable date of composition is between 80 and 90, probably in the latter half of that decade.[85] Though the Aramaic Gospel was said to be composed in Judea, Viviano suggests that the Greek Gospel was composed in Caesarea Maritima.[86]

The final Greek version of Matthew has several thematic emphases:

- **Jesus** is the heavenly Son of Man (from Dn 7:13–14) sent by God to judge humankind, but He is more than that; He is the Son of God (the Emmanuel, "God with us"), which is revealed by God in the baptism (see Mt 3:17) and the Transfiguration (17:5), by Jesus (27:43, as reported by the chief priests), by Peter in his confession (16:16), and by the centurion after the earthquake (27:54).[87]

- **Jesus' mission** is to bring the kingdom of God to the world, which has its culmination in the eternal kingdom of justice, peace, and joy.[88]
- **Justice/Righteousness** signifies obedience to the will (particularly the moral will) of God.[89]
- **The law** (Torah) has continuing significance, but the Pharisaic interpretation is rejected in favor of Jesus' interpretation, which emphasizes moral teachings — such as the Ten Commandments, the Beatitudes and the Sermon on the Mount, and teachings on marriage and divorce.[90]
- **Church governance and structure** are explained in this Gospel, particularly Peter's (and his successors') place as supreme teacher and juridical authority in the Church (16:17–19) and the apostles' (later bishops') authority (18:18).[91]

As can be seen, many of these concerns do not overlap with those of Luke, though both Gospels derive much of their eyewitness material/oral traditions from the Gospel of Mark and the Q Source. This reflects not only the different theological emphases of the authors but also the different concerns of the communities they led and served. Matthew's is a Jewish-Christian community trying to find its place within Judaism after being harshly removed by the Synagogue at Jamnia in AD 80; Luke, on the other hand, is writing to a predominantly Gentile-Christian community in Syrian Antioch, which is beset by a myriad of problems with pagan churches and secular governments and moral viewpoints.[92]

Conclusion

Richard Bauckham and his collaborators and members of the Third Quest for the Historical Jesus have altered the foundation of biblical historiography and exegesis. Their enormous contribution includes:

- The negation of form-critical assumptions about eyewitnesses and oral transmission, which implied that the transmission of oral traditions in the early Christian Church was informal, uncontrolled, frequently inaccurate, and mostly anonymous. Bauckham and his collaborators show that these assumptions are almost entirely wrong. Contemporary evidence reveals that the oral traditions were formal, controlled, checked for accuracy, and mostly named.

- The re-establishment of eyewitness testimony using not only historical sources, such as Papias but also historical-exegetical methods, such as the *inclusio* of eyewitness, the significance of apostolic lists, eyewitnesses named within the narratives they witnessed, first person plural ("we") translation into third person plural ("they") in narratives, the requirements of ancient historiography, and modern studies of the transmission, oversight, and control of oral traditions within modern oral cultures, which are applied to the apostolic Church.

By correcting the errors of form-critical assumptions and using the above methods for determining eyewitness testimony, Bauckham and his collaborators have concluded that all four Gospels are the result of eyewitness testimonies that go back to Peter, the Twelve Apostles individually and collectively (in the Jerusalem Church), the beloved disciple, and other eyewitnesses named in the Gospel traditions. As we shall see in NT#3, these eyewitnesses (particularly in the Jerusalem Church) were not only exceedingly careful to accurately record and check these eyewitness accounts but also to control the transmission and retelling of the oral traditions based on those accounts. As such, we can know with reasonable certainty that the Gospel narratives accurately reflect the events surrounding the ministry, passion, and resurrection of Jesus. Yes — the authors of the traditions and the Gospel writers blend accurate eyewitness accounts with theological interpretation and thematic emphases, but these do not detract from the overall historical reliability of the Gospel accounts of Jesus' ministry, sayings, miracles, self-designation as the exclusive Son of the Father, glorious resurrection, and gift of the Holy Spirit.

NT#3: How Were the Oral Traditions Transmitted?

How can we be sure that the testimony of the eyewitnesses was *accurately transmitted* between the years AD 33 and 70 — the time of Christ's resurrection to the formation of Mark's Gospel? As we have seen above, form critics (primarily Rudolf Bultmann) held that these oral traditions were decoupled from the eyewitnesses and underwent a very informal, layered development.[93] Birger Gerhardsson,[94] James Dunn,[95] Kenneth Bailey,[96] N. T. Wright,[97] and Bauckham have shown conclusively that every major tenet of the form-critical view of oral transmission is mistaken.[98] Four areas of research have uncovered the major problems of form criticism:

1. **Studies of ancient historiography:** These studies show that form-critical assumptions grossly underestimate the role of eyewitnesses (particularly the Twelve Apostles), not only in the development of oral traditions (see NT#2)[99] but also in ongoing control of the transmission of those traditions.
2. **Studies of Middle Eastern oral transmission:**[100] Kenneth Bailey shows that form-critical assumptions about the transmission of oral traditions do not reflect how the Gospel traditions would have occurred in first-century oral cultures.[101]
3. **Studies of stability and variability in Gospel traditions:**[102] N. T. Wright and J. D. G. Dunn show that the variability of transmission assumed by form critics is "too variable" to match contemporary scholarly assessments,[103] because form criticism attributes little value to eyewitnesses' and the apostolic Church's ongoing control of the transmission of oral traditions. Evidence for this is manifest in the stability of those traditions over time, which can be seen in similarity of traditions in earlier and later Gospels.
4. **Studies on how notebooks and writing led to control of formal transmission:** Gerhardsson shows that if Christians followed customs of the Rabbis in oral transmission, it is likely they used notebooks to control the content of oral traditions of high importance. These notebooks could have been the beginnings of collections of Jesus' actions and

sayings, which may have inspired Mark to write his Gospel from the dictation of Peter.[104]

Perhaps the best way of explaining the above studies is to use Kenneth Bailey's three kinds of oral transmission: (1) informal and uncontrolled; (2) informal and controlled; (3) formal and controlled. The word *formal* refers to having specially designated teachers who can retell the oral tradition at community gatherings. *Informal* would mean that qualified teachers are not authoritatively designated. *Controlled* refers to the content being transmitted. If content is valuable (deemed important to the identity of a people, their religion, or their way of life), then that content is memorized according to its initial formulation. Further control is frequently exerted by two elders, who also memorize the traditions and are put in charge of checking newer teachers in the exact retelling of those traditions. *Uncontrolled* refers to content that is not deemed highly valuable (such as rumors and hearsay about tragedies, etc.) and is allowed unrestricted latitude in the retelling of traditions.

According to Bailey, form criticism viewed oral transmission as informal and uncontrolled,[105] which led to the idea that New Testament oral traditions changed considerably over the course of time, one changed layer giving rise to an even greater changed layer, until the resultant tradition had almost no connection with the actual events or witnesses themselves. This led most form critics to judge the Gospel narratives to be historically unreliable.[106] Gerhardsson, Wright, Bailey, and Bauckham show that this judgment about the transmission of oral tradition was highly inaccurate.

1. Controlled or Uncontrolled?

For Bailey, Gerhardsson, Dunn, and Bauckham, in oral cultures around the world today, if the content of a tradition is deemed valuable by the community for its identity, religion, and way of life, then that content is highly controlled. The same would have been true for rabbis from the second century BC to the second century AD. There is certainly no reason why the words and actions of Jesus would not be viewed as valuable — indeed essential — by the early Christian community, so we should expect that if the oral culture of the New Testament were similar to that of ancient Jewish rabbis and modern oral cultures, the eyewitness content of Jesus' deeds would be highly controlled.[107] The above four groups of studies indicate control in three areas:

1. Words of the eyewitnesses would have been judged as of highest value, and therefore those words would have been carefully preserved, being shared with men of the highest capability and repute for memorization and preservation.[108]

2. Though the Christian community in towns in which an event of Jesus occurred might have preserved the name of the witness and the text of his or her testimony according to the standards of the local church's elders, the events witnessed by the apostles and fashioned into a tradition by them (with theological interpretation) would have been overseen and controlled by the mother church in Jerusalem.[109] When a tradition was formulated or approved by the apostolic leaders, it would have been committed to memory by initial transmitters and entrusted to others with the capability to transmit that story accurately.

3. Some of the apostolic traditions were probably written down in notebooks to ensure that later oral traditions could be checked against an approved version. These notebooks may well have been the origin of the first collections of Jesus' sayings as well as small collections of the events in Jesus' life.[110] Such collections may have inspired Mark in his desire to write a full Gospel narrative.

In sum, if contemporary studies are correct about the high control of valuable material by community authorities in ancient rabbinical and modern oral cultures, and if the apostolic Church in Jerusalem functioned as such a community authority in the early Church, then form-critical assumptions are highly inaccurate and should be revised in favor of these contemporary scholarly studies. Such studies indicate that the Gospel narratives are generally faithful to the eyewitnesses who testified to them.

2. Formal or Informal Transmission?

With respect to formal versus informal transmission, form critics believed that the Gospel traditions were transmitted informally, with little restriction about the capability or knowledge of transmitters who retold the stories. Conversely, Gerhardsson believes that transmission was formal, having restrictions and criteria for who could transmit valuable content and how they were to do it. As Bauckham, J. D. G. Dunn, and N. T. Wright show, transmission of eyewitness accounts in the early Church was formal, being entrusted to elders (for example, John the Elder), who had the capability, knowledge, and desire to be highly accurate. However, the degree of formality was less restricted than Gerhardsson implies, because teachers were allowed some flexibility in the telling of *details* (but not core material) to enhance pedagogical, catechetical, or apologetical effectiveness. So, an elder would not have to recount a particular tradition in the exact way he memorized it in every preaching or teaching setting. Like ancient rabbis or modern storytellers, he would have been allowed flexibility in how he told the story to unconverted people he was trying to evangelize versus converted students he was trying to instruct.

In sum, an approved teacher would not have been allowed to change what was considered essential or valuable material about Jesus' deeds. But he would have been allowed to emphasize some deeds or words, de-emphasize other deeds or words (if it did not change the meaning), or add theological interpretation about the meaning of deeds and words (so long as it did not change the core message).[111] We can see this flexibility in the small variations of the same tradition in different Gospels.

Notwithstanding these variations, there is an impressive amount of consistency and stability of oral traditions in various Gospels and epistles. This shows that the essential oral traditions were transmitted in a formal, controlled manner, allowing for some flexibility and informality among individual teachers. We might say then that transmission was informal enough to allow for contextual adaptation, but since the content was highly controlled, teachers had to be qualified enough to keep this adaptation from changing the essential message.

Conclusion

The Gospel traditions are generally reliable — and highly reliable in the eyewitness accounts of Jesus' deeds and sayings. This reliability is ensured by the eyewitness origins of those traditions; the central role of the apostolic Church in the formulation, oversight, and transmission of those traditions; and the formal control over that transmission. There are few historical documents that can boast of such a direct, formal, and controlled connection between eyewitness testimony and its publicly manifest proclamation.

When we combine this formal controlled transmission with what was said above (NT#2) about the predominance of eyewitness testimony in the Gospels and the role of the Twelve in overseeing the formulation and transmission of these eyewitness testimonies, we can have reasonable certainty that the Gospel narratives accurately reflect the events surrounding the ministry, passion, and resurrection of Jesus. The theological interpretation contributed by the four evangelists can much of the time be rapidly detected because the preservation of eyewitness material in the oral traditions on which they depended was so well controlled for accuracy. Therefore, most of the core material about Jesus' ministry, sayings, miracles, self-designation as the exclusive Son of the Father, glorious resurrection, and gift of the Holy Spirit can be reasonably and responsibly affirmed as historical.

In the following units, we will further validate the historical reliability of these accounts by using several criteria of historicity (explained in NT#4) as well as scientific investigation of the Shroud of Turin and contemporary miracles associated with Jesus.

NT#4: How Can We Validate the Truth of the Gospel Narratives and Their Eyewitness Authors?

Up to this point we have shown through the arguments of Bauckham and his collaborators the high likelihood that the Gospel narratives were the result of eyewitness testimony from the apostles and other disciples individually and collectively. Some may ask how we can know that the apostles were telling the truth in their eyewitness testimonies. Is there any way of reaching through history to ascertain whether their testimony was true? Of course, we can presume that the apostles loved, trusted, and respected Jesus so much that they would have been exceedingly careful to be accurate in their eyewitness testimony so that they would describe the events of Jesus' ministry, passion, resurrection, and gift of the Spirit in precisely the way He would have wanted — *truthfully*.

This presumption can be indirectly validated by comparing the four canonical Gospels with the post-first-century Gnostic gospels, which are highly inflated in their miracle claims and almost opposite of the canonical Gospels in their portrayal of Jesus, showing Him as arrogant and insulting instead of "gentle and lowly in heart." For example, the Gnostic gospels portray Jesus performing miracles for astonishment and aggrandizement instead of love for the recipient and the desire to bring the kingdom of God into the world. Furthermore, many of the Gnostic infancy narratives are laughable — Jesus turning clay pigeons into real ones, cursing a child to death for accidentally bumping into Him, and striking His neighbors blind when they complain.[112]

Is there another, more objective way of reaching through history to confirm the truth of the apostolic eyewitness testimony of Jesus? The Third Quest for the Historical Jesus (E. P. Sanders, N. T. Wright, and John P. Meier) has proposed a highly probative argument based on the exponential growth of the Christian Church amidst persecution and martyrdom during the first three centuries after Jesus. Wright examined this phenomenon in comparison with other Messianic movements before and after the time of Jesus, and the contrast was overwhelming — while other Messianic movements soon faded away, Jesus' movement kept accelerating in its growth.[113]

Why would Christianity contrast so profoundly with these other Messianic movements by growing exponentially throughout two centuries? E. P. Sanders,[114] N. T. Wright,[115] and John P. Meier[116] all arrive at the same conclusion: the apostles and many others witnessed the Risen Christ in His glory (see the Pauline list in 1 Cor 15:3–8) and began performing miracles through the power of the Holy Spirit *in the name of Jesus*. Those who witnessed the miracles done in Jesus' name saw them as evidence of Jesus' resurrection and the truth of the apostolic preaching. As Meier puts it:

There was a notable difference between the long-term impact of the Baptist and that of Jesus. After the Baptist's death, his followers did not continue to grow into a religious movement that in due time swept the Greco-Roman world. Followers remained, revering the Baptist's memory and practices. But by the early second century A.D. any cohesive group that could have claimed an organic connection with the historical Baptist seems to have passed from the scene. In contrast, the movement that had begun to sprout up around the historical Jesus continued to *grow* — amid many sea changes — throughout the 1st century and beyond. Not entirely by coincidence, the post-Easter "Jesus movement" claimed the same sort of ability to work miracles that Jesus had claimed for himself during his lifetime. This continued claim to work miracles may help to explain the continued growth, instead of a tapering off, of the group that emerged from Jesus' ministry.[117]

There is well-documented historical evidence of the exponential growth of Christianity amidst persecution, which implies the efficacy of miracles worked by the apostles in the name of Jesus. If the apostolic preaching about the resurrection and ministry of Jesus was essentially false, why would God have empowered Jesus' disciples to work an extensive ministry of miracles in Jesus' name throughout two centuries? The Acts of the Apostles and Pauline letters testify to these miracles, but the exponential growth of Christianity also gives extratestamental validation of their likelihood. Without some kind of supernatural intervention, it seems likely that the Jesus Messianic movement would have faded away, along with that of John the Baptist and all the other pretenders to the title of Messiah (the anointed by God). The fact that Christianity experienced precisely the opposite — exponential growth — is a significant sign of divine approbation of Jesus as the Messiah, Risen, and Lord.

We now proceed to the validation of the historicity of *specific* Gospel narratives (and parts of narratives) by means of seven criteria of historicity (section 1). We will then proceed to a subjective approach to the truth of the Gospels manifest in the hearts of individual believers (section 2).

1. Objective Evidence and Criteria of Historicity: Affirming the Truth of the Gospels

The following seven criteria of historicity have been utilized for the last sixty years to demonstrate the likely historicity of particular sayings and narrated events in the New Testament. The study of criteria of historicity was brought to the fore by Joachim Jeremias (responding to Rudolph Bultmann)[118] and was brought to its current state by members of the Third Quest for the Historical Jesus, particularly E. P. Sanders,[119] N. T. Wright,[120] and John P. Meier.[121]

(1) **The Criterion of Multiple Attestation:** This criterion refers to the principle that the more often a narrative event or saying appears in *independent* sources, the more probable its historicity. Note that the converse statement cannot be deduced from the former ("The less often a story or saying appears in independent sources, the less probable its historicity"). Silence does not indicate probability or improbability — only silence. Appearance in multiple independent sources strongly suggests that those sources go back to a common source — presumably one or more of the eyewitness accounts addressed in NT#2 and NT#3.

Prior to modern biblical criticism, it was thought that each Gospel represented an independent source. This meant that multiple attestation consisted in the occurrence of the same narrative in different Gospels. However, since the time of modern Scripture scholarship, this earlier view could no longer be sustained. As noted in NT#2, modern Scripture scholarship shows that Mark was very likely the first Gospel and that Matthew and Luke relied very heavily upon it. Furthermore, it was also shown that Matthew and Luke shared another common source (which Mark did not use or know): the Q Source (an early collection of Jesus' sayings).

Luke and Matthew had their own special sources, which are not found in either Mark or Q. We know that these sources are not mere inventions of the evangelists because many of them have the characteristics of an oral tradition developed prior to any literary tradition, and many of them do not follow the literary proclivities of the evangelists (e.g., some of Luke's sources write in a far less sophisticated and stylized way than Luke himself — and the fact that Luke does not correct them indicates that he is being respectful of his sources). The Johannine source has long been recognized to be independent of the Synoptics (Matthew, Mark, and Luke). Thus contemporary biblical criticism has been able to identify five independent sources for the four Gospels: Mark, Q, M (Special Matthew), L (Special Luke), and J (the independent Johannine tradition).

We may now retranslate our principle thus: The more often a story appears in the five *independent* Gospel sources, the more probable its historicity. So, if a story appears in all five sources, it very likely goes back to an eyewitness account. If it appears in three or four independent sources, its historicity is likely. If it appears in only one or two sources, this does *not* indicate non-historicity[122] but only that its origin as an eyewitness account cannot be demonstrated by this criterion.

(2) The Criterion of Embarrassment: This refers to actions or sayings that the early Church would have found embarrassing, apologetically unappealing, disrespectful to Jesus, or disrespectful to the apostles. Evidently, no evangelist would want to include such statements in the Gospels, which are written to instruct and edify the community and potential converts. So, we can safely assume that they are included in the Gospel only because they are true.

For example, with respect to the empty tomb, Matthew reports the accusation of the religious authorities that the disciples of Jesus stole His body. Why would Matthew have reported such an accusation — with all of its unappealing implications — unless it was true? Another example is the Gospels' report that the Pharisees accused Jesus of casting out demons through the power of Beelzebul, the prince of demons. Why would the Gospel writers include such a repugnant accusation unless the charge had really been leveled against Jesus, was known by many in the general public, and required a response?

This criterion can be extended to many Gospel narratives: Peter's denials, mistakes, and embarrassing comments; Jesus being ridiculed by onlookers or villainized by hostile parties; John the Baptist asking if Jesus really is the one who is to come; and other sayings or events that would have been embarrassing to Jesus, the apostles, or the early Christian Church.

If Bauckham and his collaborators are correct about most, if not all, the Gospel narratives being grounded in eyewitness testimonies and controlled in their transmission by those eyewitnesses (particularly the Twelve in the Jerusalem Church), we do not need this criterion to demonstrate the likely historicity of those narratives. Nevertheless, this criterion does add to the demonstrability of the historicity of those narratives, giving greater credence to Bauckham's (and his collaborators') contention about their eyewitness origins.

(3) **Coherence with the Environment of Palestine at the Time of Jesus:** Béda Rigaux in 1958[123] recognized that the evangelists' accounts conform almost perfectly with the Palestinian and Jewish milieu of the period of Jesus, as confirmed by history, archaeology, and literature. Latourelle summarizes several of Rigaux's examples as follows:

> The evangelical description of the human environment (work, habitation, professions), of the linguistic and cultural environment (patterns of thought, Aramaic substratum), of the social, economic, political and juridical environment, of the religious environment especially (with its rivalries between Pharisees and Sadducees, its religious preoccupations concerning the clean and the unclean, the law and the Sabbath, demons and angels, the poor and the rich, the kingdom of God and the end of time), the evangelical description of all this is remarkably *faithful* to the complex picture of Palestine at the time of Jesus.[124]

Richard Bauckham has added considerably to this criterion in his study of names in the New Testament.[125] Using the huge database of names of Palestinian Jews from 330 BC to AD 200 (of which a very large portion comes from the first century and the early second century) compiled by the Israeli scholar Tal Ilan,[126] Bauckham compared the popularity (incidence) of the names of eyewitnesses in the Gospels to the incidence of names in Ilan's database. He discovered that the names given in the Gospels and Acts correlate well with those given in the general population of Palestine at or slightly after the time of Jesus:[127]

- 18.2 percent of men in the Gospels/Acts have one of the two most popular male names, Simon or Joseph.

- 40.3 percent of men in the Gospels/Acts have one of the nine most popular male names.
- Only 3.9 percent of men in the Gospels/Acts have a name that is attested only once (Agabus, Bartimaeus/Timaeus, or Caiaphas).
- 38.9 percent of women in the Gospels/Acts have one of the two most popular female names, Mary or Salome.
- 61.1 percent of women in the Gospels/Acts have one of the nine most popular female names.
- 2.5 percent of women in the Gospels/Acts have a name that is attested only once (Drusilla or Rhoda).

The significance of this becomes clear when we recognize that the names of Jews in the diaspora changed significantly. This means that it would have been very difficult after AD 70 to put in new names of Gospel characters that would not fall outside of the mainstream of the Palestinian list. As Bauckham puts it:

> Thus the names of Palestinian Jews in the Gospels and Acts coincide very closely with the names of the general population of Jewish Palestine in this period, but not to the names of Jews in the Diaspora. In this light it becomes very unlikely that the names in the Gospels are late accretions to the traditions.[128]

In view of the fact that names in the Christian community changed significantly after AD 70, it is unlikely that authors after that time would have created narratives with names like those in our canonical Gospels. Hence, our Gospel traditions were almost certainly drawn from the area of Jerusalem and environs before 70 (the destruction of the temple and the beginning of the diaspora). This agrees with the evidence of eyewitness authorship of the Gospel traditions given by Bauckham and his collaborators (discussed in NT#2 and NT#3).

In sum, the environment of the early Church, with its post-Resurrection faith and extensive ministry to the Gentiles, became progressively detached from the ethos of Palestine at the time of Jesus, and by the time the Gospels were written, much of this ethos was obscure to many Christians. Remarkably, the Gospel narratives preserve not only the customs and actions of Palestinian Judaism at the time of Jesus but also the names of individuals used before the diaspora. Furthermore, the Gospels maintain first-century Jewish expressions (such as "Son of Man," "Son of David," "Rabbi," or "He is a prophet") superseded by other more suitable titles or expressions in the post-Resurrection Church. This demonstrates the historicity not only of the Gospels in general but of the specific narratives within the Gospels where these customs, names, and expressions occur.

(4) Coherence with the Unique Style of Jesus: Some expressions, attitudes, and actions of Jesus diverge significantly from those of the milieu in which He lived and constitute a style distinctive or unique to Him. For example, the way Jesus worked miracles is completely different from that of Jewish or Hellenistic miracle workers[129] (see NT#5). This unique style of miracle-working is present in all five independent sources (Mark, Q Source, John, Special Matthew, and Special Luke), which leads to the question: If the evangelists did not derive this unique style from the teachings, expressions, and actions of an original common source (Jesus), how could it occur so consistently in all five independent sources?

Jesus also had a unique style of praying, addressing God as *Abba* — a child's name for a loving, trusted, protective, affectionate father. This exceedingly familiar and intimate expression is virtually unique to Jesus in the whole of Old Testament and rabbinical literature, with very few exceptions.[130] Additionally, Jesus has a unique way of making a solemn declaration of a moral injunction or a solemn truth — what Joachim Jeremias calls the "emphatic *ego*." This generally occurs with the verb "say" (*lego*, "*I* say to you"). The use of the superfluous first-person pronoun *ego* is Jesus' way of showing that He, by His divine authority, is declaring something new in the moral or salvific order.[131] He also expresses it as "Amen, I say to you." As Jeremias notes, this expression for solemn (divinely authorized) declarations is virtually unique to Jesus.[132] There are other unique expressions and mannerisms of Jesus identified by Jeremias throughout *New Testament Theology*.[133]

(5) Specific Identifiable Names and Places: As we saw above in

NT#2, when non-apostolic individuals are named in a Gospel narrative, they very likely indicates the eyewitnesses who formulated and oversaw the transmission of the oral traditions behind those narratives. Specific place names and sites are also thought to be accurate, because the oral traditions portraying these events were written within living memory of Jesus. This would have enabled people at the time to verify them. A spectacular event such as raising the dead or curing blindness or paralysis would certainly be known and remembered by people in a particular small town or village, which could have been easily verified. If such a spectacular event were not remembered, it would have cast doubt not only on the oral tradition but also on the formulators (mostly the apostles) themselves.

(6) **Criteria of Semitisms:** The New Testament Gospels were written in Greek; however, the oral and written traditions underlying their many narratives were formulated in Aramaic. If these traditions can be identified from the Greek text, it shows a probable origin within a Palestinian community near the time of Jesus. Aramaic does not translate perfectly into Greek, so when linguists identify strange or awkward Greek expressions, they look for possible underlying Aramaic expressions. Much of the time an awkward Greek expression reveals a very common Aramaic expression of Palestinian origin. Additionally, there are Palestinian expressions that would have been virtually unknown to post-AD 70 audiences, such as *tal'itha cu'mi* (see Mk 5:41), and so their occurrence in our Gospels shows an earlier Palestinian origin.

(7) **Departures from Second Temple Judaism:** N. T. Wright shows that prior to the banishing of Christians from the Synagogue in Jamnia in AD 80, Christians adhered closely to an informal body of Jewish doctrines referred to generally as "Second Temple Judaism."[134] When Christians reluctantly parted from this body of doctrine, they did so because they felt it contradicted *something they had witnessed* in Jesus' life, death, and resurrection. Wright points out that two of the few times radical departures were made from Second Temple Judaism were with respect to the idea of the Messiah and the Resurrection. As will be explained in NT#13, every Christian mutation of the Second Temple Jewish notion of the Resurrection can be explained by the unique resurrection of Je-

sus in Spirit, power, and glory — instead of the bodily resuscitation held by Second Temple Judaism. The apostles' experience of the glorious and spiritual body of the Risen Jesus would explain why the Christian community would make such a radical departure from the doctrine on which it depended.

2. Subjective Evidence of the Truth of Jesus Christ and the Gospels

Those who have read the New Testament with care will probably have discovered the worthiness of its authors. There are several indications of the evangelists' faithfulness to sources, apologetical restraint, honesty about themselves, care to report the words of Jesus faithfully, and concern for the salvation of readers. A brief overview of these indicators, which stand in contrast to later Gnostic gospels, provides an intuitive sense — evidence of the heart — that the Gospel writers intended to convey the truth about the life, activities, and words of Jesus.

As we read the Gospel stories, we may notice that their authors could have embellished the accounts of miracles and the Resurrection beyond their rather prosaic form. Indeed, they seem to underplay these "deeds of power" so much so that the miraculous event or resurrection appearance appears somewhat anticlimactic. When we compare the exorcism stories (which are dramatic) with the miracle stories (which are quite subdued), we get the impression that an editor went through the miracle stories to take out the exciting parts. Recall the above comparison of the four canonical Gospels with the post-first-century Gnostic gospels, which showed the former to be quite reserved in their presentation of miracles and the Resurrection and the latter to be hyperbolic and frequently ridiculous.

Furthermore, the canonical Gospels portray Jesus as the beloved Son of the Father, who came into the world to teach us, heal us, sacrifice himself completely for us, and give us His Spirit and the Church for the sole purpose of saving us. In contrast to this, the Gnostic gospels frequently portray Jesus as self-interested, impatient, and on a "power trip." The authors of the canonical Gospels are respectful, reserved, and humble — even to the point of being self-critical — clearly attempting to follow their teacher, Jesus. The inclusion of insults leveled at Jesus by the religious authorities (e.g., "He casts out demons by the prince of demons"), the failings and weaknesses of the apostles — such as Peter's denials, Thomas's doubts, Matthew's former profession as tax collector (a traitor to Israel), Philip's naivete, and the accusation that the apostles stole Jesus' body — shows the Gospel writers' interest in the truth before the reputation of Christianity's foundational leaders. If those leaders had not had the humility to tell the whole truth, wouldn't they have asked the evangelists to use their editorial pens a little more assiduously? Humility speaks convincingly about the reliability of witnesses and authors.

Furthermore, the tone of the Gospel texts is "just right." The Gospels manifest an almost exclusive interest in our salvation, telling us the whole truth even if it is difficult to bear, such as the inevitability of the cross, the power of the Devil, the difficulties we are likely to encounter on our journey, and warnings about the possibility of hell. They are the opposite of the "prosperity gospel," which tries to mitigate difficulties and challenges in the Gospel message to make it more palatable and easier to accept. The canonical Gospels were written not to gain readers' approval but rather in a challenging — almost "off-putting" — way, to help us toward salvation, to call us out of self-delusion and darkness into the light of Christ's love. If the evangelists had been more interested in winning converts instead of helping souls, the Gospels would have been written quite differently, avoiding the challenges of authentic love. The evangelists' interest in authentically following Jesus, helping us to salvation, telling the truth, and remaining humble-hearted in the face of embarrassment and lack of apologetical appeal reveals that they wanted to tell the Good News in the way that Jesus instructed — truthfully.

CHAPTER 7
The Life and Miracles of Jesus: History and Science

NT#5: How Can We Validate Jesus' Miracles?

Jesus' miracles are central to His mission. As acts of healing and deliverance, they were integral to bringing His divine kingdom into the world and dispelling the power and darkness of evil. By performing these miracles through His personal power (unlike the earlier prophets, who asked God to heal), Jesus demonstrates His divine authority and validates His claim as Emmanuel, "God with us." Given the importance of the miracles in Jesus' mission and revelation of His true identity, we will want to explore the evidence for their historicity.

We will examine this in three sections:

1. The Purpose and Distinctiveness of Jesus' Miracles (section 1)
2. The Historicity of Jesus' Exorcisms and Healings (section 2)
3. The Historicity of Jesus Raising the Dead (section 3)

1. The Purpose and Distinctiveness of Jesus' Miracles

Recall from NT#1 that two non-biblical sources acknowledge Jesus' miracles: the Jewish historian Josephus, who puts them in a positive light, and the Babylonian Talmud, which attributes them to sorcery. Since these Jewish sources had nothing to gain and everything to lose by attributing miracles to Jesus, it is very likely that Jesus had a widespread reputation for a prolific ministry of miracles.

Jesus' enemies also validated the historicity of His exorcisms. The Gospels report that the Pharisees attributed Jesus' exorcisms to demonic power ("the power of Beelzebul"). The idea of associating Jesus with Satan would have been utterly repugnant to any Christian, and it is scarcely imaginable that Christian writers would have included this accusation in the text of the Gospels unless it was true. This provokes the question of why the Jewish authorities accused Jesus of casting out demons by the power of Beelzebul (which on the face of it is self-contradictory and ridiculous). If Jesus had not had an undeniably successful and prolific ministry of exorcisms, there would have been no need for the Pharisees to make such an accusation; they simply could have denied that He had such a successful ministry. Therefore, it is likely that Jesus' reputation for successfully exorcising demons was so widespread that a denial would have seemed patently false and ineffective.

We may now examine the miracle stories in the New Testament. Miracles are documented extensively in the New Testament, with specific verifiable references to public places and times, and are mentioned in the earliest *kerygmas* ("proclamations," which were very early creedal statements) of the Church. These documented miracles are distinctive in several ways:

- Jesus does miracles by His own authority. The Old Testament prophets prayed to be intercessors or mediators of *God's* power. However, Jesus claims and proves that the divine power to heal and raise the dead comes from within himself alone, implying His divinity.
- Jesus' miracles are not intended to astonish the audience or aggrandize himself. Rather, their purpose is to actualize the

kingdom of God and vanquish evil by compassionately free-
ing faith-filled petitioners from sickness, disability, and pain.

- Jesus is not a wonder-worker or magician in either the pagan or Jewish sense. Raymond Brown has made an extensive
study of the *rare* miracles of pagan magicians and Jewish
wonder-workers, which emphasize superstition, magic, and
frivolous displays of power. Jesus' miracles are focused on
compassion, faith, the kingdom, and the vanquishing of evil.[1]
No Hellenistic or Jewish wonder-worker ever asked that his
astonishing deeds be kept secret.

- Jesus combines teaching with His miracles. Lessons on faith,
forgiveness of sins, giving thanks to God, and the like are often integrated into the performing of miracles.

- The faith and freedom of the recipient are integral to the miraculous deed. Before working miracles, Jesus frequently asks
recipients if they believe He can heal them.

These five distinctive aspects of Jesus' miracle working are reflected in
how the Gospels report on them. As mentioned in NT#4, the Gospels
show marked restraint in reporting miracles, with no hyperbolic aggrandizement, and no frivolous or punitive miracles, as are frequently found
in the Gnostic gospels.

2. The Historicity of Jesus' Exorcisms and Healings

John P. Meier has one of the very best analyses of the historicity of Jesus'
miracles in *A Marginal Jew, Volume 2: Mentor, Message, and Miracle.*[2] I
will only summarize his very thorough analyses of exorcisms and miracles, leaving the reader to obtain a more detailed analysis from his comprehensive work.[3]

- **Exorcisms:** Exorcisms are frequently cited in the Synoptic
Gospels (seven non-overlapping cases are narrated, in addition to several "summary" mentions of exorcisms), indicating that they formed a significant part of Jesus' ministry.
Recall that there are five non-overlapping sources of the

Gospel narratives that can show multiple attestation of particular events and sayings: Mark, the Q Source, John, Special Matthew, and Special Luke (see NT#4, criterion number one). John P. Meier has identified the seven non-overlapping accounts of Jesus' exorcisms in four independent sources — Mark, the Q Source, Special Matthew, and Special Luke — which strongly attest to their historicity:[4]

1. The possessed boy (Mark 9:14–29)
2. A passing reference to the exorcism of Mary Magdalene in Special Luke (Luke 8:2)
3. The Gerasene demoniac (Mark 5:1–20)
4. The demoniac in the Capernaum synagogue (Mark 1:23–28)
5. The mute and blind demoniac in the Q tradition (Matthew 12:22–24/Lk 11:14–15)
6. The mute demoniac in Special Matthew (Matthew 9:32–33)
7. The Syrophoenician woman (Mark 7:24–30/Matthew 15:21–28)

Meier concludes, "That there should be seven individual 'specimens' of a very specific type of miracle, namely, exorcism, supports the view that exorcisms loomed large in Jesus' ministry."[5]

- **Healing:** References to healing are more frequent than exorcisms in the Gospels. Meier has identified fifteen unique cases in four out of five non-overlapping Gospel sources: Mark, the Q Source, John, and Special Luke. The number of non-overlapping narratives attests very strongly not only to the historicity but to the frequency of miracles in Jesus' ministry. The breakdown of miracles in each of the four non-overlapping sources is as follows:
- Mark relates *eight* miracle accounts: two concerned with cures of paralytics (see Mk 2:1–12 and Mk 3:1–6), two con-

cerned with cures of blindness (Mk 10:46–52 and Mk 8:22–26), one concerned with the cure of leprosy (Mk 1:40–45), and three concerned with various diseases mentioned only once (fever of Peter's mother-in-law in Mk 1:29–31, the woman with a hemorrhage in Mk 5:24–34, and the deaf-mute in Mk 7:31–37).[6]

- The Q Source relates only *one* account of a healing miracle, which is the cure of a centurion's servant (at a distance). The presence of this miracle in both Q and John indicates multiple attestation of sources for a single healing account. Q also has a list of miracles (see Mt 11:2–6/Lk 7:18–23), which include healing of the blind, the lame, lepers, and the deaf.
- Special Luke relates *four* healings: one paralytic (see Lk 13:10–17), one concerned with leprosy (Lk 17:11–19), and two cures of various ailments mentioned only once (the man with dropsy in Lk 14:1–6 and the ear of the slave of the High Priest in Lk 22:49–51).
- John relates *two* healings: one concerned with the cure of a paralytic (see Jn 5:1–9) and one concerned with the man born blind (Jn 9:1–41).[7]

Evidently, healings enjoy wide multiple attestation. Furthermore, healings of paralytics, the blind, and lepers also have independent multiple attestation. Additionally, there are dozens of references to healing miracles in other contexts, including the accusations that Jesus performs miracles by the power of demons and the account of Jesus conferring the power of healing on His disciples. Again, the accounts of these miracles illustrate Jesus' healing by His own power.

Many of the healing miracles are connected with place names, personal names, and unusual details that would be easy for a contemporary reader to verify or refute. It is difficult to imagine that anyone in the Gerasene territory would forget Jesus' exorcism of Legion, which caused an entire herd of swine to rush down the hill and drown in the sea. Exorcisms of demoniacs in the synagogues of small towns would also have been unforgettable. Likewise, the healing of blind Bartimaeus near Jericho (Mk 10:46–52), and the paralytic in Capernaum (Mk 2:1–12), would have been well remembered and verifiable. As we shall see, these place names and specific witnesses are significant in all three raisings of the dead.

3. The Historicity of Jesus Raising the Dead

Raising the dead is rarer in the Gospel accounts than other kinds of miracles. There are three specific stories that are reported in three different narrative traditions: Mark (the raising of Jairus's daughter), Special Luke (the raising of the son of the widow of Nain), and John (the raising of Lazarus). These particular miracles have considerable historical substantiation:

- The narratives of Jesus raising the dead have multiple attestation in three non-overlapping Gospel sources: Mark, Special Luke, and John.
- All three narratives have Semitisms (e.g., *tal'itha cu'mi* and Greek translations of Aramaic expressions) indicating Palestinian origins, showing composition near the time of Jesus[8] (see criterion #6 in NT#4).
- All three narratives contain either proper names of people, names of places, or both. With respect to the names of people, Mark, reporting Peter's testimony, indicates that the daughter of Jairus, a synagogue leader, was raised (see Mk 5:21–43). A Galilean synagogue leader named Jairus would have been well known in the region, and a raising from the dead would have been widely remembered. Additionally, John reports three names in connection with the raising of Lazarus: Lazarus and his sisters Martha and Mary. He also mentions that the raising occurred in Bethany — a small town in which this miracle would have been remembered by almost everyone (Jn 11). Special Luke reports the raising of the son of the widow of Nain. Though no personal name is mentioned in connection with the miracle, the town of Nain is so small that again almost everyone would have known

and remembered this remarkable miracle. Interestingly, the town of Nain was unidentified until the actual gate of the town (where Jesus performed the miracle) was discovered in a recent archaeological excavation.[9]

- The raising of Jairus's daughter has several features confirmable by the criterion of embarrassment: Jesus being laughed to scorn and Jesus healing the daughter of a synagogue leader, who would not have been popular at the time of the Gospel's writing because of Jewish encouragement of persecution.

These stories of raising the dead should be distinguished from the story of Jesus' resurrection, because they are not a transformation in glory and divine power, like the resurrection of Jesus, but only a restoration of the person's former embodied state. Furthermore, raisings of the dead are only temporary, while spiritual resurrection is eternal. Despite these differences, the incidents of raising the dead are significant in demonstrating Jesus' power over life and death and thus illustrating His divinity, since this power is reserved to God alone, and Jesus' power originates from within himself.

It should be noted that the three non-overlapping traditions of Jesus raising the dead were formulated by three *different* authors grounding their stories in three *different* historical incidents originating in three *different* locations. All of these traditions have Palestinian origins and all of them have identifiable features that could have been easily validated within living memory of Jesus: Jairus's daughter (synagogue leader in small town), the widow of Nain (very small town), and Lazarus (brother of Mary and Martha in Bethany). In view of this, it is likely that the raisings actually occurred of the named individuals in the places mentioned.

The Seeming Necessity of Miracles to Explain the Church's Initial Exponential Growth

In NT#4, we addressed N. T. Wright and John P. Meier's argument for the seeming necessity of miracles to explain the early Church's exponential growth amidst continuous persecution after the ignominious death of her Messiah, Jesus. As Wright shows, every Messianic movement (including that of John the Baptist) from 200 BC to AD 200 quickly faded away after the death of its Messiah, while Christianity enjoyed an explosive growth amidst continuous persecution. How did the Church accomplish such a unique and naturally inexplicable feat?

Wright and Meier suggest that it was the combination of Jesus' glorious resurrection as well as the gift of the Holy Spirit enabling the disciples to do the same miracles as Jesus did, except this time through His name (see NT#4). If the disciples had not continued to work miracles in the name of Jesus throughout the first and second centuries, what other explanation could there be for the exponential growth of this little Israelite clan amidst continuous persecution? How could it have established itself over the entire Greco-Roman world within two and a half centuries? The apostles and later disciples worked the same miracles as Jesus in His name, which would explain why so many people believed in the truth of their proclamation. After all, why would God work miracles in the name of Jesus if His apostles were lying about His resurrection, His miracles during His ministry, and His claim to be the exclusive Son of the Father?

Conclusion

We can conclude that Jesus' prolific ministry of exorcisms, healings, and other miracles is one of the best-established facts in history. Consider all that has been discussed: the strong likelihood of apostolic miracles, implying the truth of the apostles' preaching; the evidence of hostile, non-Christian sources (Josephus and the Babylonian Talmud); the multiple attestation of Jesus' miracles, exorcisms, healings, and raising the dead; and the abundance of place names, person names, and historical details that could be easily checked within living memory of Jesus. Combine this with the work of Bauckham and his collaborators on the strong likelihood of eyewitness testimony for the vast majority of Gospel narratives. Based on all of this, we can safely conclude that Jesus was the greatest documented worker of miracles in history, followed only by His apostles, who worked their miracles through His name.

NT#6: Are There Miracles Today Like Those of Jesus and the Apostles?

Some are under the impression that miracles are a thing of the past, implying that they were the reports of overactive, prescientific imagination before and during the time of Jesus that cannot stand the test of scientific scrutiny today. Nothing could be further from the truth. This can be demonstrated by the comprehensive medical records of thousands of scientifically and naturalistically inexplicable healings connected with Jesus as well as His mother and the saints. These miracles include the instantaneous and permanent regeneration of bone, organ tissue, nerves, and brain tissue, as well as the instantaneous and permanent cure of blindness, atrophied muscle, severe tubercular peritonitis, cancer, and diseases of every kind. If thousands of contemporary, scientifically inexplicable healings connected with Jesus happen today, why couldn't they happen at the hands of Jesus in the first century? Why would they have to be attributed to overactive, prescientific imaginations? Evidently, such miracles could have occurred in abundance through the hands of Jesus and His apostles working miracles through His name.

The following is a partial accounting of the thousands of contemporary, scientifically investigated phenomena connected with Jesus that were found to be naturalistically inexplicable.[10] We will begin with the Lourdes Bureau of Medical Investigation and then proceed to the scientific panels for the beatification and canonization of Catholic saints.

The Lourdes Medical Bureau (now called the Lourdes Office of Medical Observations) was initiated in 1905 to use modern medical procedures and instruments to investigate extraordinary and instantaneous healings occurring at the Lourdes grotto. The directors of the medical bureau are well-known physicians who work in concert with the bureau's consulting physicians as well as the physicians of the patients cured at the grotto. The procedures used to investigate these extraordinary cures are well defined and stringent.[11] There are approximately seven thousand naturalistically inexplicable (near instantaneous and permanent) cures recorded in the Lourdes Office of Medical Observations[12] between 1858 and 2018.[13] The number of remarkable cures at Lourdes is about five to ten times higher than the seven thousand registered and recorded in the Lourdes Office of Medical Observations, making the actual number closer to between thirty-five thousand and seventy thousand cures.[14] The primary reason for the significant understatement of officially recorded cures is that many of those cured do not want to go through the extensive process of being physically examined, submitting records before and after the cures, multiple interviews, and follow-up examinations.[15] As noted above, these scientifically inexplicable cures include instantaneous regeneration of bone, tissue, and nerves, as well as instantaneous cures of blindness and severe diseases of every kind.[16] This clearly establishes that "miracles" connected with Jesus are occurring in large numbers today.

We now move to the scientifically investigated miracles connected with the process of canonization (declaration of sainthood by the Catholic Church). There are many well-documented, medically confirmed miracles by objective scientific panels that occurred in the twentieth and twenty-first centuries in connection with the canonization of some well-known saints, including St. Padre Pio, Pope St. John Paul II, Pope St. John XXIII, Ven. Fulton J. Sheen, and many more.[17] Note that for each of these individual saints, two scientific panels had to be convened (for each of the two required miracles), all of whose members had to collectively agree that there was no scientific explanation for the healing. The Church requires one such miracle for the beatification of a holy individual and a second miracle for canonization. The diocese in which a miracle occurred is responsible for convening an objective scientific panel to judge whether a miracle is beyond any natural explanation. As at Lourdes, such miracles are frequently instantaneously cured long-term malignancies, the instantaneous regeneration of dead tissue, instantaneous cure of blindness or long-term paralysis, and the like.

In recent times Pope John Paul II canonized 482 saints,[18] Pope Benedict XVI canonized 45,[19] and Pope Francis 68.[20] In addition to these 595 saints, there were several thousand individuals beatified. For the saints alone, this would amount to 1,190 miracles certified by the same number of scientific panels in the dioceses where the miracles occurred. Complete scientific and medical records along with analyses by the physicians on the panels are available through the dioceses or the religious orders of the saints in question. Of course, there are many more miracles than the ones documented between the pontificates of St. John Paul II and Pope Francis.[21]

Conclusion

When we consider the thousands of scientifically inexplicable healings occurring at Lourdes and through the intercession of canonized saints (as determined by independently established medical-scientific panels), it is exceedingly likely that miracles connected with Jesus are occurring in modern times to almost the same degree they did during the ministry of Jesus and the early Church.

NT#7: Did Jesus Claim to Be Divine?

Though Jesus reveals His divine nature to His apostles (in the famous *Q Logion* — Matthew 11:25–27; Luke 10:21–22 — explained below), He remains somewhat cryptic in revealing this identity to the crowds and religious authorities. He hints at this identity to the crowds in a variety of ways (explained below) to allow them the freedom to conclude, like Peter, that He is "the Christ of God" (Lk 9:20). Jesus has another reason for veiling His divine identity from religious authorities. He wishes to avoid an accusation and prosecution for blasphemy before His ministry is completed. Though the Pharisees built a trumped-up case to accuse Him precisely of this charge (see below), it took them about three years to do so. We will examine Jesus' self-revelation in two sections:

1. Jesus' Implicit Way of Revealing His Identity to the Crowds and Authorities (section 1)
2. Jesus' Overt Revelation of His Divinity to His Apostles and Disciples (section 2)

1. Jesus' Implicit Way of Revealing His Identity to the Crowds and Authorities

Jesus has five major ways of pointing to His divine identity: the title "the Son of Man," His prolific ministry of miracles by His own power, His claim to bring the kingdom of God in His own Person, His claim to defeat Satan by His own authority, and His claims to forgive sins and fulfill the Torah through His own authority. As we shall see, each of these deeds and claims implies His divine nature but does not explicitly proclaim it (for the reasons noted above).

(1) **"Son of Man":** Jesus uses this title in place of the first-person pronoun "I" throughout His ministry (e.g., "The Son of man has nowhere to lay his head" [Mt 8:20]). Though this title is used eighty times in the Gospels, it is used only four times throughout the rest of the New Testament, where post-resurrection titles such as "the Lord" and "the Son of God" are used in its place.[22] The only possible explanation for this massive retrojection of a title no longer used in the post-resurrection Church into the Gospels is that it was the title that the eyewitnesses of the Gospel narratives recounted Jesus using to identify himself.

Jesus selected this title because of its Messianic and eschatological significance from the Book of Daniel:

> I saw in the night visions, and behold, with the clouds of heaven there came one like a son of man, and he came to the Ancient of Days and was presented before him. And to him was given dominion and glory and kingdom, that all peoples, nations, and languages should serve him; his dominion is an everlasting dominion, which shall not pass away, and his kingdom one that shall not be destroyed. (7:13–14)

Jesus reveals that He was using "Son of Man" in precisely this Messianic and eschatological way (with its implications of divinity) during the trial before the High Priest and other members of the Sanhedrin: "The high priest asked him, 'Are you the Christ, the Son of the Blessed?' And Jesus said, 'I am; and you will see the Son of man sitting at the right hand of Power, and coming with the clouds of heaven'" (Mk 14:61–62).

We can now see that when Jesus used this title throughout His ministry, He intended it in this Messianic, eschatological, and implicitly divine way — as the One who was with God before being sent, the One who is sent by God to judge the world, and the One who has in His own right an eternal kingdom. The reason Jesus waits until the trial to reveal this is because He no longer has anything to lose. The authorities were trying to bring a charge of blasphemy against Him, and they had already used false witnesses to show this, so in the final confrontation, Jesus proclaimed that He was the divine Son of Man sent by God to judge the world and to initiate a new, eternal kingdom. The High Priest and the Sanhedrin understood Jesus' use of "the Son of Man" to be a declaration of His divine status, which precipitated the charge of blasphemy — a charge that was unique to Jesus in the history of Jewish and Roman legal proceedings. According to Wright, "Since we have no evidence of anyone before or after Jesus ever saying such a thing of himself, it is not surprising that we have no evidence of anyone framing a blasphemy law to prevent them doing so."[23]

Though Jesus was implicit about His divinity to prevent premature closure of His ministry, He revealed it explicitly, with all of its deadly consequences, when the proper time had arrived, intending to complete His mission in self-sacrificial love to redeem the whole world (see NT#8).

(2) Jesus' prolific ministry of miracles: We have already addressed the uniqueness and proliferation of Jesus' miracles (NT#5), particularly His healing, exorcising, and raising the dead by His own power and authority. This has a double implication that would not have been lost on many in Jesus' audience:

- Since Jesus did not ask God to perform the healing or ask to be an intercessor of God's power, He implies that He has the divine power to cast out demons and raise the dead within himself — a sign of His divinity.
- Jesus is much more than a prophet, for Old Testament prophets did not heal, exorcise, or raise the dead by their own authority; they asked God to perform the miracle or made themselves intercessors of *His* power.

Hence, Jesus' prolific ministry of miracles implied both His messiahship and His divinity.

(3) Jesus' claim to bring the kingdom of God in His own Person: The kingdom of Yahweh was a very well-known idea from the Old Testament during Jesus' time.[24] The fact that Jesus could say to the crowds, "If it is by the finger of God that I cast out the demons, then the kingdom of God has come upon you" (Lk 11:20) shows that He associated the kingdom of God with himself and was bringing this kingdom to the world in His own Person. His audience would have understood that the only one who can actualize the kingdom of God is God himself.[25]

Thus, without actually saying it, Jesus identified himself with God and revealed His central mission: to bring God's justice, redemption, glory, power, splendor, love, and eternity to the world so that whoever acknowledges and follows Jesus as the way, the truth, and the life would be able to inherit this glorious fulfillment. Jesus did this not only through His words and the establishment of His Church but also by every redemptive act of love, from His miracles to His passion.

(4) Jesus' victory over Satan: As will be explained in NT#8, a major part of bringing the kingdom of God is the defeat of Satan — God's and humanity's prime enemy. After His baptism, Jesus proceeded straightaway to the desert (driven by the Holy Spirit) to do battle with Satan. After Jesus' initial victory, Satan departs to return at a more opportune time. In the meantime, Jesus begins His ministry of exorcisms, building His Church, and teaching about Satan, and He plans His ultimate victory in His self-sacrificial love on the cross (explained in NT#8).

As Wright makes clear, the mission of definitively defeating the enemy of God ("the prince of this world") is reserved to God alone: "The kingdom of YHWH was itself [Jesus'] proffered solution [to the impending cosmic battle], with its component elements of *the return of the true Israel from exile, the defeat of evil, and the return of YHWH to Zion*."[26]

These three tasks were reserved to Yahweh alone.[27] Thus Jesus took onto himself the very tasks reserved by Scripture to Yahweh. If Jesus did not believe in His own divinity, He would never have attempted those tasks — particularly, an ultimate challenge to Satan and his minions.

This may explain why no one in the history of Israel — no priest or prophet — ever dared to proclaim the mission of defeating the prince of darkness by himself. The fact that Jesus had the power within himself to exorcise demons showed both friends and enemies that He had not only divine power, but the very power needed to accomplish the task of defeating evil that was reserved by Scripture to Yahweh alone. This is why He can state so straightforwardly, "If it is by the finger of God that I cast out the demons, then the kingdom of God has come upon you" (Lk 11:20).

(5) **The power to forgive sins and fulfill the Torah:** One of the main elements in Jesus' mission of bringing the kingdom of God and defeating evil is the forgiveness of sins. His adversaries recognize immediately that the claim to have such power is tantamount to blasphemy because this redemptive power belongs to God alone:

> And when Jesus saw their faith, he said to the paralytic, "My son, your sins are forgiven." Now some of the scribes were sitting there, questioning in their hearts, "Why does this man speak thus? It is blasphemy! Who can forgive sins but God alone?" And immediately Jesus, perceiving in his spirit that they thus questioned within themselves, said to them, "Why do you question thus in your hearts? Which is easier, to say to the paralytic, 'Your sins are forgiven,' or to say, 'Rise, take up your pallet and walk'? But that you may know that the Son of man has authority on earth to forgive sins" — he said to the paralytic — "I say to you, rise, take up your pallet and go home." (Mark 2:5–11)

The final phrase is tantamount to saying that Jesus ("the Son of Man") has on earth the power and authority of God. As the narrative shows, His enemies immediately consider this to be blasphemy. Jesus is claiming to be divine.

Jesus also claims to be the fulfillment of the law ("Think not that I have come to abolish the law and the prophets; I have come not to abolish them but to fulfil them" [Mt 5:17]). As the rabbis recognized, Torah (the law) comes from the heart of God. The righteousness of the law is intrinsic to Him. Thus Jesus' claim to fulfill the law is tantamount to saying that He is going to fulfill what comes from the very heart of God. Who or what can be the fulfillment of the heart of God but God himself?

Jesus also reveals that love lies at the heart of God and himself by declaring that love of God and neighbor are the highest commandments, which fulfill the Torah:

"Teacher, which is the great commandment in the law?" And he said to him, "You shall love the Lord your God with all your heart, and with all your soul, and with all your mind. This is the great and first commandment. And a second is like it, You shall love your neighbor as yourself. On these two commandments depend all the law and the prophets." (Matthew 22:36–40)

In the above two passages (Jesus as the fulfillment of the law, and love as the essence of the law), Jesus signals to the religious authorities and others that He is the power and authority of God, that the fulfillment of the law is perfect love, and that God and He are the perfect love that fulfills the law. In these passages, Jesus is not only signaling His divinity but the essence of that divinity: perfect love.

Conclusion

Though Jesus does not say to the crowds and religious authorities, "I am the unconditionally loving Son of God," He implies it unmistakably for those who have eyes to see and ears to hear (see Mt 13:10–15) by calling himself the eschatological, implicitly divine Son of Man (of Dn 7:13–14); doing exorcisms, healings, and raising the dead by His own power; claiming to bring the kingdom of God in His own Person; claiming to be the conqueror of Satan by His salvific work (reserved to Yahweh alone by Hebrew Scripture); forgiving sins by His own power; and fulfilling the Torah by His own power and authority. The authorities were well aware of what Jesus was claiming about himself, as shown by the fact that they were already preparing to prosecute Him for blasphemy (a unique charge in Judaism) prior to Jesus' revelation at the trial before the High Priest. In the above ways, Jesus revealed himself to be not only the Messiah but the Son of the Blessed One, sharing His power, authority, unconditional love, and eternity.

2. Jesus' Overt Revelation of His Divinity to His Apostles

The famous *Q Logion* (see Mt 11:25–27 and Lk 10:21–22) expresses in a first-century Semitic way Jesus' divinity and intimate relationship with God, His Father. This prayer/declaration so evidently points to Jesus' divinity that He reserves it for His apostles alone.* The Lukan version slightly rephrases the Matthew version (which probably follows the Q Source more exactly) to help his predominantly Gentile audience. We will use this version because it may prove more lucid to contemporary audiences:

> At that same hour Jesus rejoiced in the Holy Spirit and said, "I thank you, Father [*pater*], Lord of heaven and earth, that thou hast hidden these things from the wise and understanding and revealed them to babes; yea, Father [*ho pater*], for such was thy gracious will. All things have been delivered to me by my Father [*tou patros mou*]; and no one knows who the Son is except the Father [*ho pater*], or who the Father [*ho pater*] is except the Son and any one to whom the Son chooses to reveal him." (Luke 10:21–22)

Most scholars agree that this passage is of ancient Palestinian origin, very probably from Jesus himself, because it is filled with His vocabulary and style. Since Matthew and Luke took the passage from the Q Source (see NT#2, section 5), we may infer that the likely sources of this passage were the apostolic eyewitnesses in the Jerusalem church.

We can confirm that the apostles reported accurately that Jesus proclaimed these words in their presence because it is filled with references to His Father within the context of prayer, as well as *pater mou*. As Jeremias notes, both of these expressions refer to Jesus' address to God, *Abba*, which is virtually unique to Jesus in Jewish sacred texts.[28]

In the above passage, there are five references to *pater* in a prayer and *ho pater/tou pater* within the context of a prayer. Additionally, there is specific reference to *pater mou*. Jeremias notes in this regard: "We have every reason to suppose that an *Abba* underlies every instance of *pater* (*mou*) or *ho patēr* in his words of prayer."[29] This means that there are five uses of Jesus' unique expression for His Father in this short passage.

---

* Recall from section 1 that Jesus continuously risks the charge of blasphemy, which would have put an end to His ministry before it had accomplished what Jesus wanted. Hence, Jesus could not have used this expression in front of the crowds or the religious authorities. Instead, He uses "the Son of Man" or one of the other expressions listed in section 1. However, Jesus trusts the discretion of His apostles and close disciples, and so we have this text, which almost certainly originated with Him.

Hence, it is likely that this Q *Logion* originated with Him, and that the apostles preserved this declaration of His divinity with great care.[30]

What does this passage mean? The expression "all things" (*panta*) refers to the whole of creation as well as all Revelation.[31] John L. McKenzie indicates that this shows that Jesus is aware of the knowledge of God, making Jesus superior to the law.[32] This is what authorizes Jesus to "upgrade" and fulfill the law (see section 1, #5). This awareness of God's knowledge points to Jesus' sharing in the Father's divine nature.

Jesus goes on to say, "No one knows who the Son is except the Father." The word *knows* has a Semitic meaning, which goes beyond abstract knowing. It refers to knowledge of the person interiorly and completely. Matthew's Semitic audience would understand this, and so he stays with the simpler expression, "No one knows the Son except the Father, and no one knows the Father except the Son." Luke has to translate this expression for his Gentile audience, and so he adds, "who is," rendering the proclamation as follows: "No one knows who the Son is except the Father, and no one knows who the Father is except the Son." This slight change in the Q text suggests personal knowledge ("who") as well as complete knowledge ("is" — being). Thus Luke's Greek translation of Jesus' Hebrew prayer/teaching might be, "No one knows the Father interiorly and completely except the Son."

Thus we might translate the Q *Logion* as: "All things [the whole of creation and Divine Revelation] have been given to me by my Father, and no one knows the Son interiorly and completely except the Father, and no one knows the Father interiorly and completely except the Son."

This passage strongly implies that the Son has interior and complete knowledge of the Father as the Father has interior and complete knowledge of the Son, which further implies not only an intimate relationship between the two but also a sharing of divinity. As noted above, Luke tries to bring this out in his slightly revised version of the *Logion*. Jesus' apostles and disciples would have understood the implications of equality of knowledge between the Father and the Son. How could there be equality of knowledge between them unless Jesus' knowledge of the Father was as divine as the Father's knowledge of Him? For this reason, scholars view this *Logion* as strongly implying Jesus' divinity, making it very much like the Gospel of John's high Christological proclamations. McKenzie calls it "a meteor from the Johannine heaven."[33]

Let us now return to N. T. Wright's assertion that Jesus proclaimed His mission to be the three tasks reserved by Hebrew Scripture to God alone: the return of the true Israel from exile, the defeat of evil, and the return of Yahweh to Zion (see above, section 1, #4).[34] Wright asks, if Jesus did not understand himself to share in His Father's divinity, how could He possibly see himself as completing the three tasks reserved by Hebrew Scripture to YHWH alone? The *Q Logion* confirms that Jesus did view himself in exactly that way: sharing in the Father's divine knowledge, action, and mission.

There is one other passage that shows Jesus' understanding of being the one beloved Son of the Father (see Lk 20:9–18). Though Jesus could not say that He was the one beloved Son of His Father in front of the religious authorities without being accused of blasphemy, He points to this in the parable of the wicked tenants. This parable portrays the history of Israel, where the owner of the vineyard (symbolizing God) sends several servants (symbolizing the prophets) to the tenants of the vineyard to obtain his fair share of the produce. The tenants beat the servants and even kill some of them. Finally, the owner sends his "beloved son" (*huion agapēton*), whom they also kill. The implication is that the owner had only one son ("he had one" — *ena eichen*), whom the parable later describes as being "the heir." Wright believes that this parable was not only spoken by Jesus, but was deliberately self-referential.[35] Would Jesus have risked being accused of blasphemy by telling this parable, implying that He was the only begotten Son of the Father (God), unless He really wanted to engender that thought in His audience (the religious authorities and crowds)? What would be the point if He did not think it to be true?

Conclusion

Now let us review the evidence we have set out in sections 1 and 2. When the *Q Logion* is combined with Jesus' claims to bring the kingdom of God in His own Person, to have divine power within himself (in the way He performed miracles), and His claim to be the beloved Son of the Father (see Lk 20:13), we can see why the apostles became convinced that Jesus claimed to be not only the Messiah but divine.

Jesus was careful not to be explicit about His divinity beyond the group of His apostles and disciples. Yet the implications of exorcising, healing, and raising the dead by His own power and authority and His preaching about bringing the kingdom of God, defeating Satan through His own authority, forgiving sins, and fulfilling the law by His own authority became increasingly suggestive of His divinity to both the crowds and religious authorities. When Jesus told the parable of the wicked tenants quite publicly and proclaimed He could rebuild the temple in three days, the authorities began to recognize that He was taking on himself the mission reserved to Yahweh alone. So they began to plot His trial for blasphemy — a unique charge in Jewish legal proceedings. As noted above, Wright sees this as the authorities' recognition of Jesus' unique claim in the history of Israel to being divine in knowledge, action, and mission: "Since we have no evidence of anyone before or after Jesus ever saying such a thing of himself [to be divine], it is not surprising that we have no evidence of anyone framing a blasphemy law to prevent them doing so."[36]

In view of the above, it is reasonable to affirm that Jesus claimed not only to be the Messiah but also the exclusive Son of His Father, sharing in His divine knowledge and reality.

NT#8: What Did Jesus Say About Love, His Mission, and Satan?

As Jesus initiated His ministry, He had in mind not only the Messianic mission described in Isaiah (to preach good news to the poor, release to captives, recovery of sight to the blind, and to free those who are oppressed [Lk 4:18–19]), but also a new mission consisting of three parts:

1. The Bringing of the Kingdom of God to the World (section 1)
2. The Defeat of Satan and All His Minions (section 2)
3. The Founding of a Church that Would Last Beyond Himself (see NT#18)

These three objectives had one major purpose: to pave the way for us to eternal salvation with Him and His heavenly Father.

1. Bringing the Kingdom of God to the World

We need to understand Jesus' distinctive view of love if we are to grasp the eternal kingdom He promised, and so we will begin here (section 1.A), and then proceed to the two dimensions of the kingdom He brought: the eternal kingdom (section 1.B) and the present kingdom in this world (section 1.C).

1.A. Jesus' Distinctive View of Love (agapē)

Jesus' view of love lies at the center of His identity, mission, and kingdom and is quite distinctive in the history of religion and philosophy. When the Catholic Church began to practice it, it had a transformative effect on culture and the social order (see below). Some of Jesus' principles that guided this transformation are:

- Jesus uniquely identified love as the highest of the commandments, indicating that love of God and love of neighbor summed up the entire law (Torah) and the prophets (see Mt 22:37–40).
- Jesus moved from the Silver Rule, which is in every religion (do no unnecessary harm to others), to the Golden Rule, which is unique to Christianity (do the optimal good to others that you would want done to you).[37] He then says that the Golden Rule sums up the law and the prophets — thereby equating it with His view of love (see Mt 7:12).
- Jesus uniquely taught that every person has co-responsibility for every other person, regardless of whether one is slave or free, woman or man, Gentile or Jew. He insists that this has salvific significance — "as you do to one of the least of these my brethren, you do to me" (see Mt 25:31–46).[38]
- Jesus uniquely defined "love" through the Beatitudes, other prescriptions in the Sermon on the Mount, and the Parables of the Good Samaritan and the Prodigal Son.

So how did Jesus define His unique view of love (*agapē*)? It comes from the recognition of the unique goodness, lovability, and mystery of all human beings, which incites compassion — a desire to help and support others, both temporally and spiritually. It is indifferent to reciprocity (*philia*/friendship), good feelings or sentiments (*storgē*), and romantic or sexual feelings (*eros*) because it does the good for others solely for their sake — without expectation of emotional, physical, or other rewards.[39] Thus it is self-giving and self-sacrificial. The essence of *agapē* is captured in four passages:[40]

1. **The Beatitudes (Mt 5:3–11):** "Poor in spirit" (humble-heartedness), "meek" (gentle-heartedness), "hungering for righteousness" (desiring to be like God in goodness and holiness), "merciful" (forgiveness from the heart and compassion toward others — even strangers and enemies), "pure of heart" (authentic), and "peacemakers"

2. **Other prescripts in the Sermon on the Mount (Mt 5–7):** Tempering anger, turning the other cheek, replacing retaliation with forgiveness, avoiding adultery and remaining faithful to marriage, and loving and praying for enemies

3. **The Parable of the Good Samaritan (Lk 10:25–37):** The Jewish man by the side of the road is a stranger and an enemy of the Samaritans, yet the Good Samaritan is moved with compassion for this suffering man and goes out of his way to care for him until he is cured.

4. **The Fourth Suffering Servant Song (Is 52:13–53:12):** This is the text to which Jesus refers in His Eucharistic words. The text portrays an innocent man who turns himself into a self-sacrificial offering for the good of all sinners throughout the world. It reflects Jesus' view of unrestricted, self-sacrificial love.

Building on the foundation of this new view of love (*agapē*/charity), Jesus reveals that God (His Father) is unrestricted, completely self-giving love. This is clearly expressed in four passages:[41]

1. **The Parable of the Prodigal Son (in which the son's father represents God the Father):** Notice that the son is as profligate as anyone could be in first-century Judaism. He betrays and shames his father, the family, his country, the law, and above all, God himself. When he has a change of heart and returns to his father, the father (symbolizing God) rushes out to meet him, kisses him (expressing his forgiveness), gives him sandals (showing that he has been restored from the status of a slave to a free man), a robe (symbolizing high birth and dignity), and the family "signet" ring (indicating that he has been completely restored to the family without any conditions), and then kills the fatted calf (celebrates with bounty and joy). In sum, Jesus is saying that His Father responds to even a most egregious sinner's repentance with complete restoration of dignity, family privilege, and overwhelming joy.

2. **His address of God as *Abba*:** This was a child's term for his affectionate, trusted, protective, and compassionate father — like "daddy."

3. **His elevation of love to the highest commandment:** The Rabbis believed that *Torah* was the reflection of Yahweh's heart; so, when Jesus says that the commandment to love sums up all of *Torah*, He is saying that love reflects Yahweh's heart: God is love.

4. **His equating of perfection with forgiveness:** In Matthew 5:43–48, Jesus implies that the Father's perfection consists in His unrestricted forgiveness and His love of enemies.

So, who is God? According to Jesus, the Father is the perfection of love as Jesus has redefined it. Thus He is perfectly humble-hearted, perfectly gentle-hearted, perfectly forgiving, perfectly compassionate, perfectly authentic, and perfectly peacemaking.

Jesus then applies His new notion of love and God to himself. This is evident in four passages:[42]

1. His love for the greatest sinners — tax collectors, prostitutes, and even those who unjustly persecuted Him and others
2. His love for the sick, the possessed, and the poor
3. His love of His apostles even when they falter (e.g., Peter denying Him and Jesus forgiving those denials — see Jn 21:15–17)
4. Above all, His completely self-sacrificial death, His act of unconditional love for all humankind: "Greater love has no man than this, that a man lay down his life for his friends" (Jn 15:13). (This is explained in section 1.C, #5. See also NT#9 and NT#11.)

Jesus' unique teaching on love, God, and himself was taken by the early Church far beyond the community of Christians, particularly to slaves, widows, orphans, prisoners, and the oppressed. From the Church's very inception, she transformed the availability and extent of healthcare, welfare, and education *for everyone*, particularly the needy.[43] Today, the Catholic Church is still the largest healthcare, education, and welfare institution in the world by far:

- **Education:** The Church provides services in 43,800 secondary schools and 95,200 primary schools.[44]
- **Healthcare:** The Church oversees 26 percent of all worldwide healthcare facilities and hospitals.[45]
- **Public welfare:** The Church provides services in 15,722 homes for the elderly, chronically ill, and disabled; 9,552 orphanages; 13,897 marriage counseling centers; and 11,758 nurseries — not including any healthcare facilities.[46]

Jesus' unique view of love, God, and himself — and the effects it has created through the agency of the Catholic Church around the world throughout history — has provided a significant "reason of the heart" not only for belief in God and Jesus but also in the Church He established. It gives an authentication of the heart to the evidence of eyewitnesses, miracles, His glorious resurrection, His gift of the Holy Spirit (the power of God), and above all, His unrestricted love given in His complete self-sacrifice and the holy Eucharist.

1.B. The Eternal Kingdom

We here turn to Jesus' teaching about the eternal kingdom, which may now be understood as the kingdom of unrestricted love (*agapē*). This kingdom of unrestricted and eternal love will put an end to pain, will be like a banquet, and will have many rooms — one of which is made especially for each of us. When we are in this eternal kingdom, we will be like the angels and will experience loving communion with the Father, Son, and Holy Spirit in perfect joy.[47] Though Jesus does not give much specification to these general themes, their result is captured in John 15:10–12:

> If you keep my commandments, you will abide in my love, just as I have kept my Father's commandments and abide in his love. These things I have spoken to you, that my joy may be in you, and that your joy may be full.
>
> This is my commandment, that you love one another as I have loved you.

The meaning is clear: by following Jesus' commandment to love, we will be able to purify our love by tempering our ego, sensuality, and desire for power. This purification will enable us to give ourselves generously, which is the key to eternal joy with God and others in the kingdom of heaven.

1.C. The Present Kingdom Brought to the World

Jesus left us with five divine gifts indispensable for our salvation (which He included in His notion of "kingdom"):

1. The gift of the Holy Spirit
2. His preaching and teaching, which He anticipated would be recorded in Scripture, liturgy, and Tradition
3. The Church He instituted with supreme teaching and juridical authority

4. The sacraments He instituted
5. His unconditional, unrestricted, enduring act of love given in His completely self-sacrificial passion and death, which becomes the loving power that will break the grip of evil, sin, and death for all time

We will discuss each of these five points in turn and give a detailed discussion of Jesus' victory over Satan (in section 2) and the founding of Jesus' Church (NT#18).

(1) The gift of the Holy Spirit: When Jesus gave the gift of the Holy Spirit to His apostles (and to the Church) in John 20:22 and Acts 2:1–12, the apostles received all of the charismatic and interior gifts needed for their preaching, purification, and evangelization of the world (see NT#15). We have already seen how the power of the Holy Spirit worked through the name of Jesus so that the apostles could work miracles (NT#5). The Gospel of Luke and the Acts of the Apostles also emphasize the guidance, protection, and inspiration of the Holy Spirit so necessary for the apostles' evangelization efforts — particularly their high level of preaching and teaching.[48] The Holy Spirit is also given to the Church to help with making decisions and governance.[49] Without the Spirit, the apostolic preaching would have been at the level of fishermen. Furthermore, there would have been an absence of divine inspiration, guidance, protection, and interior and charismatic gifts (including miracles) in the Church, which would have enervated her capacity for evangelization, disallowing the incredible success she evidently enjoyed (see below, NT#15).

(2) The preaching and teaching of Jesus: Throughout His ministry, Jesus was confident that His apostles were being transformed by not only His deeds but also His words. As noted in NT#3, in oral cultures, leaders are accustomed to hold in memory — and often to memorize — significant words and deeds. Therefore, it should come as no surprise that Peter remembered in detail a large number of Jesus' sayings, which he dictated to Mark (see NT#2, section 1) and that the other apostles and eyewitnesses precisely remembered other sayings and deeds (given in the Q Source, Special Luke, Special Matthew, and John). The collective efforts of the apostles and other disciples (who traveled with Jesus — see

NT#2) gave rise not only to the Gospel narratives and sayings but also to baptismal, Eucharistic, and reconciliation liturgies and ministries. These efforts also provided much of the early tradition not recorded in Scripture, including moral teachings, liturgical practices, governance practices, and Christian devotions that were part of early Church life. Some of these early, non-scriptural traditions are recorded in catechetical documents, such as the *Didache* (composed around AD 70–80). Thus the words of Jesus lie at the heart of Scripture, Tradition, liturgical practices, and Christian community. Jesus' teachings on morality (see, especially the Sermon on the Mount, Mt 5–7, and the Sermon on the Plain, Lk 6:20–49 and Mk 7:20–23) and on marriage (Mt 5:31–32 and 19:3–12) are of particular importance because they provide countercultural guidance leading to significantly better spiritual, emotional, relational, and marital health.[50]

(3) **The institution of the Catholic Church:** As we shall see in NT#18, Jesus gave us the community-institutional gift through which His preaching and teaching would be interpreted and disseminated to the world: the Catholic Church. Jesus was well aware that a Church with both teaching and juridical authority would be needed to keep the community unified, faithful to His teaching, and capable of adapting to new challenges. As such, He bestowed special spiritual leadership charisms on all the apostles (see Mt 18:18) and the keys to the kingdom on Peter alone (Mt 16:17–19). This Church would become the community that would grow exponentially, safeguard the unity and truth preached by Jesus, and transform secular culture in the Roman Empire and to the ends of the earth.

(4) **The Seven Sacraments:** The seven sacraments were instituted by Jesus as signs and vehicles of His special graces for salvation.[51] These indispensable gifts of grace impart the Holy Spirit (baptism and confirmation), protect us from evil, forgive sins, help with moral conversion and transformation of heart (reconciliation and the holy Eucharist), enable the Church to grow through special leadership charisms (holy orders), and give graces to help strengthen and meet challenges in marriage (matrimony) as well as sickness and death (Sacrament of the Sick).[52] This is explained more fully in NT#18.

(5) **The unconditional redemptive love in the self-sacrificial pas-**

sion and death of Jesus: In John's Gospel, Jesus says, "Greater love has no man than this, that a man lay down his life for his friends" (Jn 15:13). If we understand this in the context of Jesus' Eucharistic words ("This is my blood of the covenant, which is poured out for many for the forgiveness of sins" [Mt 26:28]), we can better appreciate the significance of Jesus' self-sacrificial act. When Jesus was dying on the cross, He intended that His act of unconditional and unrestricted love be not just momentary but last throughout eternity.[53] This act of love was meant to overpower the evil spirit and his dark effects over each of us, individually and collectively. When Jesus' unconditional and unrestricted act of love overpowered and outshone evil, it released us from the grip of Satan by forgiving our sins, paying the indebtedness of our sinfulness, healing us from the effects of sin, and healing those who were adversely affected by our sin. This eternal and unrestricted love stays in the world to empower every priest's absolution and is integral to the holy Eucharist we receive. It is, therefore, the ultimate defeat of Satan (see section 2).

Conclusion

When the Son of God became incarnate as Jesus Christ, He intended to leave a legacy of enduring grace and love through the Holy Spirit, His preaching, His Church, the sacraments, and His unrestricted love. The combined effects of these graces and gifts are not only the defeat of Satan but also Jesus' pathway from this world to the next. He refers to this pathway as "the kingdom He is bringing into the world" — the kingdom that is in our midst to this very day. When Jesus died on the cross, rose in glory, and gave His Spirit to individual apostles and the Church, His mission was completed. Now it is incumbent upon us to enter into His present kingdom in our world by following His spirit and teaching, participating in His Church and sacraments, and trusting in the unrestricted love He has bestowed on the world. We will then be on the path to His eternal kingdom.

2. Jesus' Defeat of Evil

As noted above, Jesus' mission had three interrelated parts: bringing the kingdom of God in His own Person (section 1), defeating the dominance of Satan in the world (section 2), and initiating His Church, which would withstand the gates of the netherworld until the end of time (NT#18). We now turn to Jesus' defeat of Satan, which is integral to bringing His kingdom to the world.

We can say with total certainty that Jesus taught the reality of Satan and his dominant influence in the world,[†] and came into the world to do battle with and defeat him. Jesus had a fivefold plan to defeat the dominance of Satan in the world:

1. To do battle with him in the desert immediately after His baptism
2. To carry out a prolific ministry of exorcism
3. To give His apostles through His Church the power to exorcise demons, forgive sins, and teach His way
4. To teach His apostles about the temptations, deceits, accusations, and dangers of Satan
5. To give an eternally enduring gift of unrestricted redemptive love to the world through His passion and death

We can only briefly explain these five parts of His plan here, and fuller explanations can be found in other works.[54]

(1) Jesus' battle with Satan in the desert: Luke 4:1–12 and Matthew 4:1–11 recount Jesus' confrontation with Satan in the desert immediately after His baptism. Satan knows that Jesus is the Son of God and tries to use His divine position against Him by tempting Him to disobey His Father's will. Though the temptations are overtly about satisfying appetites, obtaining worldly power, or showing off His divine power (spiritual pride), there is a continual undercurrent of trying to convince Jesus to disobey His Father. Essentially, the Devil is telling Him, "You have the power and the equality with God. Why don't You just go for whatever You want (regardless of what Your Father wants)? Eat some bread when You are hungry, enjoy an abundance of worldly power, and let everybody

---

† Jesus uses the expression "ruler of this world" to refer to Satan (see Jn 14:30). Though God has authority over Satan, Satan has achieved a position of dominant influence through his dark arts. Satan himself tells Jesus after showing Him all the kingdoms of the world, "To you I will give all this authority and their glory; for it has been delivered to me, and I give it to whom I will. If you, then, will worship me, it shall be all yours" (Lk 4:5–7).

know You are the most important Person that ever lived." Of course, Jesus sees right through him and is so much in love with His Father that He would not, under any circumstances, disobey His will. When Jesus resists these temptations, He proves His dominance over the Prince of Darkness and then exercises that power by carrying out His prolific ministry of exorcisms.

(2) **Jesus' prolific ministry of exorcisms:** In Mark and Matthew, Jesus' first work after leaving the desert is to go to a Galilean synagogue and exorcise a man with an unclean spirit (see Mk 1:21–28). Notice that on Jesus' mere approach, the demons know who He is and that He has the power to destroy them: "What have you to do with us, Jesus of Nazareth? Have you come to destroy us? I know who you are, the Holy One of God" (Mk 1:24). Without making recourse to God (as all other prophets did), Jesus orders the demons by His own authority (Mk 1:25–28). Jesus' apparently unprecedented authority astonishes the crowds. This event begins a systematic and prolific ministry of exorcisms, which the Pharisees implicitly acknowledge by accusing Him of "casting out demons by the Prince of Demons" (a transparently self-contradictory rationalization). For Jesus, each exorcism is a diminishing of Satan's power, limiting his sphere of influence, which makes the kingdom of God more present.

(3) **Jesus empowers His apostles to exorcise demons and later to forgive sins through His Church and sacraments:** In Mark 6:7, Jesus gives His apostles power to exorcise unclean spirits, and in Luke 10:17, He confers the same power on an additional seventy disciples. As we shall see in NT#18, Jesus gives special charisms to a three-layered hierarchical Church:

- The office of the keys to the kingdom of heaven (given to Peter as first officeholder), which has supreme magisterial and juridical authority (see Mt 16:18–19) as well as the power to bind and loose, to preach the kingdom, to heal, and to cast out demons.
- The office of the apostles (which becomes the office of bishops), where Jesus gives the apostles the power to bind and loose but not the keys to the kingdom of heaven — supreme

magisterial and juridical authority (Mt 18:18). He also confers on them the power to preach the kingdom, to heal, and to exorcise demons.

- The seventy disciples (who may be predecessors to the presbyteral office — office of priest), to whom He gives the power to heal, exorcise demons, and preach the kingdom (see Lk 10:8–9 and 17).

Jesus was well aware that He needed a hierarchical Church to extend His mission beyond His death and resurrection. He intended to give special charisms to those who held offices within that Church. His objective was to create the best defense against Satan, not only through the power of exorcism but also through His spirit in teaching, administration, and evangelization.

This gives rise to the question of why Jesus had to create this ongoing defense against Satan. After all, if He has defeated Satan in His completely self-sacrificial death, then why would Satan continue to have any power over people in the world? Jesus has certainly defeated Satan in an *ultimate* way — that is, Satan can never be victorious if people freely turn to Jesus in sincere faith. However, Jesus does not prevent people from being tempted by Satan, because that would deprive them of free will. If our virtue is to be our own, we must *choose* that virtue over the real possibility of sin and temptation (by Satan or any other means). If Jesus takes away the possibility of temptation, our choice is mere illusion; virtue would then come not from us but from God's absolute protective wall around us. So Jesus creates a middle path: He allows us to be tempted while giving us the Holy Spirit, the sacraments, His teaching, the Church, and His enduring love to help us in our choices, and to heal and forgive us when we choose poorly.

(4) Jesus teaches His apostles and disciples about Satan's tactics: Jesus teaches His disciples about Satan's temptations and deceits and how the Devil is bent on tempting us to choose hell. He reveals Satan's true character: a liar and a murderer (see Jn 8:44) who recruits his own disciples to live side by side with the children of the kingdom (Mt 13:24–26). If he can, Satan causes unbelief on every level: unbelief in God, Jesus, the Church, the Eucharist, and the preaching of Jesus. He does this by appealing to sensual appetites, greed, lust, sloth, vanity, envy, anger, and pride. Jesus' teachings and parables are quite extensive and are presented in other works.[55]

(5) **Jesus' unconditional, unrestricted, eternal act of love:** Recall from section 1.B (#5), that Jesus' complete self-sacrificial love on the cross was not meant to be a *momentary* act of unconditional and unrestricted love but a *permanent* one. This unconditional love remains in the world to release us from the grip of Satan by forgiving our sins, paying the indebtedness of our sinfulness, healing us from the effects of sin, and healing those who were adversely affected by our sin. Even though Satan can still tempt and deceive us into committing sin, he can never have the last word if we sincerely call upon the Lord's unconditional love for forgiveness and healing — particularly through the Church, the Sacrament of Reconciliation (see Jn 20:23), and the holy Eucharist (Lk 22:20).

Though Jesus considered all five steps of His plan to be vital to the defeat of Satan, the last step — the outpouring of unconditional, unrestricted, eternal love through His self-sacrificial passion and death — was the definitive end of Satan's reign. After that, every sincerely repentant sinner would be able to break free from Satan, and at the end of time, Satan would be completely separated from God and the blessed. Ironically, Satan participated in his own demise because he did not recognize that Jesus was creating this eternal, unrestricted act of love through His self-sacrificial death. So Satan entered into Judas's heart, encouraged the chief priests and the elders to persecute Jesus, and no doubt attempted to influence the Roman authorities to put Him to death. However, when Jesus began to utter the words of Psalm 22 on the cross ("My God, my God, why have You forsaken me"), Satan might have recognized that this was a psalm of trust, victory, and redemption for everyone — past, present, and future. Thus, as Jesus breathed His last, and His unrestricted love poured forth into the world, Satan felt his ultimate defeat and realized that he had participated in his own undoing. Checkmate.

CHAPTER 8
The Passion of Jesus and the Eucharist: History and Science

NT#9: What Is the Historical Evidence for Jesus' Passion and Crucifixion?

We now turn to the historicity of the passion narratives as they are given in the four Gospels. Most contemporary biblical exegetes agree that the narratives of the passion, crucifixion, and burial of Jesus are, in general and in most details, historically reliable. There are many reasons for this that will be only briefly summarized here:

1. The Testimony of Non-Christian Hostile Historical Sources (section 1)
2. The Number and Veracity of Eyewitnesses (section 2)
3. The Criterion of Embarrassment (section 3)
4. The Recently Rehabilitated Shroud of Turin (NT#10)

1. The Testimony of Non-Christian Hostile Historical Sources

Recall from NT#1 that all three non-Christian hostile witnesses living close to the time of Jesus testify to His crucifixion:

- The first-century Roman historian Cornelius Tacitus[1]
- Flavius Josephus, a Jewish historian writing a history of the Jewish people for a Roman audience in approximately AD 93[2]
- The Sanhedrin text (43a) of the Babylonian Talmud (written between 73 and 250)[3]

As shown in the texts of these writers (quoted in NT#1), there are three circa first-century non-Christian witnesses hostile to Jesus who agree on the time (during the reign of Tiberius on the eve of Passover), the principal hostile parties (Pontius Pilate and the Jewish priests and elders), and the implied place of Pilate's jurisdiction (Jerusalem). This provides a strong historical ground for the *fact* of Jesus' crucifixion in first-century Jerusalem, in which both Pontius Pilate and the Jewish elders participated.

2. The Number and Veracity of Eyewitnesses

Recall (from NT#2) Richard Bauckham's evidence for the major eyewitnesses of the events described in the passion narratives of the four Gospels:

- **Peter:** He is the major eyewitness for Mark's Gospel, including elements of the passion narrative — the agony in the garden, the arrest of Jesus, the trial/denials, and the empty tomb — but he is not a witness of the Way of the Cross and Jesus' crucifixion (see NT#2, section 1).
- **The women who followed Jesus:** According to all four Gospels, the women who followed Jesus remained with Him throughout the events of the crucifixion. Luke's secondary *inclusio* of eyewitness makes explicit that many of these

women were eyewitnesses not only to many events in Jesus' ministry but also to His crucifixion, burial, and the empty tomb described in his Gospel (see NT#2, section 6). Differences in the lists of the women witnesses in the Gospels can be reasonably explained by the fact that there were many more than three women following Jesus in His ministry and passion. Mark makes this explicit when he says, "There were also women looking on from afar, among whom were Mary Magdalene, and Mary the mother of James the younger and of Joses, and Salome … and *also many other women* who came up with him to Jerusalem" (Mk 15:40–41, emphasis added). Each Gospel writer selected three women (the number needed for official witness) who were best recognized or known by his community.[4] In view of this, it is almost certain that more than three women were eyewitnesses and gave eyewitness testimony to Peter and the other apostles about the events surrounding Jesus' crucifixion, burial, and the empty tomb.

• **The beloved disciple:** As noted in NT#2 (section 4), the beloved disciple was, along with Peter, the primary eyewitness of the Gospel of John. As noted there, he had connections with the High Priest (to gain admittance to his courtyard), was probably from Jerusalem, and was well educated in both Jewish religious and secular areas of study. Unlike the other apostles, he was well positioned in religious circles around Jerusalem. This enabled him to be part of the procession that followed Jesus to the cross and remain with Him at the cross without risking arrest. He twice asserts that he witnessed all the proceedings of the passion:

1. John 19:35: "He who saw it has borne witness — his testimony is true, and he knows that he tells the truth — that you also may believe."
2. John 21:24: "This is the disciple who is bearing witness to these things, and who has written these

things; and we know that his testimony is true."

- **Other eyewitnesses to the passion:** In addition to Peter, the women followers of Jesus, and the beloved disciple, there are six other named eyewitnesses: Mary the mother of Jesus, Simon of Cyrene, Alexander and Rufus (Simon's sons), and two members of the Sanhedrin — Joseph of Arimathea (in all Gospels) and Nicodemus (in John's Gospel).

We can be sure that the apostles (who avoided the public proceedings because of the possibility of arrest) received news of what happened to Jesus after His trial. This is corroborated by the fact that all four Gospels indicate that the women did make such reports to the apostles (see Mk 16:7; Mt 28:7; Lk 24:8–9; Jn 20:2 and 20:18). This agreement between the Synoptics and John (independently formulated traditions and narratives) points strongly to the historicity of these events.

3. The Criterion of Embarrassment
The passion narratives are replete with embarrassing events that manifest historicity:

- Peter, who is the undisputed leader of the early Church, lies and curses in his denials of Jesus — his beloved master — three times. Why would any Christian include these events in the passion narratives if they were not true?
- Peter and the other apostles run away to avoid possible arrest, missing the events of Jesus' passion. Though they had a good reason (avoiding arrest), it diminishes their reputations.
- The insults leveled at Jesus by the soldiers and the crowds, the rejection by religious authorities, the degradation of the tortures inflicted by the soldiers, and the humiliation of Jesus' near-nakedness on the cross would not only have been embarrassing to Jesus' followers but also apologetically unappealing. Why would these details be included in the passion narratives unless they were true?

Why were the passion narratives as a whole (which are everywhere filled with embarrassments) included in all four Gospels if they were not true?

Conclusion

When we combine the testimony of hostile non-Christian sources writing near the time of Jesus with an abundance of eyewitnesses who give amazingly similar accounts of the passion events, and the proliferation of humiliating, insulting, degrading, repugnant, and embarrassing details throughout the passion narratives, it is reasonable and responsible to affirm that the passion narratives are historically reliable in general and in most of their details. This is further confirmed by a remarkable ancient artifact — the Shroud of Turin, which we will discuss in the next unit (NT#10).

NT#10: What Does the Shroud of Turin Tell Us about the Passion and Crucifixion of Jesus?[5]

The Shroud of Turin is a linen burial cloth fabricated by means of a herringbone, three-to-one twill pattern, measuring roughly fourteen feet by three and a half feet. It bears a perfect, three-dimensional, photographic negative image of a crucified man, an image executed in such accurate anatomical detail that modern medicine can diagnose many of the crucified man's injuries by analyzing it. Most intriguing of all, scientific tests have revealed that the image was not produced by any kind of paint, dye, chemical, vapor, or scorching but by intense radiation (see NT#14). The Shroud has 372 bloodstains (159 on the front image and 213 on the back image) with AB blood type and enzymes, indicating polytrauma, which were embedded on the Shroud prior to the creation of the image. It tells the story of a crucifixion that resembles the unique crucifixion of Jesus of Nazareth by Roman authorities (see section 2). The Shroud has the distinction of being the most unique image produced in human history and is by far the most scientifically investigated historical artifact.

In 1988, a carbon dating was performed that indicated the Shroud was produced between 1260 and 1390. As will be shown, this carbon dating has been debunked by several methods. New dating tests place the Shroud between AD 55 and 74, and other evidence indicates that it spent much of its time in Jerusalem and Northern Judea. We will here examine two issues:

1. The Dating of the Shroud (section 1)
2. The Blood Stains on the Shroud and the Crucifixion of Jesus (section 2)

1. The Dating of the Shroud

As noted above, a C-14 dating was done on the Shroud in 1988, showing a date between 1260 and 1390, implying that the Shroud has existed for only seven hundred years. If this carbon dating were true, it would disqualify it from being the Shroud of Jesus. But is it true? Five areas of evidence show that the Shroud almost certainly originated many centuries earlier, near the time of Jesus.

1. Dr. Ray Rogers showed that the sample taken for the C-14 dating (which came from a seriously compromised corner burned in the fire of Chambery in 1532) had cotton fibers dyed to make them look like the linen on the cloth. This disqualified the sample from being adequate to date the actual linen fabric throughout the Shroud. A C-14 test has not been done on any pure linen sample from the Shroud.[6]

2. Tristan Casabianca and colleagues, publishing in the Oxford journal *Archaeometry*, performed a statistical analysis of the raw data from the C-14 dating, which revealed significant heterogeneity within and among the samples. This shows that there are problems with the C-14 dating and that there may have been materials added to the place from which the sample was taken. This probably happened when religious sisters repaired the cloth after the fire of Chambery using cotton thread dyed to match the color of the linen. The heterogeneity itself disqualifies the sample. At this point, the C-14 dating has been debunked.

3. Several dating tests have been performed since the C-14

dating that are not based on carbon isotope content. First, Giulio Fanti and colleagues performed three tests: a Fourier transformed infrared spectroscopy, a Raman laser spectroscopy, and a mechanical compressibility and tension test. These tests combined give a dating of AD 90 ± 200 years at a 95 percent confidence level. Secondly, in 2022, Liberato De Caro and colleagues peer-reviewed a new dating test based on wide-angle X-ray scattering, which dated the Shroud between 54 and 75. Scientists believe this test is equivalent in accuracy to C-14 dating.

4. The bloodstains on the face and head of the man on the Shroud have 120 points of congruence with the bloodstains on the Facecloth of Oviedo (thought to be the facecloth used to transport Jesus from the cross to the tomb, mentioned in John 20:7), which has a documented provenance dating back to AD 616. If the two cloths had to touch the same bloodied face in order to produce 120 points of congruence in the irregular bloodstains on both cloths (which seems to be required), then the Shroud would have to go back to at least 616 or before. The bloodied face and head that the two cloths touched show a man who has been crowned with thorns — Syrian Christ thorns native to the Mediterranean region. This is quite similar to the *unique* crucifixion of Christ — the only crucifixion known to have had a crowning with thorns.

5. There are a considerable number of pollen grains embedded in the Shroud. Three-fourths of them are from the region of Jerusalem and Northern Judea, with thirteen being indigenous and four unique to that region. This means that the Shroud had to have been in Jerusalem and Northern Judea for a long time in the open air, probably for several centuries. Furthermore, there are pollen grains indigenous and unique to Edessa and Constantinople (in Turkey), which means the Shroud must have been in those cities for a significant time. But this conflicts with the carbon dating. If the Shroud is

only seven hundred years old (as determined by the C-14 dating), then it could not have been anywhere except in France and Italy throughout its lifetime, for it has a documented provenance in France and Italy starting in 1353, in Lirey, France, announced by Geoffroy de Charny. However, this conflicts with the fact that it was in Jerusalem/Northern Judea, Edessa, and Constantinople for several centuries. This undermines the C-14 dating.

The above five areas of scientific evidence show almost definitively that the C-14 dating test was flawed and could not have accurately determined the age of the Shroud. This evidence goes on to show the high likelihood that the Shroud originated about the mid-first century AD (close to the time of Jesus) in the area of Jerusalem/Northern Judea, after which it took a journey to Edessa, then to Constantinople, then to Lirey, France (1353), and finally to Turin, Italy (1578), where it remains today.

2. The Bloodstains on the Shroud and the Crucifixion of Jesus

There are 372 bloodstains on the Shroud. The image was formed after the bloodstains congealed on the cloth.[7] This means a potential forger would need to place all the bloodstains on the cloth before there was an image on which to place them — highly unlikely, even before we add the question of how the image itself was put on the Shroud without any paints, dyes, chemicals, vapors, or scorching (see NT#14). The bloodstains on the Shroud are genuine, containing real human hemoglobin, bilirubin, AB blood type, plasma-serum differentiation, human albumin, human whole blood serum, and human immunoglobulins.[8] These typical characteristics of blood are not present in paints or dyes or any other non-blood chemical, which assures that the stains on the Shroud are in fact human blood.

We now turn to the remarkable correspondence between the man on the Shroud and the unique crucifixion of Jesus. There are five major areas of correspondence: (1) the crown of thorns, (2) the wound from a lance thrust, (3) the wounds from the scourging, (4) the dislocated shoulder, and (5) the nail wounds in the hands and feet. We will discuss each in turn.

(1) **The crown of thorns:** The man on the Shroud was crowned with thorns, which left irregular wounds pointing to the Syrian Christ thorn, which is specific to the Mediterranean region. The Romans wove this crown over the top of the head as well as the forehead, temples, and back of the head, which inflicted more pain on the victim as the large thorns penetrated the scalp and bone. This feature (over the top of the head) would have been unknown to a potential medieval forger. The crowning with thorns is recounted in three Gospels (see Mt 27:29; Mk 15:17; and Jn 19:2) and is unique to Jesus in the history of crucifixion (who was accused of being "King of the Jews").[9]

(2) **The wound from a lance thrust:** Jesus was pierced with a lance (see Jn 19:34), which is another unique feature of His crucifixion. Romans preferred to let crucifixion last for as long as possible, but in Jesus' case there was pressure from the Sanhedrin to take Him down from the cross before Passover. This is so unusual — as well as the blood *and water* flowing from His side — that the beloved disciple had to insist that he had witnessed it, and it was true (Jn 19:35).

The Shroud shows a wound on the right side between the fifth and sixth ribs at an upward angle by a spear with an elliptically shaped tip, resembling the lance carried by Roman militia. The wound exuded both blood and a watery substance (detectable at the wound site on the Shroud), which was produced by piercing the right atrium of the heart and then piercing the pleural cavity (next to the lung), causing pleural effusion. How would a medieval forger be able to produce this elliptically shaped wound at the correct angle and replicate on the wound site both blood and pleural fluid? It seems highly unlikely.[10]

(3) **The wounds from the scourging:** Jesus was scourged a great number of times (see Mt 27:26, Mk 15:15, Jn 19:1, and implicitly in Lk 23:16). The number of lashes was beyond the norm, apparently because Pilate wanted to show that Jesus was sufficiently punished and would not need to be executed (Lk 23:16 and Jn 19:4–16). The man on the Shroud was scourged approximately thirty-nine times by two individuals, one on his left and a slightly taller individual on his right, using the Roman fla-

grum. The flagrum had three strands with a dumbbell-shaped lead pellet at the end of each strand. This left 117 lash marks (thirty-nine strikes times three strands per strike), which covered the man's back, thighs, and calves and reached around to his sides and the lateral parts of his chest.[11]

The scourging would have literally torn the flesh off the back and sides of the man, causing him to bleed profusely. Examining pathologists believe that this blood loss was the main reason why Jesus died after only three hours on the cross (a highly unusual feature of Jesus' crucifixion). The flagrum is precisely the instrument used by Roman legionaries for torture and execution for serious crimes. The flagrums used on the man on the Shroud are almost identical to those found in archaeological digs at Pompeii and Herculaneum. How would a medieval forger know how to replicate this Roman whip perfectly (without ever having seen one) and know how to replicate the effects on a man's body? Once again, it seems highly unlikely.

(4) The dislocated shoulder: Several pathologists have identified on the man in the Shroud a lowering of the right shoulder 10 to 15 degrees, hyperextension of the arms, a left twist in the neck, and the retraction of the right eye in its orbit. These injuries indicate that the man on the Shroud had a large object on his shoulder, and when he fell to his knees (identified by knee abrasions), the object hit him so hard that it caused a dislocated shoulder and paralysis on the upper right side. When this occurred, the man's head was twisted violently to the left, his right eye was sucked into its orbit, and he suffered hyperextension of the arms — a feature that, when first discovered on the Shroud, was thought to be anatomically incorrect but is now shown to be consistent with the dislocation of the shoulder and other injuries. The hyperextension of the arms would have exacerbated the pain of the man when he hung from the cross, and it would have made his breathing difficult, thereby shortening his life.

The dislocation of the shoulder and the paralysis of the right side would have prevented the man from carrying the large object on his right shoulder (probably the horizontal beam of the cross) any farther. This explains a curious feature of Jesus' crucifixion — namely, that Simon of Cyrene was summoned to help carry the cross. Given that the Romans would not have done anything to ease Jesus' burden, the summoning of

Simon in this scenario appears to be necessary for Jesus to reach Golgotha.[12]

(5) The nail wounds in the hands and feet: The Gospel accounts speak about the nail wounds in Jesus' hands (see Lk 24:39–40 and Jn 20:20, 25, 27) as well as His feet (Lk 24:39–40). These wounds were visible on His risen body. The man on the Shroud had a nail go through his left hand (and probably his right hand, though this is not visible because the left hand is covering the right). Pathologists think that the angle of the nail, judged from the exit wound, proceeded from his palm (in the thenar furrow region) angled 10 to 15 degrees downward toward the back of the wrist, which naturally guided the nail toward the area created by the metacarpal bones of the index and second finger and the capitate and lesser multiangular bones of the carpus (wrist), called the "Z" area. This would have strongly affixed the man's hand to the cross, causing considerable pain to the victim when he tried to lift himself to breathe, because this region contains a large network of nerves. This also explains the lengthening of the Shroud man's fingers.

It appears that the Shroud man's feet were also nailed to the cross. It is difficult to determine whether the feet were nailed side by side to the stipes or one foot on top of the other by a single nail. The feet were probably strapped flush to the stipes and then nailed to the upright through the top of the foot, going through the heel. No support was necessary for criminals to push themselves up — the feet would have felt glued to the upright. Once again, the pain would have been excruciating.[13]

Conclusion

The latest dating evidence of the Shroud of Turin shows the 1988 C-14 dating to be flawed and places the origin of the Shroud with high probability to mid-first-century AD in the region of Jerusalem/Northern Judea. This correlates well with the crucifixion of Jesus. The blood on the Shroud is certainly human blood, and the 372 bloodstains (relative to the perfect anatomical image of a man's body) show such striking resemblances to Jesus' unique crucifixion that it can scarcely have been produced by anyone other than Jesus. The anatomically perfect placement of the bloodstains relative to the body, the fact that the bloodstains were placed on the cloth *before* the image, and the distinctively Roman methods and weapons of crucifixion, make the medieval forger hypothesis highly unlikely, if not insupportable. In NT#14, we will show that the cause of the image must be intense radiation, which cannot be explained as coming from a corpse naturalistically, seemingly requiring supernatural causation.

Given the veracity of this analysis, the Shroud shows the high reliability not only of the Gospel narratives in general, but also all of the details about the tortures and crucifixion themselves. Furthermore, it heightens our awareness of the pain and suffering endured by Jesus to rescue us from the power of darkness and bring us into the eternal kingdom of His light and love.

NT#11: Did Jesus Intend to Give Us His *Real* Body and Blood in the Holy Eucharist?

Jesus' intention to give us His real Body and Blood in the holy Eucharist has been obscured significantly by erroneous exegetical analyses since the time of the Protestant Reformation and has grown vague in the minds of many Catholics today. If we are to extricate ourselves from this misleading exegetical analyses, we must return to Jesus' mindset, which was Jewish, prophetic, Messianic, and imbued with His divine Sonship (see NT#7).

We may summarize Jesus' intention as follows. At the Last Supper, He placed himself at the center of a ritual self-sacrificial act, separating His Body (given before the Supper) and His Blood (given after the Supper) precisely as would be done with a sacrificial animal offered for the forgiveness of sins. His intention was not only to give us His Body and Blood but also His whole self, crucified and risen, in an act of unrestricted love that would redeem our sins, protect us from evil, heal and transform our hearts, and lead us to eternal life with Him. We will explain this in three sections:

1. The Meaning of Jesus' Eucharistic Words (section 1)
2. The Double Collapse of Time and Jesus' Real Presence in the Eucharist (section 2)

3. The Eucharist in Saint Paul and Early Church Fathers (section 3)

1. The Meaning of Jesus' Eucharistic Words

If we are to enter into this celebration of unrestricted love more fully, we will first want to understand Jesus' Eucharistic words. When He said, "This is my body which is given for you" (Lk 22:19), the Greek word used to translate His Hebrew (*zeh baśari*) or Aramaic (*den bisri*) was *sōma* rather than *sarx*. *Sarx* means "flesh" and would certainly refer to Jesus' corporeal Body given on the cross, while *sōma* is much broader and refers to the whole person (mind, soul, will, as well as corporeal Body). It might, therefore, be roughly translated as "person" or "self." If we substitute the word *self* for *Body* in the Eucharistic words, we obtain, "This is my whole self given up for you." This is remarkably close to Jesus' definition of love ("gift of self") given in the Gospel of John: "Greater love has no man than this, that a man lay down his life for his friends" (Jn 15:13). Thus, in the Eucharist, Jesus is giving us not only His whole self — His whole Person — He is also giving us His love, indeed, His *unrestricted* love — that is, a love that cannot be exceeded.

This unrestricted love is confirmed by the gift of His Blood (which, according to Jewish custom, is separated from the body of the sacrificial offering[14]). When Jesus offered His Blood separately from His Body, He showed himself to be an intentional self-sacrifice, which He interpreted to be an offering of unrestricted love.

Blood (the principle of life for the Israelites[15]) was the vehicle through which atonement occurred in sin or guilt offerings.[16] Jesus' reference to His sacrificial Blood would be seen as the blood of a sin-offering — with the notable exception that the sin-offering is no longer an animal but rather Jesus himself, the exclusive, beloved Son of the Father. Jesus humbled himself (taking the place of an animal — a sacrificial sin offering) as the Beloved One of the Father, to take away the sin of the world forever. The Eucharistic words Jesus uses in both Mark/Matthew and Luke/Paul are "poured out" (and in Mark/Matthew alone, "for the forgiveness of sins"). This is an allusion to Isaiah 53:12, which is a Messianic prophecy indicating that the Messiah would give up His life for the forgiveness of sins (see OT#24) — "He [the Messiah] poured out his soul to death, and was numbered with the transgressors; yet he bore the sin of many, and made intercession for the transgressors." Thus Jesus, in His Eucharistic words, is taking the place of Isaiah's Messianic innocent suffering servant to redeem the sins of the world.

Jesus goes beyond identifying himself with the new sacrificial sin-offering and further identifies himself with the Paschal lamb. His use of the word *blood* within the context of the Passover supper shows that He intended to do this. He loved us so much that He desired to *become* the new Passover sacrifice, replacing an unblemished lamb with His own Messianic Divine Presence.

Recall that the blood of the Passover lamb, put on the doorposts of every Israelite household in Egypt, was the instrument through which the Israelite people were protected from death, as the Angel of Death passed over those houses. This enabled them to move out of slavery in Egypt to freedom in the promised land. When Jesus took the place of the Paschal lamb, He transformed a merely temporal and conditional freedom given through the Passover ritual into a *trans*temporal freedom from slavery to sin and death, which is the entryway into an eternal life of unrestricted love. Thus He made His self-sacrifice the new vehicle for protection from death itself for all eternity by outshining sin and darkness with His unconditionally loving eternal light.

There is yet a third dimension of Jesus' use of blood, which He explicitly states as "the blood of the covenant" (Mt 26:28 and Lk 22:20). A covenant was a solemn promise that bound parties to an unbreakable agreement. When Jesus associates His Blood with the covenant, He is *guaranteeing* the covenant with His life (because blood is the principle of life). When He sheds His Blood on the cross (the following day), He elevates His guarantee from word-based to action-based. By shedding His Blood, He has guaranteed His covenant absolutely; there can be no higher proof of the guarantee.

So, what is this covenant or contract about? In addition to guaranteeing the forgiveness of sins and the freedom and protection from evil and death, Jesus' blood covenant makes those who receive the Eucharist His family. As McKenzie notes, "[The covenant of blood makes] the contracting parties one blood, one family (Ex 24:3–8)."[17] When Jesus makes us family members through His Blood covenant, He intends that it be this way throughout eternity, so long as we do not reject Him and break the covenant with Him.

We may summarize by saying that Jesus' Blood of the covenant is a guarantee of His unrestricted love (by giving us His whole self); a guarantee of the forgiveness of our sins (by making himself a sin offering); a guarantee of freedom from darkness, emptiness, and slavery to sin and evil (by taking the place of the Paschal lamb); and a guarantee of eternal life (by making us members of His divine family). This is why the Eucharistic discourse in John 6 repeats again and again that whoever eats Jesus' Flesh and drinks His Blood will have eternal life (see Jn 6:39, 40, 44, 47, 50, 51, 54, and 58).

2. The Double Collapse of Time and Jesus' Real Presence in the Eucharist

How do we know that Jesus intended to give us His *real* Body and Blood — His *real* crucified and risen self — rather than a merely symbolic presence in the bread and wine? We begin with the implications of John's Eucharistic discourse (see Jn 6:30–66). Consider the following:

> I am the living bread which came down from heaven; if any one eats of this bread, he will live forever; *and the bread which I shall give for the life of the world is my flesh.* He who eats my flesh and drinks my blood abides in me, and I in him. (John 6:51, 56)

The beloved disciple here could not be more clear: The bread that comes down from heaven *is* the bread that Jesus gives in the holy Eucharist, which *is* His flesh for the life of the world. This bread which is Jesus' flesh has real power to bestow eternal life on those who receive it and to bind those who receive it to Him (in His family), enabling Him to live in us and us to live in Him.

It is a real stretch to interpret this passage to mean that the bread Jesus gives has only symbolic significance, because *is* (*estin*) indicates identity in predication. If the beloved disciple wanted to indicate mere symbolic significance, he could have used many other expressions, such as, "is like," "represents," "points to," or even "symbolizes" — but he did not. Furthermore, how does a mere symbol bind us to Jesus so that He is living in us and we in Him? Where in Israelite literature does a mere symbol have life-giving power and the power to unite divine and human beings? If the Johannine grammar and the absence of precedent indicating that mere symbols have power over life and death are not enough to convince the skeptic, the end of the Johannine discourse should make the beloved disciple's intention clear. In John 6:60 and 66, many of Jesus' disciples leave Him after hearing His discourse: "Many of his disciples, when they heard it, said, 'This is a hard saying; who can listen to it?' ... After this many of his disciples drew back and no longer went about with him." If Jesus meant only that the bread was a mere symbol of His Body and Blood, it would hardly have scandalized His disciples enough to cause them to abandon Him *en masse*.

We now move to the distinctively prophetic-Messianic meaning and power of Jesus' Eucharistic words and actions. Jesus' action at the Last Supper is prophetic — that is, it reaches into the future toward its fulfillment and, in accordance with Jesus' intention, brings the future fulfillment into the present.[18] The first-century Jewish view of time is quite different from our physical view of time. While we view time as physical, objectively determinant, and measurable, first-century Judaism viewed it as sacred, malleable, and collapsible — particularly with respect to prophetic utterances about the future and ritual reenactments of past events.[19]

Recall that the prophet's word is the living word of God, which has power (apart from the prophet who uttered it) to transcend and negate the effects of time. As such, it could collapse the time between a future event (existing in the mind of God) and the present. Accordingly, when Jesus says, "This is my body which is given for you" (Lk 22:19), He means it *is* really His Body, on the cross at Calvary on Friday, transforming the bread He is handing to His disciples at the Last Supper on Thursday. Thus, through His prophetic word and action, He is bringing His future sacrificed Body (existing in the mind of God, which transcends time) into the bread He is giving to His disciples at the Last Supper.

This transcendence of time is implied in Luke's account of Jesus' Eucharistic words, which uses the present passive participle *didomenon*, which means "is being given." Hence, Jesus' words over the bread that He gave to His disciples were, "This is my Body which is *being given* for you." The implication is "being given for you — *now*." This corresponds precisely to the prophetic word going into the future to bring a salvific event into the present — the real Body of Jesus on the cross on Friday being brought into the bread being handed to His disciples on Thursday.

The same holds true for the cup of wine. Again, Jesus uses a present passive participle in Hebrew/Aramaic, which is translated into Greek *ek-chunomenon*, which means, "is being poured out." Thus Jesus' word over the cup of wine should be translated, "This cup which *is being poured out* for you [*now*] is the new covenant in my blood" (Lk 22:20). In the first-century Jewish view of time, Jesus is collapsing the time between the future pouring out of His Blood on the cross (on Friday) and the time of the Last Supper, when He hands the cup to His disciples (on Thursday).

In sum, when Jesus uttered His prophetic words at the table, He made present His *real* future Body and Blood, sacrificed in love for humankind on the cross. For Him, the separation of time was transcended by His prophetic word and divine power — and therefore, the reality of His future Body sacrificed on the cross was just as real at the Last Supper as it would be in the future.

It is important to note here that first-century Judaism did not have a view of a merely symbolic (abstract) prophetic utterance, but rather, the living and powerful word of God, which had a life of its own.[20] This is particularly the case for Jesus, the divine Messiah. In view of this, we should interpret Jesus' words as He meant them: that what appeared to be bread was His real crucified Body being given on the cross, and that what appeared to be wine was His real Blood being poured out for us on the cross.

Jesus did not expect the bread to turn into the appearance of His Flesh or the wine to turn into the appearance of His Blood. Though these appearances are very important to our scientific mindset, they were considered only incidental by the first-century Jewish mindset, which understood what appeared to be bread as the medium through which the future salvific event was present — really present — irrespective of what it looked like.[21]

We now move to the second collapse of time, which is manifest in Jesus' command to His disciples, "Do this in remembrance of me." It is essential to note that Judaism (in the first millennium BC and into the first century AD) shared with other ancient cultures the view of sacred time in which the reliving or reenactment of a sacred event causes time between the present reenactment and the past event to collapse.[22] This would enable the reenactors to enter into the sacred moment of the past, in which they could share the fruits of its saving action.[23] Ancient Judaism had several rituals in which designated prophets or others would reenact past sacred moments, enabling the Divine Presence and salvific action of the past to become present and efficacious at the moment of reenactment. For example, in the Jewish celebration of the Passover, the reenactment of the Passover event brought the Divine Presence and saving power of that event into the lives of those celebrating it.[24]

This background sheds light on what Jesus was asking of His apostles at the Last Supper. When Jesus commissioned His disciples to "do this in remembrance of me," He and they would not have thought that this meant merely to call it to mind. This simplistic view of ritual reenactment did not exist in first-century Judaism, and it would not have occurred to either party. Rather, the apostles would naturally have thought that Jesus was asking them to do a ritual reenactment (with which they were familiar from their Jewish background) that would make His Person and saving action present in the bread, wine, and ritual words being reenacted. They would also have recognized that He was commissioning them and empowering them to do this very special reenactment to bring His Person and efficacious saving action to all future generations.

When Jesus commissioned the apostles to do the rite of Eucharistic remembrance, He simultaneously created a special charism for this celebration, which was given to apostles and prophets — the two highest offices in the Church.[*] The *Didache* (composed around AD 70–80) indicates that the apostles and prophets were set aside to celebrate the Eucha-

---

[*] Saint Paul lists the ranking of charisms/offices in the early Church in 1 Corinthians 12:28, "God has appointed in the church first apostles, second prophets, third teachers, then workers of miracles, then healers, helpers, administrators, speakers in various kinds of tongues."

ristic remembrance.[25] It is not surprising that those who had the charism to bring the past salvific event into the present were called "prophets," because the word they uttered was not their own but the living divine word that could make past saving actions real in the present.

In sum, a ritual reenactment was understood as a re-presentation of a *real* — not merely a symbolic or cognitive — saving event in which God's Presence and saving action are manifest. In the case of the holy Eucharist, the Divine Presence is Jesus' Person (*whole self*, including His crucified and risen Body and Blood), bringing His unrestricted love and salvific action into the world through the self-sacrificial crucifixion and the Eucharistic celebration at the Last Supper. Johannes Betz synthesizes this complex act of "remembrance" (*anamnesis*) as follows:

> *Anamnesis* [remembrance] in the biblical sense means not only the subjective representation of something in the consciousness and as an act of the remembering mind. It is also the objective effectiveness and presence of one reality in another, especially the effectiveness and presence of the salvific actions of God, in the liturgical worship. Even in the Old Testament, the liturgy is the privileged medium in which the covenant attains *actuality*. The meaning of the logion ["Do this in remembrance of me"] may perhaps be paraphrased as follows: "do this (what I have done) in order *to bring about my Presence*, to make really present the salvation wrought in me."[26]

In conclusion, the Eucharistic remembrance (reenactment) brings the real, objective Presence of Jesus and His saving power and action of the past event into the present moment. So, when Jesus said, "Do this in remembrance of me," He meant that the apostles (and their successors, the "prophets"[27]) should engage in a ritual reenactment of His Eucharistic words, which would make His Person (whole self, including His crucified and risen Body and Blood) and saving action and power really present under the appearances of bread and wine.

We may now synthesize the double collapse of time initiated by Jesus at the Last Supper, which actualizes Jesus' whole Person, including His crucified and risen Body and Blood, whenever the Eucharistic remembrance is celebrated:

- **First collapse of time:** Jesus' prophetic utterance brings His real crucified Body and Blood (on Friday) into the present in Jesus' ritual during the Passover supper (on Thursday).
- **Second collapse of time:** Future priests collapse the time between the Last Supper (in which Jesus' Body and Blood are really present under the appearances of bread and wine, which He offered to His disciples) and the present moment through the consecration at Mass — the ritual reenactment of Jesus' Eucharistic words.

It might be objected that time, according to science, does not collapse. While it is true that *physical* time is not viewed by science as collapsible, time itself (with its earlier and later components) can only be held together by a transcendent mind that is not conditioned by time (i.e., a divine mind).[28] If God is beyond all time (and time exists through the mind of God), then He can bring a future event into the present (as Jesus expects He will do in His prophetic utterance), and He can bring the reality of a past event into the present, which Jesus expects He will do when He commands His disciples to "do this in remembrance of me."

Assuming that Eliade, Jeremias, von Rad, and Betz are correct about the temporal implications of Jesus' prophetic utterance and His command to ritually reenact the institution of the Eucharist, then when we receive a consecrated Eucharistic Host, we receive the whole Person of Jesus (His Body, Blood, soul, and divinity) within the saving events of His crucifixion and resurrection. This gift is divinely redemptive, protective, transformative, and life-giving unto eternity. If we take Jesus at His word, understood through a first-century Jewish hermeneutic, there could be no greater gift, no greater love, and no greater hope than the holy Eucharist.

3. Saint Paul and Early Church Fathers and the Real Presence of Christ in the Eucharist

What did Saint Paul and the early Church Fathers believe about the Eucharistic bread and wine? As we shall see, they universally proclaimed that they were the *real* Body and Blood of Christ. Let us first begin with two passages from 1 Corinthians that show Saint Paul's belief in the Real Presence of Jesus' Body and Blood in the Eucharist.

> The cup of blessing which we bless, is it not a participation in the blood of Christ? The bread which we break, is it not a participation in the body of Christ? Because there is one bread, we who are many are one body, for we all partake of the one bread. (1 Corinthians 10:16–17)
>
> Whoever, therefore, eats the bread or drinks the cup of the Lord in an unworthy manner will be guilty of profaning the body and blood of the Lord. Let a man examine himself, and so eat of the bread and drink of the cup. For any one who eats and drinks without discerning the body eats and drinks judgment upon himself. (11:27–29)

Beyond the fact that Paul identifies the bread and wine unqualifiedly with the Body and Blood of Jesus, he asserts that the Body and Blood have the power to unify us and that their unworthy reception jeopardizes our salvation. How can a mere symbol have such power and salvific consequences?

Let us now turn to the early Church Fathers, who follow the beloved disciple (see Jn 6:32–59) and Saint Paul very closely. St. Ignatius of Antioch, in his Letter to the Romans (AD 110), wrote: "I have no taste for corruptible food nor for the pleasures of this life. I desire the bread of God, which is the flesh of Jesus Christ ... and for drink I desire his blood, which is love incorruptible."[29]

We see the same conviction about the bread becoming the Body of Christ and the wine becoming the Blood of Christ, which produces the effects of self-transformation, healing, unity, and eternal life, in additional Church Fathers:

- St. Justin Martyr (AD 151), *First Apology* (6)
- Saint Irenaeus (189), *Against Heresies* (4:33 and 5:2)
- Tertullian (210), *The Resurrection of the Dead* (8)
- Hippolytus (217), *Commentary on Proverbs* (9:2)
- Origen (248), *Homilies on Numbers* (7:2)
- St. Cyprian of Carthage (251), *The Lapsed* (15–16)
- St. Cyril of Jerusalem (350), *Catechetical Lectures* (19:7)
- St. Ambrose of Milan (390), *The Mysteries* (9:50, 58)
- Saint Augustine (405), *Explanations of the Psalms* (33:1:10)

Evidently, virtually every early Church Father, from St. Ignatius of Antioch to Saint Augustine, expressed his conviction about the Real Presence of Christ in the Eucharist. If this had not been a well-defined part of the apostolic tradition, it would never have become such a universally strong part of the ongoing, living Tradition through Saint Augustine.

Conclusion

In light of the above, we conclude that Jesus intended that His whole Person (manifest through His crucified and risen Body and Blood) be really present under the appearances of bread and wine at the Eucharistic remembrance He instructed His disciples to celebrate. This is evident in all known New Testament and early Church sources, including Jesus' Eucharistic words (when understood through the hermeneutic of sacred time intrinsic to first-century Jewish thought); John's Eucharistic discourse (see Jn 6:30–66); Saint Paul's Eucharistic declarations (in 1 Cor 10:16–17 and 11:27–29); the apostolic Tradition; and the ongoing living Tradition until this very day. The interpretation of the Real Presence as "transubstantiation" first occurred at the Fourth Lateran Council in 1215, and St. Thomas Aquinas gave it a metaphysical explanation, which continues to be professed to the current day.[30] This conclusion is further corroborated by three contemporary, scientifically investigated Eucharistic miracles to be discussed in the next unit.

NT#12: Are There Scientifically Investigated Eucharistic Miracles Manifesting Jesus' Body and Blood?[31]

Though a Eucharistic miracle occurs during every Mass, there are some scientifically inexplicable manifestations of living cardiac tissue growing out of a consecrated Eucharistic Host that may provide a scientifically oriented world with evidence of Jesus' intention to give us His real Body and Blood at the Last Supper. The first recorded Eucharistic miracle to undergo scientific investigation occurred at Lanciano, Italy, in the eighth century, and was tested by Dr. Edoardo Linoli in 1971 and 1981. His tests indicated that the tissue growing out of the Host resembled cardiac tissue, and no artificial preservatives were used to cause its remarkable longevity. However, the Host was quite old, and the chain of custody uncertain, so we will focus on three contemporary Eucharistic Hosts with a secure chain of custody that have undergone considerable scientific investigation in several laboratories:

1. **The Host of Buenos Aires (1996):** The primary scientific investigators were Dr. Ricardo Castañón Gomez and Dr. Frederick Zugibe. Ecclesiastical oversight was provided by Archbishop Jorge Bergoglio — now Pope Francis (section 1).
2. **The Host of Tixtla, Mexico (2006):** The primary scientific investigator, Dr. Ricardo Castañón Gomez, was supported by eight other scientific experts (section 2).
3. **The Host of Sokolka, Poland (2008):** The primary scientific investigators were Dr. Maria Łotkowska and Dr. Stanislaw Sulkowski of the Medical University of Bialystok (section 3).

We will here give only the major scientifically validated highlights of these Hosts showing the strong likelihood of supernatural origin.

1. The Host of Buenos Aires (1996)[32]

In 1996, a Host was abandoned at the back of the church of Santa Maria y Caballito Almagro in Buenos Aires. It was placed in a glass of water and put into a tabernacle and remained in water for over three years. Instead of the Host dissolving, tissue began to grow out of the substance of the Host, which was later revealed to be *living* cardiac tissue. The Host was examined by Dr. Ricardo Castañón Gomez, a former adamant atheist who, after examining the Host, converted to a fervent Catholic. It was also examined by Dr. Frederick Zugibe, one of the world's foremost pathologists and experts in diagnostic histochemistry at Columbia University; Professor John Walker, histopathologist at the University of Sydney; and Dr. Edoardo Linoli, professor of histology and clinical microscopy in Rome. They found the Buenos Aires Host to be scientifically inexplicable in three ways.

1. First, the Host/tissue did not decompose after three years of being immersed in water, for which there is no natural explanation (validated by Zugibe and Castañón Gomez).
2. Second, the tissue was identified by Drs. Linoli and Zugibe as being heart tissue from the myocardium (left ventricle) near the valve area. This was further corroborated by Dr. Walker, who identified muscular cells in the blood, and Dr. Lawrence, who indicated that the tissue could be inflamed heart tissue.
3. Third, according to Drs. Linoli, Walker, and Zugibe, there are intact living white blood cells in the heart tissue, indicating that the heart tissue was alive at the time of testing. Thus the Host was transformed into *living* heart tissue, for which there is no known natural explanation. Inasmuch as the samples tested by Drs. Walker, Linoli, and Zugibe originated on or before September 6, 1996, and there were intact white blood cells, indicating that the heart tissue was alive at the time of testing (between 2001 and 2004), it must be concluded that this tissue is beyond natural explanation, for how can heart tissue remain alive separate from an embodied circulatory system for eight years?

There is another enigma: Despite remnants of DNA molecules in the blood and two attempts to amplify a profile (through polymerase chain reaction), no profile could be obtained. This also occurred with the Host of Tixtla — see below.

2. The Host of Tixtla, Mexico (2006)

On October 22, 2006, a religious sister looking at a Host in a pyx at the Church of St. Martin of Tours in Tixtla, Mexico, saw that it was effusing a reddish substance that looked like blood. After being shown to several priests, the Host was secured in a tabernacle, after which a scientific investigation was initiated by the bishop, who appointed Dr. Ricardo Castañón Gomez to oversee it. Several laboratories in the United States and Latin America were commissioned, and several scientific experts joined the investigative team. The team included an anatomical pathologist; two experts in surgical histopathology; experts in DNA biotechnology, forensic genetics, biochemistry, and pharmacy; an expert in legal and forensic medicine; and two computer imaging experts.[33] Scientific testing took place between 2009 and 2012, and Dr. Castañón Gomez documented all the laboratory results in appendices 1–19 in his volume on the miracle.[34] Since the evidence of scientific inexplicability was so well-documented and overwhelming, Bishop Alejo Zavala Castro of Chilpancingo-Chilapa declared the Host to be miraculous on October 12, 2013. A scientific team concluded that three aspects of the Host were scientifically inexplicable:

1. Human blood with living red blood cells and white blood cells is issuing from the Host. These blood cells usually die within one hour of being removed from a living circulatory system. The white blood cells (e.g., macrophages) are engaged in healing activities — phagocytizing lipids (engulfing and digesting harmful fat cells) — indicating that the blood is *living* blood and that the tissue is injured. There are four indications of human blood: AB blood type, human hemoglobin, immunoglobulins, and whole blood. Since fresh blood continued to issue from the Host during testing in 2010, we must ask how a consecrated Host (unconnected to an embodied circulatory system) could produce fresh blood.

2. There is living cardiac tissue in the interior of the Host from which the blood is issuing, provoking the question of how living cardiac tissue is integrated with the substance of a consecrated Host, which is molecularly and structurally distinct from that Host. Since fresh living blood is effusing from this tissue, it must be *living* tissue (like the Buenos Aires Host). Inasmuch as the bleeding from the Host began in 2006 and the activity of the white blood cells was taking place during testing in 2010 (indicating that the tissue and blood were still alive), we must ask how the tissue and blood could remain alive for four years when the tissue and blood of the Host are not connected to a living circulatory system. This is not scientifically or naturalistically explicable.

3. The blood is moving from the interior of the Host to the exterior (surface) of the Host, which is conclusively shown by pressure tests as well as the fresh blood being underneath coagulating (older) blood. This implies that new blood is being created in the interior of the Host and pushing outward. These effects exclude the possibility of someone fraudulently placing blood in the interior of the Host. This has no naturalistic explanation.

Like the Host of Buenos Aires, the blood and tissue samples used for DNA analysis showed evidence of DNA molecules, but after multiple attempts, researchers could not amplify a profile through polymerase chain reaction. This is a real conundrum because the blood and tissue were alive at the time of the testing (meaning they can't be too old to produce a profile), and the sample size was more than adequate. Why can't a DNA profile be found on the Tixtla and Buenos Aires Hosts?

3. The Host of Sokolka, Poland (2008)[35]

On Sunday, October 12, 2008, during a Mass at Saint Anthony's Church in Sokolka, Poland, a Host was dropped by a vicar who was distributing Communion. He picked up the Host and, after examining it, placed it into a glass of water and secured it in a safe. After one week, the sacristan checked on the state of the Host and found that it had a bright red stain, which was later discovered to be cardiac tissue growing out of the Host (see below). The Host remained in water for forty-eight days, after which the archbishop asked that it be removed and kept on a corporal in a dry place. After two and a half years, the archbishop requested a scientific study be done, and samples of the Host were given to two histopathologists at the Medical University of Bialystok for *independent* examinations — Professor Maria Elżbieta Sobaniec-Łotkowska, M.D., and Professor Stanislaw Sulkowski, M.D. They concluded that the consecrated Host was scientifically inexplicable in three ways:

1. The Host remained in water for forty-eight days without notable decomposition of either the substance of the Host or the cardiac tissue growing out of it.
2. The tissue growing out of the Host is *living* cardiac tissue. The indicators of cardiac tissue are cellular nuclei in the fibrils resembling contraction nodes as well as inserts that typify damaged *cardiac* muscle. The indications of the tissue being alive (non-necrosed) are segmentation and fragmentation that are typically produced by rapid beating of the heart shortly before death. These phenomena do not occur in necrosed fibers.
3. The substance of the Host and the substance of the living heart tissue are inextricably integrated with only a few microns of separation — on the level of the outlines of the communicating junctions and the thin filaments of the myofibrils. This was observed through both a light microscope and a transmission electron microscope. This is not only scientifically inexplicable but, as Dr. Sobaniec-Łotkowska declared: "Even NASA scientists, who have at their disposal the most modern analytical techniques, would not be able to artificially recreate such a thing."

Conclusion

The combined scientific analysis of the Hosts of Buenos Aires, Tixtla, and Sokolka indicate through many different tests in many different laboratories with many scientific experts that living cardiac tissue is found to be growing out of consecrated Eucharistic Hosts. In the case of Tixtla, fresh blood continues to issue from the Host, and in the case of Sokolka (where transmission electron microscopic analysis was done), the integration of the substance of the Host and the substance of the cardiac tissue was so complex and refined as to be unreplicable by the best technologies today. Despite the presence of DNA molecular structures in the samples from the Buenos Aires and Tixtla Hosts, no DNA profile was amplifiable by polymerase chain reaction, which is highly unusual given that the tissue was alive at the time of testing. Is this linked to the fact that Jesus had no genetic contribution from a human father?

One last consideration: The cardiac tissue from all three Hosts was wounded. This is evidenced in the living white blood cells performing healing functions in the Buenos Aires and Tixtla Hosts, as well as the fragmentation and segmentation in the tissue, caused by rapid beating from trauma to the heart prior to death, in the Sokolka Host. What better sign of the Real Presence of Jesus' Body and Blood given on the cross at Calvary could there possibly be? The irony is that science has not undermined this miracle but has brought its supernatural character to light.

CHAPTER 9
The Resurrection, Holy Spirit, and Catholic Church: History and Science

NT#13: What Is the Historical Evidence of Jesus' Resurrection?

As will be seen, there is considerable historical evidence for Jesus' glorious resurrection, which is complemented by the scientific investigation of the Shroud of Turin. Jesus' resurrection, manifesting His divine power and will to bring us into His risen glory, is central to Christian faith. Saint Paul says that if Jesus did not rise from the dead, then the Christian's faith would be in vain, the apostles' preaching useless, and all those who have died in Christ would have perished in their sins, making Christians the most pitiable of all people (see 1 Cor 15:12–19).

The vast majority of New Testament scholars believe that Jesus appeared to His disciples in a transformed, glorious, bodily form. A recent survey of New Testament scholars by Gary Habermas[1] indicates: "*Most* contemporary scholars agree that, after Jesus' death, his early followers had *experiences* that they at least believed were appearances of their risen Lord. Further, this conviction was the chief motivation behind the early proclamation of the Christian Gospel."[2]

We examine this evidence in three sections:

1. The Common Elements in the Gospel Narratives of Jesus' Risen Appearances (section 1)
2. The Historical Evidence of the Resurrection in the Writings of Saint Paul (section 2)
3. N. T. Wright's Historical Analysis of the Resurrection (section 3)

1. Common Elements in the Gospel Accounts of Jesus' Risen Appearances

The Gospel accounts of Jesus' risen appearances to the apostles share many common elements, and one of the most telling is that the apostles were not expecting what they saw, which shocked and amazed them. They were so overwhelmed by His transformation that they thought they were witnessing a divine appearance — not the same corporeal Jesus they had worked with during His ministry. In the midst of His glorious appearance, He reveals His former bodily characteristics with the wounds of His crucifixion.

Contrary to their expectations, Jesus appeared so transformed that Saint Paul had to coin a new term to describe it: a *soma pneumatikon*, or spiritual body. Matthew, Luke, and John put different emphases on this transformation, but all of them point to Jesus having powerful, spiritual characteristics proper to God himself. We will examine the accounts of Matthew, Luke, and John in turn.

Matthew: The Gospel of Matthew emphasizes Jesus' transformation in divine power and glory. There are three manifestations of this:

- First, when Jesus first appears, the apostles bow down and worship Him (see 28:17). The term *worship* is reserved almost exclusively for God (see the temptations of the Devil, 4:9–10). What could have provoked the apostles to do this? Jesus must have appeared in such power, glory, and beauty that worship was the only thinkable response. He looked like God.
- Second, Jesus says to His apostles, "All authority in heaven and on earth has been given to me" (28:18). This is clearly an assertion of divine power, because God alone has "*all* authority in heaven and on earth."
- Third, some of the apostles doubted (28:17). Evidently, they are not doubting that something resembling God is appearing, because they are overwhelmed by and worshiping the divine power and glory before them. So, what are they doubting? It seems that they do not recognize Jesus in the theophany (the appearance of God). It is not until Jesus missions them that they become cognizant that the divine power is actually He (28:20). Note that the "I" in 28:20 ("all that *I* have commanded you") indicates recognition of Jesus.

Luke: Luke's account of Jesus' appearance to His apostles has two parts: (1) when He initially appears, and they mistake Him for a spirit (see 24:36–48), and (2) Jesus' ascension (24:49–53). There are indications of Jesus' divine appearance in both:

- In the first part (24:36), Jesus seems to appear out of nowhere, standing among the disciples, implying that He did not enter their midst in an ordinary way.
- Again in the first part (24:37–38), Jesus shocks the apostles. Three different verbs are used to indicate fright, doubt, and amazement.
- Again in the first part (24:37, 39), Jesus is identified twice as having the form of a spirit (indicating transformation). This transformation is so significant that Jesus has to show the apostles His hands and feet to assure them that it is truly He,

and then He eats a fish to demonstrate continuity with His former embodiment. At this point, Jesus' spiritual transformation is revealed, but Luke reserves the revelation of His divinity to the second part.

- In the *second part* (24:51–52), Jesus ascends into heaven, showing that He has the power to enter the heavenly domain (proper to God) on His own. The apostles recognize this, and so "they *worshiped Him.*" Again, the term *worship* is used, which is reserved for God alone (4:7–8).

John: The Gospel of John has three Resurrection appearances to the apostles in two narratives (see 20:19–31 and 21:1–25): (1) the appearance to ten apostles in the closed room without Thomas (20:19–25); (2) Jesus' appearance to the Eleven with Thomas in a closed room (20:26–29); and (3) Jesus' appearance to seven of the apostles at the Sea of Tiberias (in chapter 21). There are five indications of Jesus' divinity in these narratives:

- In the first occurrence (20:19), Jesus appears out of nowhere in a closed room (without going through doors), manifesting transphysical characteristics.
- Again in the first appearance (20:22), Jesus breathes on the apostles, giving them the Holy Spirit by His own power. Note that the Holy Spirit was viewed as "the power of God" by the early Church, so this shows that Jesus by His own authority can give the power of God to whomever He wishes.
- In all three appearances, the narrator uses the name "Jesus," but the apostles only use the name "the Lord." This indicates that what the apostles are seeing and hearing is "the Lord." This title (*ho Kyrios* — with the definite article) is the Greek translation of God's name revealed to Moses — *Yahweh*. It is evidently used here to indicate Jesus' divinity, because prior to the Resurrection, Jesus is never referred to as "the Lord" (with the definite article), but only as "Lord," which can mean "Sir," "Master," or "Lord" (in a secular sense). So, what is John saying? After the Resurrection, the apostles saw and

heard a Person not appearing in physical form but appearing like the God of spirit, glory, and power — Yahweh. This explains why Jesus shows them His hands and side when He first appears (20:20).

- The confession of Thomas, *ho Kyrios mou, ho Theos mou,* means literally, "the Lord of me; the God of me." As explained before, Thomas's use of the definite article with *Kyrios* refers to the personal God — Yahweh. However, his use of *Theos* (God) with the definite article harkens back to the Christological hymn at the beginning of John's Gospel (1:1): In the beginning was the Word, and the Word was with/toward (*pros*) God, and the Word was God. The "Word" refers to the Son (Jesus), who explicitly shares in the divine nature (*pros ton theon*).[3]

- In the third appearance, at the Sea of Tiberias (21:12), we read the curious passage, "Now none of the disciples dared ask him, 'Who are you?' They knew it was the Lord." If the apostles knew very well it was the Lord (the one appearing in divine spirit, power, and glory — like Yahweh), why would they want to ask, "Who are you?" In light of the above, it seems clear that they did not recognize Jesus in the theophany (the Presence and power of God) until He revealed himself to them — in the feeding with bread and fish (Eucharistic signs) in 21:13 and in His love for Peter (21:15–17). Note that in John 20 Jesus resolves the recognition problem by first showing the apostles His hands and side (20:20), and then He does the same for Thomas (20:27).

The above textual evidence shows that the beloved disciple (the author of John's Gospel) asserts that Jesus appeared in a divine form and that the apostles saw (witnessed) Him in that form. Though they did not clearly perceive Jesus in the Divine Presence and power that appeared to them, He resolved their lack of recognition by showing them His hands and side as well as His love in feeding them with the sign of Eucharistic bread.

The authors of Matthew, Luke, and John reveal that Jesus after His resurrection was transformed in divine spirit and power and that in His initial manifestation to His apostles, He appeared like God while maintaining continuity with His former human embodiment. After manifesting His divinity, He revealed himself as Jesus by showing the wounds in His hands, feet, and side (see Lk 24:39–40; Jn 20:20; and Jn 20:27), by missioning His apostles (Mt 28:19 and Jn 21:15–19), and by giving the apostles the sign of the Eucharistic bread (Jn 21:13).

No doubt, Jesus' divine spiritual and powerful Presence after the Resurrection was a foundation for the apostles' unyielding proclamation of His divinity, which caused the early Church to lose converts, be banned from the Synagogue, and be persecuted, frequently unto death (see NT#16).

2. Paul's Testimony to the Resurrection of Jesus

One of the earliest New Testament traditions from the First Letter of Paul to the Corinthians contains a list of witnesses to the Resurrection:

> For I delivered to you as of first importance what I also received, that Christ died for our sins in accordance with the scriptures, that he was buried, that he was raised on the third day in accordance with the scriptures, and that he appeared to Cephas, then to the twelve. Then he appeared to more than five hundred brethren at one time, most of whom are still alive, though some have fallen asleep. Then he appeared to James, then to all the apostles. Last of all, as to one untimely born, he appeared also to me. (15:3–8)

Paul offers this list with an eye to its value as legal evidence. He mentions the five hundred, most of whom "are still alive," implying that his audience could still consult the witnesses to corroborate the story. The reason the list does not include the women at the tomb — the earliest witnesses mentioned in the Gospel narratives — is because Jewish law of the time did not acknowledge them to be valid witnesses.[4]

Paul's witness dilemma: Having offered the evidence of these witnesses, Paul probes the value of their evidence by laying out a dilemma in 1 Corinthians 15. Either the witnesses believe in God, or they do not believe in God. In either case, Paul argues, they had everything to lose and nothing to gain by falsely claiming to have witnessed the Resurrection. This shows that the witnesses to the Resurrection were internally motivated to tell the truth, because the consequences of lying were quite significant. Let's examine each side of the dilemma:

- **False witnesses who believed in God:** If a believer told a public lie about the resurrection of Jesus to gain a new convert to Christianity from Judaism, he would have falsely and unjustly undermined the Jewish religion. If the Resurrection were untrue, then the Jewish religion would continue to be the ultimate Revelation and religion of God. Falsely and unjustly undermining this ultimate Revelation and religion of God would jeopardize the salvation of this believer. As Paul states, "We are even found to be misrepresenting God" — a most grave offense in Judaism and Christianity (see 1 Cor 15:14–15). Why would believers risk their salvation to undermine God's Revelation and religion for a false religion (in which there is no resurrection)? Paul believes that this would be contrary to believers' best interests in both this life and the next — a lie that gains nothing but risks everything.
- **Witnesses who did not believe in God:** Those who did not believe in God would also lose much and gain nothing by lying about the Resurrection. Preaching Jesus' resurrection set the early Christians at odds with the Jewish tradition they lived in, causing them to get expelled from their synagogues and ostracized by their communities. Soon, it led to harassment by the Roman authorities as well. Ultimately, it meant active persecution, torture, and death. Indeed, Paul himself suffered repeatedly from these harassments and would soon die for the Faith. If the Resurrection were a lie, all that suffering would be for nothing. As he states: "If for this life only we have hoped in Christ, we are of all men most to be pitied. Why am I in peril every hour? What do I gain if, humanly speaking, I fought with beasts at Ephesus? If the dead are not raised, 'Let

us eat and drink, for tomorrow we die'" (15:19, 30, 32).

Paul uses this dilemma to show (in a legal fashion) that he and the other five-hundred-plus witnesses have everything to lose and nothing to gain by bearing false witness to the resurrection of Christ. Therefore, they are the best kind of witness.

3. N. T. Wright's Two Arguments for the Historicity of Jesus' Resurrection

N. T. Wright argues from the historical record that two aspects of the early Church are quite enigmatic if the Resurrection did not occur: the remarkable success of Christian Messianism (section 3. A) and the Christian mutations of Second Temple Judaism (section 3.B).

3.A. *The Remarkable Success of Christian Messianism*

As noted in NT#4, there were many Messianic movements in the time of Christ. Wright lists several of these: Judas the Galilean, Simon, Athronges, Eleazar ben Deinaus and Alexander, Menahem, Simon bar Giora, and bar-Kochba.[5] In every case, a charismatic leader would attract an enthusiastic following, the leader would die (usually at the hands of the authorities), the followers would scatter, and the Messianic movement would shortly die. One example of this pattern is even found in the Gospels: John the Baptist.

Christianity is the one dramatic exception to this pattern. After the public humiliation and execution of their leader, the disciples don't fade away but instead begin preaching throughout the surrounding countries that their crucified leader is in fact the Messiah and that He has somehow succeeded in fulfilling the ancient prophecies, is risen from the dead, and in fact is divine. Even more shockingly, the Messianic movement grew exponentially, and in a few generations, Christianity would be the dominant religion of the Roman Empire.[6] Where did this momentum come from? What inspired the early Christians with such conviction?

As explained in NT#4, John P. Meier and N. T. Wright believe that the apostles would have had little credibility with this message among the Jewish or Gentile people were it not for three extraordinary occurrences:

1. Jesus' resurrection appearance in glory turned their dejection into an exceedingly strong conviction, individually and collectively.
2. The apostles were able to perform healings and miracles on a regular basis through the Holy Spirit.
3. They worked these miracles through the name of Jesus.

As the apostles imply: If Jesus is not risen from the dead as we have preached, then how could we work miracles through His Spirit *in His name*? No other Messianic movement worked regular miracles in the name of their Messiah (including the movement of John the Baptist).[7] This explains how Christianity's preaching of the Resurrection was so credible and therefore how the early Church grew so rapidly.[8] This gives evidence not only of the power of the Holy Spirit in the ministry of the apostles but also of the resurrection of Jesus. We might all ask ourselves why God would have worked miracles through the hands of the apostles, in the name of Jesus, if the apostles were lying about Jesus' resurrection and divinity. This seems to have been recognized by many early converts in the Church, catalyzing Christianity's exponential growth.

3.B. The Christian Mutation of Second Temple Judaism
The second historical argument for the Resurrection presented by Wright is in the teaching of the early Church. Whenever possible, the early Christians tried to maintain continuity in teaching with the broader Jewish community, whose teachings were developed in a period called Second Temple Judaism (516 BC to AD 70).[9] They did so because Jesus cited these teachings, and they believed they were generally the will of God. Given this great reluctance to depart from the doctrines of Second Temple Judaism, we must ask why the early Christians made such an explicit exception to their doctrinal loyalty in one area: the Resurrection. It should be noted that this doctrinal departure was in part responsible for the Christians' expulsion from the synagogues (which they definitely did not want).

The following are the specific changes that early Christians made to

Second Temple Judaism's doctrine of the resurrection:

SECOND TEMPLE JUDAISM	CHRISTIANITY
Resurrection means return to the same kind of physical body.	Resurrection means transformation into a spiritual and glorified body (the *soma pneumatikon*).
No one will rise before the end times.	Jesus and others are risen already.
The Messiah is not associated with resurrection.	The hope for a Messiah and the hope of a resurrection are both fulfilled in Jesus.
The end times (*parousia*) are in the future.	The end times have begun with Jesus and will be completed in the future.
Resurrection is a minor doctrine.	Resurrection is the central doctrine that justifies and connects the entire Faith.

Historians have tried to theorize where these mutations of Second Temple Judaism came from — perhaps from paganism or the Christians' own desire to come to terms with the death of their leader. The problem with these theories is that the ideas are unprecedented; no one had proposed them within or outside of Judaism, so it's hard to find a plausible source other than the one given in the Gospels — namely, that Jesus really did rise from the dead and appeared to the disciples in a spiritual, powerful, glorified body. (Remember that Paul even had to make up a new term to describe the idea of a spiritual and glorified body; they literally didn't have a word for it prior to Him.) When we combine how unique these mutations were with the fact that they were just about the only areas where Christians departed from the prevailing Jewish doctrine, we must again ask where this conviction came from, if not from a powerful, glorious risen appearance of Jesus that the early Christians witnessed.

Conclusion

In light of the apostles' power to work miracles in the name of Jesus, the exponential growth of Christianity after the humiliating execution of its Messiah, the highly unusual Christian mutations of Second Temple Judaism, and the large number of witnesses to the Risen Christ (who had everything to lose and nothing to gain by falsely preaching His resurrection), it is reasonable to conclude that the historical basis of the early Church's proclamation of Jesus' resurrection in the spirit, power, and glory of God is exceptionally strong. This implies that the Church's proclamation was true and that hundreds had witnessed it. When we combine this mutually corroborating evidence with the fact that Jesus' tomb was empty (and that the Jewish religious authorities, contrary to their best interests, were not able to deny it), it shows why the members of the early Church preached Jesus' resurrection and divinity even though it meant the loss of their financial status, social status, religious status, and in many cases, their lives.

NT#14: What Is the Scientific Evidence of Jesus' Resurrection?[10]

In NT#10, we showed the high likelihood that the Shroud of Turin is the authentic burial cloth of Jesus, which validates the Gospel accounts of His crucifixion. We now turn to the scientific analysis of the three-dimensional photographic negative image appearing on a non-photographically sensitive linen cloth. As we shall see, there is a very high likelihood of that image having been produced by an intense form of radiation accompanied by the mechanical transparency ("spiritualizing") of the radiating body of the deceased man.

Since the Shroud of Turin Research Project (STURP) investigation in 1978, radiation was thought to be the most likely explanation for image formation on the Shroud, because other physical explanations — such as liquids, rubs, vapors, and scorching — cannot explain some of the most obvious characteristics of the Shroud.[11] For example, the image is limited to the uppermost surface of the fibrils (a few microns deep) of the frontal and dorsal surfaces of the cloth and does not even penetrate into the middle of the fibers, let alone the middle of the cloth, and its precision does not "leak" into adjacent fibers. This precludes liquids, vapors, and rubs, all of which would penetrate into the middle of fibers, spangle, and diffuse to adjacent fibers. Furthermore, the cloth did not make contact with every part of the body, meaning that the source of the image would have to not only act at a distance but encode information about relative distances between the body and the Shroud. This is precisely what radiation does that other image agents do not. The consensus of the physicists who have examined the image on the cloth (Dr. John Jackson, Dr. Paolo Di Lazarro, Dr. Giulio Fanti, Dr. Jean-Baptiste Rinaudo, Dr. Kitty Little, Dr. Arthur Lind, Dr. Luigi Gonella, and many others) is that radiation is the only image agent that can explain the forty-five enigmas on the Shroud.[12] Currently, there are two hypotheses that can explain many of these enigmas:

1. The vacuum ultraviolet radiation hypothesis of Drs. John Jackson and Paolo Di Lazzaro, which can explain twenty-five out of the forty-five enigmas (section 1)
2. The particle radiation hypothesis of Drs. Jean-Baptiste Rinaudo, Kitty Little, and Arthur Lind, which explains all forty-five of the image enigmas (section 2). Evidently, the particle radiation hypothesis is favored by a large number of physicists and physical chemists who have examined the cloth.

There is another highly unusual feature that must also be accounted for: The body must become mechanically transparent so the cloth can receive image information from the *inside* of the body. The image on the Shroud not only shows information from the surface of the front and back of the body but also from the inside of the body in perfect three-dimensional proportionality to the surface. For example, the backbone (inside the body) can be seen in three-dimensional proportionality to the flesh surrounding the back, and the bones in the hands can be seen in the same three-dimensional proportionality to the flesh surrounding the bones, and so on. The vacuum ultraviolet radiation hypothesis does not explain this phenomenon, but the particle radiation hypothesis decidedly does.

1. The Vacuum Ultraviolet Radiation Hypothesis[13]

The vacuum ultraviolet radiation hypothesis was proposed by Dr. John Jackson in two papers and later confirmed by Dr. Paolo Di Lazzaro in the laboratory in 2010. These two physicists proposed that directional (collimated) vacuum ultraviolet (high frequency) radiation was responsible for the imaging on the Shroud, because it could produce a perfect, three-dimensional, photographic negative image on a non-photographically sensitive linen cloth without penetrating the uppermost surface of the fibrils. Paolo Di Lazzaro (chief of research for the Italian National Research Agency for New Technologies) produced this radiation through exceedingly short pulsations (of one forty-billionth of a second), by using ARF excimer lasers in a laboratory. Di Lazzaro indicated that in order to obtain sufficient radiation to produce the image of the whole body on the Shroud, it would require ultraviolet radiation in the order of several *billion* watts emanating from the entire body. This would require about fourteen thousand ARF excimer lasers, a number which exceeds all ultraviolet sources of radiation in every laboratory around the world today. In 2010, he reproduced the straw-yellow coloration on the uppermost surface of the fibrils in precise images on a cloth with similar spectral reflectants as the Shroud. It also resembled the Shroud's unique image features in many other ways.

As noted above, this hypothesis does not explain the mechanical transparency of the body, and only explains twenty-five out of forty-five enigmas.

2. The Particle Radiation Hypothesis[14]

As noted above, this hypothesis explains all forty-five enigmas concerned with the Shroud's image, blood, longevity, strength, and other features. It is the *only* physical explanation remotely capable of explaining all forty-five enigmas. The main proponents of this theory are Dr.

Jean-Baptiste Rinaudo (France), Dr. Kitty Little (Great Britain), and Dr. Arthur Lind (USA), among others.

In 1995, Dr. Jean-Baptiste Rinaudo and Dr. Kitty Little independently proposed this comprehensive explanation of the Shroud's image, mechanical transparency, and enigmas: Every stable atomic nucleus in the entire body (seven octillion) *simultaneously* underwent nuclear disintegration, causing a low-temperature nuclear reaction. This nuclear disintegration gave rise to a shower of particles at low temperatures (approximately 170 degrees Fahrenheit) that would not destroy the cloth. Electrical energy would be in the range of three million watts, accompanied by a very bright light (and according to Little, a nondestructive "boom"). There are two primary constituents of the shower (flux) of the particles coming from the nuclear disintegration:

1. Heavy charged particles (e.g., protons, deuterons, and alpha particles)
2. Other particles, such as neutrons (heavy, but not charged), electrons (charged, but not heavy), and gamma rays

The heavy charged particles (e.g., protons) are the ones that produce the image. Their positive charges interact with the charged particles in the cloth, causing them to stop at the uppermost surface of the fibrils (not penetrating to the middle of the fibers or the cloth). When they stop, they cause dehydration and discoloration on the cloth (from conjugating carbonyls). The intensity of the discoloration will be in inverse proportion to the distance the particle has to travel from the body to the cloth. This produces a very precise, three-dimensional, photographic negative image with straw-like coloration, similar to that on the Shroud. Drs. Little and Rinaudo have independently shown that this does in fact occur in low-temperature nuclear reactions (nuclear disintegrations) on cloths with similar spectral reflectants as the Shroud at nuclear laboratories in Great Britain and France.

The other particles, which are either not charged or not heavy (such as neutrons and electrons), do not stop at the cloth but pass right through it. When they do, they produce changes in the cloth's carbonyl structure, strengthening it. The neutrons irradiate the bloodstains, making them abnormally bright red, and cause other enigmatic effects (explained below).

The particle radiation hypothesis also explains the mechanical transparency of the body, allowing information from the *inside* of the body to be encoded as an image on the cloth. As the body is disintegrating, particles from the inside of the body (for example, from the backbone) can pass through the surface of the body (because it takes the inside particles a split second to move from the inside to the disintegrated surface). Since those particles would have traveled farther than the surface particles, their coloration would be less intense, encoding perfect three-dimensional proportionality between the inside and surface of the body. Thus the particle radiation hypothesis explains both the image and the mechanical transparency of the body.

We may now address how the particle radiation hypothesis explains some of the major enigmas on the Shroud:

- **Imaging enigmas:** We have already addressed how the particle radiation hypothesis explains the perfectly precise, three-dimensional photographic negative image on the uppermost surface of the fibrils of the Shroud and how the body became mechanically transparent so that images from the inside of the body could be recorded on the Shroud in perfect three-dimensional proportionality to the surface of the body. There is another major imaging enigma that is better explained by the particle radiation hypothesis than the ultraviolet radiation hypothesis: The images on the frontal and dorsal parts of the cloth are of equal intensity. How can this be, since the body is in a supine position with the weight of the body on the dorsal part of the cloth? In a low-temperature nuclear reaction (as occurs in the particle radiation hypothesis), a vacuum is created, and the vacuum sucks both the front part of the cloth and the dorsal part of the cloth toward the inside at equal intensity, irrespective of the weight of the body toward the dorsal part. There are about twenty-eight other primary imaging enigmas and eight secondary imaging enigmas that are explained in detail by Mark Antonacci's article cited above.[15]

- **The mystery of the body's removal from the Shroud:** Let us suppose that the body was not raised from the tomb and that, for the sake of argument, the apostles removed the Shroud from the body sometime after the Sabbath. We know that the body must have been in the Shroud for enough time to transfer the bloodstains to the cloth, but not more than two and a half days, because there is no sign of decomposition on the cloth. Scientists have long known that if a person (or some mechanical device) tried to take the cloth off the body, it would have smeared, fragmented, distorted, and/or broken a large number of the bloodstains on the Shroud. However, this did *not* happen. So how was the cloth separated from the body? The particle radiation hypothesis explains this, because as the body disintegrates, it leaves intact the bloodstains that have already been transferred to the cloth and are not part of the disintegrating body.

- **The bright red color of the bloodstains:** As blood ages, it turns brown and then eventually black, but all the Shroud's bloodstains are bright red. This cannot be attributable to bilirubin alone because bilirubin content would vary from stain to stain. The particle radiation hypothesis explains this, because the shower of neutrons irradiates all the bloodstains, and this irradiation (in the presence of sunlight, as at an exhibition) turns the blood bright red in color. This was shown in the laboratory by Dr. Carlo Goldoni and others.

- **Extraordinary strength, longevity, and pliability:** Roger and Marion Gilbert (chemical materials specialists) showed in 1978 that the Shroud is extraordinary in its longevity, strength, pliability, and resistance to oxygenation and solvents (even if it were only seven hundred years old). Dr. Kitty Little showed in the laboratory that the particle radiation hypothesis explains this. The neutrons, electrons, and gamma rays (*not* heavy *and* charged) flowing out of the body easily penetrate the linen cloth and move through it. Some of them hit the long-chain cellulose molecules in non-crystalline (weaker) regions, causing them to break, and then to crosslink with crystalline (stronger) structures, which would strengthen the cloth — making it more substantial and pliable while increasing its resistance to solubility, oxygenation, and chemical reactions.

As noted above, the particle radiation hypothesis explains all forty-five enigmas on the image, blood, and cloth itself.[16]

The particle radiation hypothesis has one final important feature: It can be definitively confirmed. If cosmogenic isotopes (such as Cl-36 and Ca-41) are found in abundance on the cloth, it would mean that the cloth was in the vicinity of a nuclear reaction. Evidently, it would have to be a low-temperature nuclear reaction, otherwise, the cloth would have been destroyed. As noted above, the simultaneous nuclear disintegration of all seven octillion stable atomic nuclei in the body of the Shroud man would produce this kind of low-temperature nuclear reaction. Thus these cosmogenic isotopes would confirm the particle radiation hypothesis definitively.

Conclusion

The particle radiation hypothesis is the best explanation of the image on the Shroud of Turin, because it explains all forty-five highly unusual enigmas of the Shroud's image, blood, and cloth. If in future scientific investigations the presence of cosmogenic isotopes is found in the Shroud (far beyond their exceedingly slight natural occurrence), it would confirm the particle radiation hypothesis.

If the particle radiation hypothesis produced the image, we are dealing with nothing short of a grand miracle, because the odds of seven octillion stable atomic nuclei in the body simultaneously undergoing nuclear disintegration is almost infinitesimally small (virtually zero). Such a miraculous event would be a sign of Jesus' resurrection in spirit, power, and glory, because it marks the definitive point at which His body moved from a physical state to a *transphysical* state, leaving in its wake a flash of bright light, a "boom," three million watts of electrical energy, and a shower of seven octillion particles producing a perfect, three-dimensional, photographic negative image while brightening the blood and strengthening the cloth on which the image would be portrayed. A more perfect relic of the Resurrection could not have been left for a skeptical scientific generation that would examine it two thousand years later.

NT#15: What Is the Scriptural and Contemporary Evidence of Jesus' Gift of the Holy Spirit?

The Holy Spirit is Jesus' major gift for humanity to dynamize, grow, guide, protect, and inspire His Church and her members. We have already seen in NT#4 how important the Holy Spirit was in the exponential growth of the Christian Church after the death and resurrection of Jesus. Indeed, as N. T. Wright[17] and John P. Meier[18] show, if the apostles had not continuously worked the same miracles as Jesus through the Holy Spirit in Jesus' name, it is doubtful that the Church would have grown exponentially after the death of Jesus. Without these miracles, Christian Messianism may well have suffered the same fate as the Messianic movements of John the Baptist and other Jewish Messianic figures.[19]

Since the time of the early Church, the gifts of the Holy Spirit have been divided into three kinds:

1. **External charismatic gifts:** working of miracles, healing, prophecy, interpretation of prophecy, speaking in tongues, and interpretation of tongues (see 1 Corinthians 12)
2. **Gifts for the purpose of evangelization** (both exterior and interior): guidance, protection, and inspiration
3. **Interior gifts for deepening relationships with God and others:** faith, hope, love, wisdom, spiritual understanding, counsel, fortitude, spiritual knowledge, piety, and fear of the Lord

Evidently, the Church and her members would be bereft of spiritual guidance, protection, inspiration, and graced relationships without this gift of our baptism. Adequate treatment of these gifts would require several volumes,[20] and so this treatment must be restricted to a brief outline and basic explanation of only the first two kinds: charismatic gifts and evangelistic gifts. This will be done in two sections:

1. The Charismatic and Evangelistic Gifts of the Holy Spirit in the New Testament (section 1)
2. The Charismatic and Evangelistic Gifts of the Holy Spirit Today (section 2)

Those seeking an explanation of the interior gifts of the Holy Spirit will want to look up each gift in the *Catechism of the Catholic Church* and a good dictionary of the Bible (e.g., John L. McKenzie's *Dictionary of the Bible*).

1. The Charismatic and Evangelistic Gifts of the Holy Spirit in the New Testament

The Acts of the Apostles, the letters of Saint Paul, and the exponential growth of the Christian Church universally attest to the continuous working of miracles by the apostles through the power of the Holy Spirit in the name of Jesus. These include healings of every kind, raisings of the dead, and even nature miracles (e.g., the releasing of chains and opening of prison doors). In addition to miracles, the evangelization efforts of the apostles and other early disciples were greatly assisted by prophecy and providential guidance, protection, and inspiration. Though all of these areas merit consideration, an overview of the first (miracles) will be sufficient to show (1) that the early Church saw the charisms as explicit manifestations of the Holy Spirit (frequently referred to as "the power of God") and (2) that the Risen Jesus was the vehicle through which the power of the Holy Spirit was manifest, for the Spirit worked through Jesus' name.

We will examine the charismatic gifts of the Spirit in two sections:

1. Jesus and the Holy Spirit (section 1.A)
2. The Charismatic Gifts of the Holy Spirit in the Acts of the Apostles (section 2.B)

1.A. Jesus and the Holy Spirit

All four Gospels assert that Jesus not only had the indwelling of the Holy Spirit but was able to impart gifts of that Spirit to His apostles and disciples. Prior to His baptism, He was certainly inspired, guided, and protected by the Holy Spirit, as implied by His conception through that Spirit (see Lk 1:35 and Mt 1:18). The descent of the Holy Spirit on Jesus at His baptism does not imply that He did not possess the Spirit from the time of His conception. Rather, it indicates that He received the Spirit in a special way to help guide Him in His mission.

As Jesus was building His Church by calling the apostles and other disciples, then commissioning Peter with supreme authority by giving him the keys to the kingdom of heaven (see Mt 16:17–19), and then commissioning the other apostles with the power to bind and loose (the power of bishops [Mt 18:18]), He would have been planning to bestow the gift of the Holy Spirit upon them after His resurrection. The Holy Spirit would give the apostles not only the three kinds of charisms mentioned above (charismatic, evangelistic, and interior charisms) but also the charisms needed specifically for leadership and governance.

After His resurrection, Jesus fulfills His plan, bestowing the Holy Spirit upon the apostles. There are two accounts of this — John 20:22 and Acts 2:1–4. John 20:22 indicates that the Risen Jesus breathed on them and gave them the Holy Spirit, while Acts portrays it as a gathering of the apostles and other disciples, where the Spirit comes in tongues of fire, manifesting the charismatic gift of glossolalia. Are these two accounts contradictory? No, because both accounts are talking about the same event, but in different ways. Though both evangelists indicate that the Holy Spirit was given after Jesus' resurrection, ascension, and final glorification, Luke's account is more detailed and differentiated than John's.

Luke makes a strong separation between the period when Jesus is visibly present (Luke's Gospel) and the period of the Holy Spirit, when Jesus is not visibly present (Acts of the Apostles); however, John does not make this separation. Thus John portrays the Risen Jesus as visibly present when He gives the apostles the Holy Spirit, while Luke does not say whether the Risen Jesus was visibly present in Acts 2:1–4 when the Holy Spirit descended upon the apostles in tongues of fire. However, Luke states clearly in his Gospel that Jesus is the source of the gift of the Holy Spirit, which will be given later: "Behold, *I* send the promise of my Father upon you; but stay in the city, until you are clothed with power from on high"[21] (Lk 24:49, emphasis added).

Furthermore, Luke puts special emphasis on the *charismatic* manifestation of the Holy Spirit (which is his usual emphasis), but John does not. This does not mean that the charismatic manifestation of the Holy Spirit in tongues of fire did not occur. John's non-inclusion of the charismatic gifts means only that this was not central to his theology, but as we shall see, Luke does include, not only because they are important to his theology but also because they occurred repeatedly in the post-Resurrection Church. In Acts 10:44–48, the Holy Spirit falls on the Gentiles in the same way as believers:

> While Peter was still saying this, the Holy Spirit fell on all who heard the word. And the believers from among the circumcised who came with Peter were amazed, because the gift of the Holy Spirit had been poured out even on the Gentiles. For they heard them speaking in tongues and extolling God. (vv. 44–46)

The implication is that a charismatic manifestation of the Spirit's power occurred frequently to believers.

So why doesn't John emphasize the charismatic gifts of the Holy Spirit? It seems that he considered them less important than the sacramental power of the Spirit (e.g., the power to forgive sins in John 20:22–23). Additionally, he is concerned with the theme of being re-created in the Spirit, which was not central to Luke's theology. By using *enephysēsen* ("breathed upon"), John refers to re-creation in the Spirit discussed in John 3:7–9. Both of these texts refer back to Genesis 2:7.[22]

What might we conclude about the two narratives (in Luke and John) concerning Jesus' gift of the Holy Spirit? They both address the *same* post-resurrection, post-ascension, and post-glorification event where Jesus bestows the Holy Spirit on His apostles. Luke emphasizes the charismatic (external and experiential) power of the Spirit while John emphasizes the sacramental and re-creative (interior) power of the

Spirit. Since all of these powers were conveyed by the one Holy Spirit, there is no contradiction in believing that all of them were part of the same event. John *states* that the Risen Jesus gave His Spirit to the apostles, while Luke *implies* this (see 24:49). Luke *states* that Jesus ascended before giving the Holy Spirit, while John *implies* that He was already ascended.[23]

In view of the above, it is reasonable to conclude that the Risen Jesus, after His ascension, gave the Holy Spirit to His apostles (and others) accompanied by a charismatic manifestation of the Spirit's external power and glory. At the same time, He gave the disciples interior, priestly, and re-creative graces, particularly to forgive sins.

1.B. Charismatic Gifts of the Holy Spirit in the Acts of the Apostles

Luke recounts a large range of healings and miracles performed by Peter, Paul, and others in the Acts of the Apostles:[24] the healing of the lame man at the temple (see Acts 3:1–10); healings and exorcisms performed by Philip in Samaria (Acts 8:4–8); Paul's healing from blindness (Acts 9:18); the healing of Aeneas's paralysis (Acts 9:33–34); the raising of Tabitha from the dead by Peter (Acts 9:36–41); the healing of a cripple in Lystra (Acts 14:8–10); Paul's restoration of Eutychus (Acts 20:9–12); and the healings performed by Paul in Malta (Acts 28:8–9).

There are some unconventional healings and miracles also recounted in Acts, for example: healings through Peter's shadow (see Acts 5:15); healings through cloths touched by Paul (Acts 19:11–12); Peter's liberation from prison (Acts 5:19–24; 12:6-11); and Paul's liberation from prison (Acts 16:26). There can be little doubt that such healings and miracles occurred in the earliest Church communities, as they are recounted not only by Luke, but also by Paul[25] (who is writing to the actual witnesses of the events).

The frequent occurrence of healings and miracles through the power of the Holy Spirit and in the name of Jesus allowed the Church to engage in a remarkably expansive missionary effort because it substantiated the apostles' claim that Jesus was raised in glory and is the exclusive beloved Son of the Father.

2. Charismatic and Evangelistic Gifts of the Holy Spirit Today

Charismatic and evangelistic gifts of the Holy Spirit are as manifest today as in the first century. These gifts are important for helping the Christian community to evangelize, grow, strengthen in faith and unity, discern the guidance of God, interact with secular culture, contend with ridicule and persecution, govern and teach with wisdom and orthodoxy, and deepen in conversion. We will explain them in two sections:

1. Charismatic Gifts of the Holy Spirit Today (section 2.A)
2. Evangelistic Gifts of the Holy Spirit Today (section 2.B)

2.A. The Charismatic Gifts of the Holy Spirit Today

The centrality of charismatic gifts of the Spirit — particularly, healing, miracles, prophecy, and speaking in tongues — in the Acts of the Apostles and some of the Pauline letters (e.g., 1 Corinthians 12) prompts skepticism among some contemporary readers because it seems so different from the activities of the Church today. Surprising as it may seem, these charismatic gifts are quite present today in the Catholic Charismatic Renewal movement, during prayer meetings, healing Masses, and other gatherings. Though these gifts may not be as central to Church life as in the first century, their considerable occurrence throughout every region of the Church shows how they could be so central to the life and evangelization efforts of the early Church.

Dr. Craig Keener, in his book *Miracles Today*,[26] has catalogued many medically investigated healings of various physical maladies, such as brain recovery, cancer, blindness, deafness, ambulatory disabilities, leprosy, and recovery from cardiac arrest. The Catholic Charismatic Renewal promotes these charismatic gifts and sponsors healing Masses and services on a regular basis. Priests, religious, and lay ministers who have the charism of healing lay their hands on the heads of the faithful, who often feel the effects of the Spirit profoundly and are sometimes healed from physical, emotional, and spiritual afflictions.[27] For example, Sr. Briege McKenna,[28] Fr. Richard McAlear,[29] Fr. Lawrence Carew,[30] and Fr. Richard Bain[31] travel throughout the country to healing ceremonies that bring about remarkable physical, emotional, and spiritual healings that build up the faith and hope of participants and their communities.

Charismatic gifts of the Spirit are not ends in themselves. They are meant to manifest the Presence of the Lord to everyone present at a healing or worship service and to edify and strengthen the faith of both individuals and the community. When healings occur, they not only bring confidence and joy to the community but even a sense of hope to those who did not receive a healing (because they can better understand that a healing is not God's will for them at that time). Above all, the evident Presence of the Lord helps the participants to recognize that same Presence in the sacraments, their prayer lives, and even their family and work lives.

2.B. Evangelistic Gifts of the Holy Spirit Today

When some read in the Acts of the Apostles and the Pauline letters about how the Holy Spirit guided the apostles, prevented them from going to various regions, inspired them in their evangelization efforts, protected them from danger, and gave them the wisdom and words to refute their adversaries, they become skeptical, because the Holy Spirit does not seem to act in these ways today. However, as we shall see, the Holy Spirit does guide, protect, and inspire anyone who asks for these graces. If we know what to ask and look for from the Holy Spirit, we will find that we too are guided, protected, and inspired, as the apostles and disciples in the first century. The more we practice asking for and following the inspiration and guidance of the Holy Spirit, the more certain and clear these gifts will be in our lives, making their reality and centrality in the New Testament patently obvious. We will focus on two major evangelistic gifts of the Spirit: guidance and inspiration.

(1) **Guidance of the Holy Spirit:** Guidance of the Holy Spirit comes both exteriorly and interiorly. With respect to exterior guidance, the Holy Spirit can orchestrate what might be called "conspiracies of divine providence," in which He opens unexpected doors of opportunity, puts impediments in front of spiritually, emotionally, or physically destructive paths, and sends messages into our lives through friends, strangers, radio and television programs, books and magazines, the internet, and every

other vehicle that might influence us. Frequently, He uses a combination of these things to direct a person toward something spiritually beneficial, or to redirect someone away from something spiritually destructive.[32] Many spiritual directors recommend writing a "spiritual autobiography" in which we articulate the combination of interior and exterior influences (many of which were unrecognized at the time of the guidance) that led us to the faith commitments and practices in our lives.

With respect to interior influences, the Holy Spirit uses consolation and desolation. Much of the time, consolation is from the Holy Spirit and desolation is from the evil spirit, but not always. The Holy Spirit can use negative feelings to dissuade us from a belief or course of action, and the evil spirit can use positive feelings to encourage us toward a destructive or sinful path.[33] For this reason, spiritual directors use rules for the discernment of spirits. One of the most widely used rules for discernment is from St. Ignatius of Loyola in his *Spiritual Exercises*.[34] These rules help immeasurably in discerning how the Holy Spirit (or the evil spirit) is using consolation and desolation to guide us.

(2) Inspiration of the Holy Spirit: The Holy Spirit inspires us in four major contexts:[35]

1. He gives us the words and arguments we need to defend the Faith, respond to critics and questioners, and confront those attacking Christ, the Church, or Christian doctrine (see Lk 12:12).

2. He gives the ideas and ideals to edify the faith of individuals, groups, and communities. This is particularly important for those who write books and give presentations, homilies, and conferences — teachers, preachers, catechists, and evangelists (see 1 Cor 12:8–11, 28).

3. He gives the ideas, ideals, wisdom, and strength for governance and use of authority within the Church (see Mt 16:17–19 and 18:18).

4. He gives pastoral inspiration to help the faithful grow in conversion, discern spirits, and console those in need (see Rom 8:26–28; 2 Cor 11:13–15; 1 Jn 4:1–2).

The interior gifts of the Spirit that help us with interior conversion and charity, such as faith, hope, and love (1 Cor 13), are exceedingly important, and there are many excellent resources explaining these gifts, and how to use them for spiritual and moral conversion.[36]

Conclusion

Jesus' gift of the Holy Spirit has been, from the inception of His ministry until today, the power, inspiration, and guiding force behind the exponential growth of the Church, the correctness of her teaching, the prudence of her governance, her zeal for evangelization, protection during persecution, and her maintenance of unity and truth in the midst of every threat. The Holy Spirit has also been the light of Christ in the life of every baptized Christian believer — bestowing guidance, inspiration, and protection beyond anything our natural abilities could produce. The Spirit also grants peace beyond all understanding, an awareness of the heart of God, a wellspring of understanding and compassion for others, and the depth of faith, hope, and love that sustains us not only in our spiritual and moral lives but in our churches, families, and workplaces. The Spirit is the fire behind our faith, hope, and love toward eternal salvation with Christ.

NT#16: Why Did the Early Church Proclaim Jesus to Be Divine at Such Great Cost to Herself?

Some skeptics have proposed that the early Church proclaimed Jesus to be divine in order to elevate Him beyond merely human prophetic status. The proclamation of divinity had precisely the opposite effect, however, because it was repugnant to the Jewish audience that the early Church was trying to attract. Indeed, the early Church could not have picked a more apologetically *unappealing* proclamation for her audience than "Jesus is the Lord." This proclamation led to the Christians' loss of religious status, social status, and financial status within the Jewish community inside and outside Jerusalem. Ultimately it led to the Christians being expelled from the Synagogue and being actively persecuted by both Jewish and Roman authorities. Why would the apostolic Church have selected a doctrine that was viewed so unfavorably by the very audience she wanted to attract, leading to her active persecution?

As Joachim Jeremias remarks, this was wholly unnecessary, because the apostolic Church did not have to proclaim or even imply that Jesus was divine in order to bestow great favor upon Him within the religious culture of the day. The early Church could have proclaimed Him to be a "martyr prophet," which would have allowed converts to worship at His tomb and to pray through His intercession.[37] This more modest claim would have made Him acceptable to Jewish audiences, who would then have ranked Him high among the "holy ones." Why then did the leaders of the apostolic Church go so unapologetically and dangerously far to proclaim that "Jesus is the Lord"? Why did they suffer social and financial loss, religious alienation, and even persecution and death, when it all could have been avoided by simply giving up the implication of His divinity? The most likely answer is that they really believed Him to be divine. So why did the apostolic Church believe Him to be divine (and even to share a unity with the Father throughout all eternity)? How could they be so sure of this radical proclamation, which had so many negative consequences, when they could have taken the easier and safer road in proclaiming Him to be a martyr prophet? Was it only because of Jesus' claim to be the exclusive Son of the Father, or was there more?

The Church proclaimed this "more" in her earliest credal statements, called *kerygmas*.[38] These kerygmas were written shortly after Jesus' resurrection and gift of the Spirit (AD 34–35) and are identifiable in the letters of Saint Paul and the Acts of the Apostles.[39] They identify the foundation upon which the Church proclaimed that Jesus is the Lord: His glorious resurrection (manifesting divinity), His gift of the Holy Spirit (identified as "the power of God"), His miracles by His own power and authority, and His unconditional, self-sacrificial love that saves us from our sins.

When these events are combined with Jesus' preaching about himself as the exclusive Son of the Father and early Church leaders' experience of the power to perform miracles in the name of Jesus, early Church leaders had no doubt that Jesus truly shared in His Father's divinity as He himself proclaimed to them.

This evidence (showing Jesus' divinity) was covered in previous units in part 2 of this book: (1) What Jesus said about himself (NT#7); (2) His resurrection manifesting divine glory (NT#13 and NT#14); (3) His miracles, particularly raising the dead by His own authority (NT#5 and NT#6); (4) His gift of the Holy Spirit (the power of God), enabling His disciples to do miracles in His name (NT#15); and (5) His total self-sacrificial death, manifesting "no greater love" for us — the same kind of love as His heavenly Father (NT#8, NT#9, NT#10, and NT#11). What follows is a brief summary of this complementary and mutually corroborative evidence.

1. What Jesus Said about Himself[40]

In His preaching to non-apostolic audiences, Jesus only implied His divinity, reserving the explicit revelation of it to His apostles to avoid an accusation of blasphemy and an early end to His mission. He gave four major, indirect indications of His divinity:

1. Doing miracles by His own power and authority (not making recourse to God)
2. Claiming to have the power to forgive sins and to amplify and expand the Torah (reserved to Yahweh)
3. Claiming to bring the kingdom of God and defeat Satan by His own authority (missions reserved to Yahweh alone)
4. Referring to himself as the "Son of Man," the divinely sent figure described in Daniel 7:13–14, who was given dominion and kingdom by God and sent by Him to judge and redeem humankind

Jesus gave *explicit* references of His divinity to his apostles (in the Q *Logion*, cited below) and to the High Priests and Pharisees before and during His trial (the claims leading to the charge of blasphemy).

Recall from NT#7 that the Q *Logion* (see Lk 10:21–22 and Mt 11:25–27) is an early text recounted by apostolic witnesses in the mother church at Jerusalem. In Luke, it reads as follows: "All things have been delivered to me by my Father; and no one knows who the Son is except the Father, or who the Father is except the Son and any one to whom the Son chooses to reveal him" (Lk 10:22).

Most scholars view this as a "meteor from the Johannine heaven," because it resembles the high Christology of the Gospel of John, though it is an early apostolic tradition, which very likely originated with Jesus. This passage strongly implies that the Son has interior and complete knowledge of the Father as the Father has interior and complete knowledge of the Son, which further implies not only an intimate relationship between the two, but also a sharing of divinity. Since there is considerable textual evidence that the passage comes from Jesus (His virtually unique use of *Abba* five times), it is highly likely that He stated to His apostles His divine relationship with His Father.

The charge of blasphemy is very probably historical (it has multiple attestation and is an embarrassing disclosure). It is a charge unique to Jesus in the history of Jewish and Roman juridical proceedings.[41] Evidently, the authorities used this unique charge because the Sanhedrin had multiple witnesses testifying that Jesus made statements implying His divinity. Mark recounts that Jesus made His divinity explicit during the trial (Mk 14:60–62). The Parable of the Wicked Tenants (Mt 21:33–46) also points to Jesus' divine Sonship, because Jesus associates "the only beloved Son" in the parable with himself (the stone rejected by the builders — see NT#7).

2. Jesus' Resurrection in Glory[42]

The evidence for Jesus' resurrection in glory is considerable in five areas:

1. **The Gospel narratives:** The Gospels of Matthew, Luke, and John indicate in several ways not only that Jesus was transformed in spirit and power but also that He appeared to be divine — so much so that His apostles bowed down to worship Him (see Mt 28:17 and Lk 24:52). The term *worship* was reserved for God alone (Mt 4:8–10 and Lk 4:7–8), indicating that the apostles thought they were "seeing God."

    Furthermore, John's Gospel indicates that Jesus' apostles only saw Him as *ho kyrios* ("the Lord" — the Greek translation of *Yahweh* in Jn 20:20, 25, and 28, and Jn 21:7, 12).

This is confirmed by Thomas's proclamation of Jesus' divinity: "the Lord of me and the God of me" (the definite article indicating divinity — Jn 20:28). There are several other indications of Jesus' divinity in John 21 (see NT#13).

2. **The letters of Saint Paul:** The letters of Saint Paul give evidence of hundreds of witnesses living within memory of Jesus. In the First Letter to the Corinthians (see 15:3–8), he gives a list of these witnesses, showing that they had everything to lose and nothing to gain by falsely proclaiming Jesus risen in glory. In the same chapter, Paul indicates that Jesus' risen appearance was transformed in Spirit, power, and glory (1 Cor 15:42–44).

3. **The exponential growth of the Christian Church amidst persecution and martyrdom:** The expansion of the Christian Church to become the predominant Church in the Roman Empire is very difficult to explain without the intervention of God to remediate the tragedy of Jesus' crucifixion through His glorious resurrection — and the power of the Holy Spirit working miracles in Jesus' name to help the apostles evangelize.[43] If the apostles were lying about Jesus' resurrection in glory, why would God be working miracles by their hands in the name of Jesus?

4. **Christian mutations of Second Temple Judaism:** N. T. Wright has identified five Christian mutations of Second Temple Jewish doctrine, all of which concern the Resurrection. In view of the fact that the Christian Church did not want to depart from Second Temple Judaism or be expelled from the synagogue, these mutations are inexplicable unless there is a significant reason for making the change. Wright believes that there is only one such significant motivation: The apostles witnessed Jesus risen in glory.

5. **Evidence of the Resurrection of Jesus' Body on the Shroud of Turin:** The image on the Shroud of Turin must have been produced by a very high level of radiation, either vacuum ultraviolet radiation or particle radiation. The particle radiation

hypothesis (which can be confirmed if there are cosmogenic isotopes in the Shroud) explains all forty-five enigmas of the Shroud's image, blood, and cloth. If validated, it would indicate that every stable atomic nucleus (seven octillion of them) constituting the man on the Shroud underwent complete simultaneous nuclear disintegration — a low-temperature nuclear reaction with a bright light and "boom" — for which there is no scientific or natural explanation.

The combination of these five areas of evidence enables us to form a strong inference that Jesus was risen in spirit, power, and glory, inciting His apostles to conclude they were experiencing God, and enabling the Church to grow exponentially through the power of the Spirit working in the name of Jesus. The Shroud of Turin's image appears to be a remnant of the scientifically inexplicable nuclear reaction and particle flux that indicates the transition from Jesus' physical Body to His transphysical, glorious Body.

3. Jesus' Miracles by His Own Power[44]
The historicity of Jesus' miracles is overwhelmingly attested by several reliable sources and arguments:

- Flavius Josephus and the Babylonian Talmud are hostile testimonies to Jesus' miraculous power, written close to the time of His ministry. The fact that Jesus' adversaries attest to this power indicates its veracity.
- There is multiple attestation in all five original Gospel sources (Mark, John, Q Source, Special Matthew, and Special Luke), two *kerygmas* (see Acts 2:22 and Acts 10:38), the Acts of the Apostles, and Saint Paul's letters (by implication from the early Church's miracles). Importantly, Jesus' adversaries accused Him of casting out demons by the prince of demons. Why did they make such a self-contradictory accusation if they could have denied that Jesus was successfully performing miracles? Evidently, His miracles were so successful that denying the fact was not possible, and so they were left only

with a self-contradictory accusation.

- Jesus worked miracles by His own authority (without appealing to God), indicating that the divine power to raise the dead, exorcise, and heal came from within himself. No other prophet in history ever dared to make such a claim.

- The fact that the apostles worked miracles through the Holy Spirit in the name of Jesus (shown by the exponential increase in the Christian Church amidst persecution) implies that Jesus worked the same or greater miracles during His own ministry.

- Jesus' miracles by His own authority confirmed His words that He shared an intimate relationship and divinity with His Father (see above, the *Q Logion*), because the divine power to raise the dead and do other miracles existed within himself.

4. Jesus' Gift of the Holy Spirit — The Power of God[45]

As noted above, after His resurrection, ascension, and glorification, Jesus, clothed in divine power, gave the Holy Spirit to His apostles and many other followers. This Holy Spirit enabled the apostles to do the same miracles (healings, exorcisms, and raisings of the dead) as Jesus did, in His name. This power was essential to the apostles' credibility and the Church's evangelizing ministry and was manifest in the early Church's exponential expansion amidst persecution and martyrdom (precisely the opposite of every other Messianic movement after the death of its Messiah). The gift of the Holy Spirit also manifested Jesus' divinity, because the Spirit was viewed as "the Power of God," and who but God himself could give the power of God to the world?

5. Jesus Has the Same Unconditional Love as the Father[46]

Throughout His ministry, Jesus uniquely redefined love as *agapē* — the self-giving, self-sacrificial love for the good of the other, which does not expect recompense or reward (see NT#8, section 1.A). He expressed this through the Beatitudes, the Parables of the Good Samaritan and the Prodigal Son, and a host of other teachings. More importantly, He demonstrated this love in His actions — His love for the most egregious sinners, the poor, the sick, and the emotionally disturbed, as well as for His apostles and disciples, whom "He loved … to the end" (Jn 13:1). Above all, He created an unrestricted act of love in His self-sacrificial gift of himself on the cross — an act of love that would endure eternally and be the power of the Eucharist, the Sacrament of Reconciliation, and the other sacraments.

When Jesus gave His very Body and Blood (His whole self) to His apostles at the Last Supper, and then allowed himself to be tortured, crucified, and killed at Calvary, He not only demonstrated His identity with His unconditionally loving Father but also showered that unconditional love on every human being who desired to be redeemed by it throughout the whole of time. We have no greater confirmation of Jesus' unconditional love and His sharing in His Father's unconditional love than this completely self-sacrificial act.

Conclusion

Let us now return to our main point. When the early Church leaders combined Jesus' proclamation of His exclusive Divine Sonship with their experience of His glorious resurrection, His gift of the Spirit of God, His miraculous power by His own authority, His unconditional love (manifest in His self-sacrifice on the cross), and the apostles' power to do miracles in Jesus' name, they had no doubt that He truly is and was the Son of God from all eternity. They proclaimed this truth boldly, though the cost was exceptionally high: the loss of thousands of potential converts; the loss of religious, social, and financial status; and, ultimately, expulsion from the Synagogue and persecution. Nevertheless, they accepted the cost because they were convinced of the truth by the above evidence, the Holy Spirit within them, and above all, their personal experience of the Lord of power and love.

NT#17: Why Do We Need a Church?

Many today believe that a church is unnecessary because anyone can have a relationship directly with God, which seems preferable. This has caused skepticism (e.g., at the time of the Protestant Reformation) and continues to cause skepticism about Jesus' intention to start not only a church but a hierarchal church with levels of greater or lesser authority. In light of this problem, it may prove helpful to first answer the question of why God would want to reveal himself through a church before answering the question (in NT#18) about which church Jesus (the Lord) started.

Most people throughout the world (84 percent) belong to a religious community and therefore explicitize their relationship with God through a church, sharing common belief, common ritual and tradition, and common worship.[47] A few decades ago, over 90 percent of the world belonged to a religious community. Why do people naturally gravitate toward a church rather than practicing private spirituality in their homes? There are four reasons:

1. The need for a source of Revelation to guide us, so we can know who God is and His path to salvation
2. The need for a spiritual community, which is a source of spiritual support, friendship, and unity
3. The need for a form of sacred ritual, worship, and symbol to bring us closer to God
4. The need for a source of spiritual and moral teaching and guidance to help us in our relationship with God through prayer and call us to moral conversion

These four dimensions of religion (Revelation, community, worship, and a guide for spiritual and moral conversion) are not self-evident. If we just sit in our rooms, we are unlikely to know what God really wants of us, where He is leading us, how He is interacting with us, and therefore, how to live, pray, and worship according to His will, which will lead to our growth and salvation. How then should we pray? What should we pray for? How do we live in accordance with the fruit of our prayer? Without some form of outward Revelation from God and authoritative teaching, we are truly lost in a haze of everything. Furthermore, we would miss out on the experience of praying to God with brothers and sisters who share our awareness and excitement for God and our reverence for His supreme love, goodness, and holiness. This would relegate us to the very narrow world of solitary thoughts in our own minds. Yes, we must make an effort to get out of the house and to join the community, but we will be the better for it, because we will grow closer to God through the community, closer to the community through God, and closer to the life and salvation to which He is calling us.

No Divine Revelation is completely self-evident, and so we need a divinely designated authority to interpret it — an authority that is given the grace and insight to know the heart of God — a church with inspired leadership. Without a definitive authority to interpret Divine Revelation, we would have virtually no way of knowing how to enter into a relationship with God, what His plan is for us, how to best enter into that plan, and what He expects from us. Without divinely revealed truth and an inspired interpretation of that truth through a church, we would be clueless about how to proceed in a spiritual life. Therefore, the claim that we can carry out a spiritual life on our own without a church seems wholly unrealistic. How can we carry out a spiritual life without knowing God beyond our very limited intuition? We might be able to intuitively know that we should be reverent and respectful toward God, but beyond that, we have little hope of probing more deeply the mysterious reality we sense interiorly. If God does not show us who He is and does not give us a means to definitively interpret His Revelation (through a church's leadership), we cannot proceed very far in prayer, in our moral lives, or toward salvation.

In sum, without a church, we lack understanding, direction, mutual support, and fulfillment in our faith on four levels:

1. Without Divine Revelation manifest through authoritative religious figures, we are lost within a myriad of untested ideas about God and salvation and are therefore left clueless about how to understand and practice our faith.

2. Without a faith community to support us, we consign ourselves to our own interior religious consciousness, devoid of interpersonal relationships, communal support, and accountability to an authority beyond ourselves. This deprives

our faith of the care, insight, and help of others.

3. Without a rite of worship (e.g., the Mass), we relegate our prayer to merely private, subjective expressions devoid of the prayers, rituals, and common beliefs given to us by Divine Revelation. This is particularly evident in Catholicism, which has a specified ritual to receive the very Body and Blood of Jesus to transform and help us (see Mk 14:22–24 and Mt 26:26–28) as well as a ritual for definitive absolution from sin originating from Jesus himself (Jn 22–23).

4. Without a church's moral teaching, we are left to our own unformed consciences for moral guidance in a complex world with literally thousands of divergent moral prescriptions, making us vulnerable to evil people and evil spirits.

This absence of church affiliation leads to religious emptiness, loneliness, and alienation, because our individual spirituality leaves us unfulfilled, unsupported, and unguided, with a profound sense that we are alone in the cosmos and not at home with the Divine.[48] Belief in God and individual spirituality are not enough. All major studies correlating religion with human happiness and fulfillment show that we need *religious* affiliation — a church community — to avoid depression and meaninglessness.[49] In fact, non-religiously affiliated people have significantly higher rates of depression, anxiety, familial tensions, substance abuse, antisocial aggressivity, suicidal ideation, and suicides than religiously affiliated people.[50] What these studies show is that without a church, we are likely to be unfulfilled and unhappy as well as depressed and anxious. This should not be a surprise, because as Saint Augustine long ago stated, "For Thou has made us for Thyself, and our hearts are restless until they rest in Thee."[51]

NT#18: Did Jesus Initiate the Catholic Church?

Though the New Testament states plainly that Jesus commissioned Peter to be the foundational rock (see Mt 16:17–19) and the chief shepherd of the Church (Jn 21:15–17), some have questioned whether this was Jesus' intention or an interpretation of the first-century Church. Furthermore, some have questioned whether Jesus' commission applied not only to Peter but also to his successors. A brief analysis of these Scripture texts, using the work of both Protestant scholars — such as W. D. Davies, Dale Allison, and Joachim Jeremias — as well as Catholic scholars — such as John L. McKenzie, Raymond Brown, and Benedict Viviano — shows the strong likelihood that Peter's commission originated with Jesus and that it does apply to Peter's successors.

Why is the primacy of Peter's office so important? The brief answer is to provide an authoritative interpretation of Scripture that will preserve the truth of Jesus' message as well as unity within the Church. Scriptural interpretation is not a simple matter. As we have seen (OT#2–4 and NT#2–4), Scripture is formed and written through the lens of times, places, and cultures quite different from our own. When Scripture passages appear to conflict with one another, the faithful can be caught up in confusion and seriously deceived. This means that there will have to be some kind of teaching authority within the Church. If there were not, the Church community would be divided into factions, each having different interpretations of the same basic books of Scripture. Such factions arose even in the early Church and especially after the Reformation movement. Over the last five hundred years since the Reformation, about 200 Protestant denominations and about 35,496 independent and non-denominational churches have been initiated.[52] This is attributable almost solely to the lack of a definitive teaching authority within Protestant churches, whose leaders had no authoritative basis to determine which scriptural interpretation was correct.

Did Jesus anticipate the possibility of such divisions and establish a church with a definitive teaching authority precisely to avoid this crisis of truth and unity? The answer is decidedly yes. This unit takes up the evidence for Jesus' intention to establish a teaching authority through Peter *and his successors* and to build one, and only one, Church on the basis of that teaching authority — the Catholic Church.

1. Jesus as the Universal Temple

Jesus was no stranger to the dangers of religious division. He lived at a time when Judaism was divided and even fragmented into many parties and schools — Sadducees, Pharisees, Essenes, Zealots, and many other subfactions and extremes. But Jesus intended to make His Body the mystical unification of a universal Church (see Jn 2:21). This would not be a "temple created by human hands" (Jn 2:19) — situated in a particular place like Jerusalem — but a temple made by God for everyone everywhere. Jesus knew He would have to leave His disciples, but He intended to give them the Holy Spirit (Jn 20:22 and Acts 2:1–4) to guide them and their successors to "go therefore and make disciples of all nations" (Mt 28:19).

In view of the above, it is highly likely that Jesus intended to start a Church that would become a universal temple in His own risen body and that He foresaw the very real possibility of factions within that Church if she did not have a definitive teaching authority. This explains why Jesus invested primary teaching authority in Peter and his successors (see Mt 16:17–19, discussed in sections 4–6).

2. Other Evidence of Jesus' Intention to Start a Church

In addition to Jesus' proclamation of being the universal temple and His commissioning of Peter in both Matthew (see 16:17–19) and John (21:15–17), Jesus recruited apostles, giving them power to heal and expel demons and to teach in His name (Mt 10:1–15 and Lk 5:1–11). Furthermore, He appointed additional disciples, such as the seventy disciples, giving them similar powers of healing and preaching (Lk 10:1–24).

Prior to His final journey to Jerusalem, Jesus' instructions to both the apostles and disciples were for missionary purposes, but as He approached the time for His final trip to Jerusalem, He spoke solely to the apostles. In these instructions, He set up the structure of His Church (see Mt 16:17–19 and 18:18), gave all the apostles special powers in that Church (Mt 18:18) and instructions for how to run the Church (Mt 18:17–19), and appointed Peter (and implicitly his successors) as the supreme teaching and juridical authority to govern that Church (Mt 16:17–19 and Jn 21:15–17).

Notice that Jesus distinguished these groups and ranked them according to three levels:

1.   Peter and his successors (the highest level)

2. The other apostles and their successors — bishops (the second level)
3. Additional disciples who were not apostles, such as the seventy (the third level)

He gave powers to the higher levels of authority not given to the lower levels. For example, Peter was given powers not given to the lower two levels: to be the foundation of the Church with the keys to the kingdom of heaven, tantamount to the highest authority of prime minister. The apostles were given powers not given to non-apostolic disciples: the power to bind and loose (to teach and govern with authority and to mitigate disputes). All three groups were given the power to preach the word, heal the sick, and expel demons.

This three-level structure, with its special powers and instructions (for higher levels), would be virtually unintelligible if Jesus had not been committed to initiating a structured hierarchical Church that would last beyond His passion and resurrection. The same holds true for His gift of the Holy Spirit to the apostles specifically for the governance of the Church (see Jn 16).

3. Did Jesus Think the Church Would Endure for Multiple Generations Beyond the Apostles?

Since Jesus instructed His disciples to proclaim the Gospel to the whole world (see Mt 28:19–20 and Mk 13:10), it would seem He intended His Church to last longer than just one generation. After all, how could His small band of apostles and disciples have preached the Gospel to *all* nations in one or two generations?

Furthermore, in every discourse about the end of the world (in all four Gospels), Jesus speaks of two sets of tribulations — one concerned with the destruction of Jerusalem and a later one concerned with the end of the world. He indicated that there would be many signs and apocalyptic events that would occur between the two tribulations, again implying more than one or two generations. Though Jesus does not specify the precise time of the second tribulation, He states, "About that day or hour no one knows, not even the angels in heaven, nor the Son, but only the Father" (Mk 13:32).

The criterion of embarrassment makes the historicity of this passage very likely. Why would Mark or the early Church have preserved this tradition, which restricts Jesus' (the incarnate Son's) knowledge of future events if it was not true? In light of this, it is highly likely that Jesus did foresee at least the possibility that the Church would last for many generations.

Inasmuch as He did anticipate this (as well as the likelihood of factions without a definitive authority to interpret His words), it is highly likely that He intended to give definitive teaching and juridical authority not only to Peter but also to his successors for one or more generations. If Jesus saw the need to have an ultimate teaching and juridical authority in Peter to prevent divisions in Peter's generation, why would He have allowed all subsequent generations to fall victim to factions and disunity? In view of this, it is very likely that Jesus intended to vest ultimate juridical authority in all of Peter's successors. We will obtain further confirmation of this in the commissioning passage itself.

4. The Historicity of Matthew's Account of Jesus' Commissioning of Peter

Let's take a look at the actual text where Jesus commissions Peter as the head of His Church:

> Blessed are you, Simon Bar-Jona! For flesh and blood has not revealed this to you, but my Father who is in heaven. And I tell you, you are Peter, and on this rock I will build my church, and the powers of death shall not prevail against it. I will give you the keys of the kingdom of heaven, and whatever you bind on earth shall be bound in heaven, and whatever you loose on earth shall be loosed in heaven. (Matthew 16:17–19)

It might seem surprising that a text so significant to the future of the Church is only found in one Gospel; however, Matthew's text here appears to be quoting an earlier Aramaic tradition that was familiar to and referenced by Saint Paul. How do we know this was an early, well-known Aramaic tradition? Matthew's Gospel was written in Greek, but this passage contains many idiomatic expressions used in Aramaic (the language Jesus used) that were likely found in His original Aramaic version, for example:

- "Blessed are you," to express Peter's inspired awareness of Jesus as Messiah[53]
- "Simon Bar-Jonah," retaining the Aramaic version of Peter's original name and ancestry[54]
- "Flesh and blood has not revealed this to you," where "flesh and blood" refers to a human being[55]

The most significant Aramaic expression occurs when Jesus renames Peter: "You are Cephas, and on this Cephas (rock), I will build my church." This doesn't work well in the Greek translation, where rock is a feminine word — *petra* — which doesn't match Peter's masculine name, *Petros*.[56]

The renaming of Peter also points to Jesus as the author of this primitive Aramaic tradition, because it requires a very high authority, like Jesus, to rename a person in Semitic culture, where the name chosen by the parents is almost sacrosanct.[57] Jesus was the only authority in Peter's life who would have been able to do that.[58]

As mentioned above, this early Aramaic tradition was also referenced by Saint Paul (see Gal 1:16–2:10). Paul's account of his own commissioning as an apostle in Galatians 1 and 2 has several parallels to Peter's commissioning by Christ. For instance, in connecting his commissioning with Peter's commissioning, Paul, who generally uses Peter's Aramaic name, *Cephas* (see, for example, Gal 1:18 and 2:9), uses the Greek translation of Peter's name, *Petros*, twice in Galatians 2:7 and 2:8. This is the only time Paul translates *Cephas* into the Greek *Petros* in all his writings.[59] Moreover, Saint Paul uses the same Aramaic expression as Matthew — "flesh and blood" — to refer to "human beings" (Gal 1:16), which Jesus used in Peter's commissioning. This is the only time Saint Paul uses this expression in all his New Testament letters.[60] Is it merely a coincidence that Paul's unique use of these terms, which precisely parallels Matthew's commissioning, is used in a passage referring to Paul's own commissioning?[61] These parallels indicate that Matthew's commissioning account was not unique to him but was also likely known by Saint Paul. Furthermore, the Aramaic background of both passages (in Matthew and Galatians) indicates a very early origin in Jerusalem well before the writing of Saint Paul's letter. As we shall see, there are several textual and phrasing indications that this Aramaic version goes back to Jesus himself.

Beyond Matthew's account of the commissioning (paralleled in Saint Paul), Saint John gives us yet another Gospel passage of Peter's exclusive commissioning to be chief shepherd of the Church by Jesus (see Jn 21:15–17). Though the Gospel of Luke does not mention commissioning, Luke's account of the early Church (in the Acts of the Apostles) frequently illustrates Peter's central role in the Church. It sets Peter in a central place (in Acts 1–15), makes him spokesman of the universal Church at the Council of Jerusalem (Acts 15:6–11), and implies his superiority to Paul (Acts 15:1–2, 6–11).

Scripture scholars have noted many other indications of Peter's supremacy over Paul, James, and the other apostles in the Acts of the Apostles.[62] How could Peter have assumed such supremacy over the entire Church community without explicit appointment from Jesus himself? The early community was quite sensitive to the need for divine authority (such as Jesus) to bestow on any individual the authority to definitively interpret *Jesus'* words and intention. What other divine authority besides Jesus could have done this to the early Church's satisfaction?

If Peter had not received this special commissioning authority, we would have expected his authority to be hotly disputed in the Acts of the Apostles and in the other writings and history of the early Church. Instead, we find this authority acknowledged consistently, not only in Matthew, John, and the Acts of the Apostles but also in the writings of popes and bishops in the early Church (see section 6).

Did Jesus' commission of Peter include his successors? From a logical standpoint alone, it would not make sense for Jesus to establish a guiding and stabilizing authority if the Church would lose this authority once Peter had died. But we can also discern clues in the words Jesus used to commission Peter that indicate Jesus' intention to establish an office of supreme authority that would be granted to Peter as well as his successors. Let's look at these significant words:

- **Rock:** A name in first-century Jewish thought represented the core identity of a person as well as his purpose in life. Thus the renaming of Simon as *Cephas* (which was unique to Peter) indicates that his purpose was to be the foundation rock of Jesus' Church and the foundational leader of the new people of God.

- **"My Church"**: Just as Jesus promised to replace the localized temple of Jerusalem with the new universal temple, Jesus used the future tense, "I will build my church," to describe the universal church He would establish.

- **"The powers of death shall not prevail against [my Church]"**: This expression has an obvious ring of permanence, which suggests that the Church structure founded on Peter might well endure beyond him.

- **Authority to "bind and loose"**: In first-century Judaism, *binding* and *loosing* were terms for a rabbi's authority to make a binding judgment on matters of faith and practice as well as the power to excommunicate. Benedict Viviano describes this power thus: "This verse gives enormous authority to Peter. ... Binding and loosing are rabbinic technical terms that can refer to binding the devil in exorcism, to the juridical acts of excommunication and of definitive decision making."[63]

Though Jesus gives the power to bind and loose to the other apostles (see Mt 18:18), He gives it to Peter definitively and absolutely by combining it with "the keys of the kingdom of heaven." He does not do this for the other apostles in Matthew 18:18. What does the expression "keys of the kingdom" mean? This phrase parallels an Old Testament expression when the prophet Isaiah announces that God has appointed a new prime minister for Israel, saying, "I will place on his shoulder the key of the house of David; he shall open, and none shall shut; and he shall shut, and none shall open" (Is 22:22). The term *keys* in this and other political/ecclesiastical contexts indicates the office of prime minister — the highest office under the king himself.[64] Notice the close parallel between Isaiah's words, "He shall open, and none shall shut, he shall shut, and none shall open," and Jesus' words, "Whatever you bind on earth will be bound in heaven, and whatever you loose on earth will be loosed in heaven." Jesus was quite familiar with the scrolls of Isaiah, so it is very likely that He had this passage in mind in His commission of Peter. If so, it is quite likely that He was initiating the highest office in the Church. Like the office of prime minister, Peter is second only to the king (Jesus) himself.

Notice that Jesus gave the office ("the keys") to Peter as if the office already existed (by Jesus' own authority). If the office existed independently of Peter and was given to Peter, then it could exist after Peter to be given to his successors.[65] The office of supreme authority that Jesus gave to Peter goes beyond any earthly political office. Through it, Jesus bestows His own divine authority — to bind *in heaven* and to loose *in heaven*. This power is so extraordinary that it must have originated with Jesus himself, otherwise it would have been seriously disputed by the other apostles and leaders in the early Church.

Can we be sure that Peter's commissioning in Matthew's Gospel really goes back to Jesus himself? We can be reasonably sure for five reasons:

1. As we have said, this commissioning passage was originally written in Aramaic (Jesus' language) and was known not only by Matthew but very likely by Paul (see Gal 1:16–2:10).
2. There are several indications in the passage that reflect Jesus' unique style, such as the use of the emphatic *ego* — that is, the use of an unnecessary first person pronoun ("I") in the expression "I tell you" (Mt 16:18).[66] This unnecessary use of the pronoun "I" for emphasis is almost exclusive to Jesus, according to Jeremias.[67] Furthermore, the use of *pater mou* (an *Abba* substitute) in Matthew 16:17 is also virtually unique to Jesus.[68] These two phrases occurring within an Aramaic passage strongly indicate that Jesus was its author.
3. As indicated earlier, renaming an individual is reserved to someone of exceedingly high authority. There is no higher authority in Peter's life than Jesus.
4. There are several other indications of the supremacy of Petrine authority in the New Testament, such as the triple commissioning in John's Gospel and Peter's central role in

the Acts of the Apostles. These passages confirm Jesus as the source of Petrine supremacy.

5. Peter's supreme authority would have been continually contested by early Church leaders if it had not been well known to have originated with Jesus.

In light of these five reasons, it is highly likely that the commissioning of Peter in Matthew's Gospel originated with Jesus. Therefore, it is also highly likely that the office of supreme teaching and juridical authority bestowed upon Peter — and implicitly upon his successors — also originated with Jesus.

5. Peter in the Acts of the Apostles and at the Council of Jerusalem

Peter plays a central role in the Acts of the Apostles (chapters 1–15). If he did not have supreme authority, the roles he played in the early Church would be inexplicable. For example, he established the succession of the apostles by proposing the election of a successor to the apostle Judas (see Acts 1:15–22); he was the spokesman for the Church at Pentecost and afterward (Acts 1:15); he made authoritative decisions like expanding the Church by preaching to Gentiles as well as Jews (Acts 10:44–48; 11:1–18; 15:6–12). The most explicit manifestation of Peter's supreme office is found at the Council of Jerusalem, the first Council of the Church, held around AD 50 (Acts 15:1–12). Many Church leaders, including Paul, James, other apostles, Barnabas, and elders, were present. Paul and Barnabas came from the Gentile lands to Jerusalem to ask the apostles to resolve the controversial question of whether new Gentile converts to the Church were required to follow Jewish law. It was Peter who first responded to the inquiry from Paul and others and did so definitively by his own authority, inspired by the Holy Spirit, assuring his audience that the Lord had made the decision — not appealing to Moses, the prophets, or any other human authority (Acts 15:2–11).

When Peter proclaimed his decision (by decree), the assembly fell silent, meaning that Peter's word put an end to all debate and discussion — it was definitive for the whole Church. By contrast, the apostle James had authority only over Jewish Christians in the Jerusalem church. He did not play a universal role as Peter did. Furthermore, Peter spoke on his own authority as inspired by God, while James appealed to Moses and the other prophets. Thirdly, James built on Peter's previous decree about the Gentiles being dispensed from much of the Jewish law — not vice-versa. It can scarcely be believed that Peter would have this unique, primary, and universal authority if it were not given to him explicitly by Jesus.

6. Were Peter's Successors Recognized as Supremely Authoritative by Bishops and Theologians in the Post-Petrine Church?

Though the intention of Jesus to create an office of supreme authority for Peter's successors can be reasonably inferred from the text of Jesus' commission of Peter (see Mt 16:17–19) — particularly in His use of "keys of the kingdom of heaven" (apparently referring to a highest *office*, such as prime minister), some non-Catholic exegetes have challenged this interpretation, obscuring Jesus' intention. The most incisive way to confirm the standard interpretation of the commissioning text (that Jesus intended supreme authority to be conveyed to Peter's successors) is to assess how the leaders of the early Church understood the authority of Peter's successors to the See of Rome. The preponderance of evidence strongly implies that a close successor (Pope Clement I), a highly placed bishop (St. Ignatius of Antioch), and theologians (e.g., Saint Irenaeus) all held that supreme authority was vested in Peter's successors in the Roman See, further implying that this is what Jesus intended.

After the Acts of the Apostles, we have only limited records of the leaders of the early Church. There are four texts we can examine that relate to the primacy of Peter and his successors (the Bishops of Rome). As we shall see, they confirm an unbroken line of thought from the death of Saint Peter to the writings of Cyprian of Carthage that the successors of Saint Peter maintained their primacy over the universal Church in matters of teaching and the resolution of juridical disputes.

6.A. Pope Clement I

Peter ordained Clement, who later became the fourth pope (after Linus and Cletus), with authority over the universal Church, according to Saint Irenaeus and Tertullian.[69] He held this high office from AD 88 to 99. During that time, factions in the Corinthian church deposed the bishop and other clergy. Pope Clement responded incisively and strongly in a letter sent to the Church in Corinth ordering them to reinstate their leaders and be "obedient to what we have written through the Holy Spirit." Clement was certain that he possessed the authority of God, as Peter's successor, to resolve disputes for the whole Church beyond the See of Rome. Indeed, he believed he could sanction the rebellious factions under penalty of sin by divine authority for their disobedience: "Should any disobey what has been said by Him [God] through us [i.e., that you must reinstate your leaders], let them understand that they will entangle themselves in transgression and no small danger."[70]

If he had not possessed supreme authority, which other local churches recognized as coming from God, the dispute in Corinth would have gone unresolved, leading to further breakdown in the Church mere decades after Christ established her.

6.B. St. Ignatius of Antioch

St. Ignatius, bishop of Antioch, wrote a letter to the Church of Rome about AD 102, acknowledging that it was superior to — and presided over — all other Christian Churches. Charles Belmonte makes a comparative analysis of the tone of Saint Ignatius's many letters to other bishops and his letter to the Bishop of Rome (the pope):

> When one compares the tone of the epistles of Saint Ignatius, one notices that the epistle addressed to the church of Rome is different. There is no doubt that the bishop of Antioch is writing to a superior. He greets the church that is "presiding in the chief place of the Roman territory;" evidently, presiding not over itself but over the other Christian communities. He calls her "the one presiding in charity," or "presiding in the bond of love." This is his way of saying "presiding over the Church universal."[71]

As can be seen, at the end of the first century there was recognition by the local churches of the supremacy of the bishop of the Church in Rome. This pervasive recognition of the supremacy of the Bishop of Rome would have to have originated with Peter himself, otherwise it would have been seriously disputed. Peter, in turn, would have traced back to Jesus his authorization to bestow primacy of authority to his successors. The recognition of the Bishop of Rome as leader of the universal Church is clarified and strengthened in the succeeding centuries, as shown in the writings of Saint Irenaeus (*Against Heresies* 3:3:2, written c. AD 189) and St. Cyprian of Carthage (*The Unity of the Catholic Church*, chapter 4).

Conclusion

The primacy of the Bishop of Rome seems to have achieved its intended role of maintaining unity and a single truth to vouchsafe the Church and her teaching amidst considerable doctrinal and juridical disputes. Without this primacy of authority, the Church would have likely disintegrated into multiple factions or disappeared altogether in her first two centuries. In view of this, it is very likely that Jesus foresaw these disputes, established a primary authority under Peter and his successors, and sent the Holy Spirit to protect His truth and the unity of His people through this office. As the former agnostic historian Arnold Toynbee comments:

> The Church in its traditional form thus stands forth armed with the spear of the Mass, the shield of the Hierarchy, and the helmet of the Papacy; and … [has the attribute] of outlasting the toughest of the secular institutions of this world, including all the civilizations. … [The institutions of the Church] are the toughest and the most enduring of any that we know and are therefore the most likely to last — and outlast all the rest.[72]

Apparently, Jesus' promise to Peter that the powers of death would not prevail against His Church has been kept, and as Toynbee implies, will continue to be kept until the end of time.

Conclusion to Part Two — The New Testament

There are many questions that remain unanswered about the rational and scientific investigation of the New Testament. The above considerations were intended solely to provide a foundation upon which to build further investigations from an exegetical, historical, and scientific perspective. It is hoped that the above eighteen responses to the most fundamental questions provide a strong, reasonable, and responsible basis to affirm the following:

- Jesus Christ is a real historical figure who performed a remarkable ministry of exorcisms, healings, and raisings of the dead. He proclaimed himself to be the exclusive Son of the Father, who shared an intimate relationship with Him and even shared in His divinity. He was crucified in a highly unusual way (with a crown of thorns, excessive whipping, and a spear wound in His side) because of a charge of blasphemy (unique in Jewish and Roman juridical proceedings). Considerable evidence points to His resurrection in glory — not only from the Gospels and letters of Saint Paul but also from His gift of the Holy Spirit, enabling His disciples to perform miracles in His name — which must have occurred in great numbers to explain the exponential expansion of the Christian Church after the condemnation and execution of her Messiah. These facts are also corroborated by the Shroud of Turin and modern miracles that have been thoroughly, scientifically investigated.
- The Gospel accounts are based in great part on the eyewitness testimonies of Peter, the beloved disciple, the other apostles who formed the core of the Jerusalem church, and other disciples who followed Jesus throughout His ministry — particularly "the women" and specifically named individuals mentioned in the Gospel traditions.
- Jesus' mission was to the bring the kingdom of God and to save humanity from Satan by His unconditional love given in complete self-sacrifice on the cross, the gift of the Holy

Spirit, the Church He initiated, the sacraments, and His words and example. If we are to enter into His kingdom, resulting in eternal salvation, we must not only believe in Him but also follow His teachings and participate in the Church — particularly the one He initiated.

- The evidence of eyewitness testimonies, the criteria of historicity, the exponential expansion of the Christian Church after the execution of her Messiah, and the investigation of the Shroud and contemporary miracles point strongly to the complementarity and mutual corroboration of science, reason, and faith in discovering the truth of Jesus Christ.

Acknowledgments

I am most grateful to Joan Jacoby, whose invaluable work brought mere thoughts into reality through her excellent editing suggestions, research, and preparation of the manuscript. I am also sincerely grateful to Jeena Rudy for her considerable help in research and preparation of the manuscript. I also want to thank Kathleen Conway and Karlo Broussard for their help in bringing the manuscript to its final form.

Notes

PART ONE: QUESTIONS ABOUT
THE OLD TESTAMENT

Chapter 1: Foundational Questions Concerned with the Methods of Science, Scriptural Interpretation, and History

1. *Catechism of the Catholic Church* (United States Catholic Conference, Inc.—Libreria Editrice Vaticana, 1994; New York: Doubleday, 2003), 159. Hereafter cited as CCC.

2. Augustine, *De Genesi ad Litteram*, bk. 1, chaps. 18–19.

3. Thomas Aquinas, *Summa Contra Gentiles*, bk. 1, chap. 7, sec. 1.

4. See Robert Spitzer, forthcoming, *Science at the Doorstep to Christ: Scientific Evidence in Support of Jesus, the Eucharist, and the Blessed Virgin* (San Francisco: Ignatius, 2024), chap. 7, § 1. Hereafter SDC.

5. See Robin Marantz Henig, *The Monk in the Garden: The Lost and Found Genius of Gregor Mendel, the Father of Genetics* (Boston: Houghton Mifflin, 2000).

6. Jens Morten Hansen, "On the Origin of Natural History: Steno's Modern, But

Forgotten Philosophy of Science," in Gary D. Rosenberg, *The Revolution in Geology from the Renaissance to the Enlightenment* (Boulder, CO: Geological Society of America, 2009), 159–178.

7. See Georges Lemaître, *The Primeval Atom* (New York: The University Press). Mauricio Livio established that Father Lemaître was the very first physicist to theorize and mathematically prove the big bang. See Mauricio Livio, "Comments," in *Nature* 479, no. 7372 (November 2011): 171–173.

8. Augustin Udías and William Stauder, "The Jesuit Contribution to Seismology," *Seismological Research Letters* 67, no. 3 (May/June 1996): 10–19, https://www.seismosoc.org/inside/eastern-section/jesuit-contribution-seismology/. See also Spitzer, SDC, chap. 7, sec. 1.

9. Augustine, *On the Literal Interpretation of Genesis*, bk. 1, chap. 19.

10. Spitzer, SDC, chap. 7, sec. 2.

11. Robert Bellarmine to Paolo Focarini, April 12, 1615, in M. Finocchiaro, *The Galileo Affair: A Documentary History* (Berkeley, CA: University of California Press, 1989),67–69, https://inters.org/Bellarmino-Letter-Foscarini.

12. John Paul II, Address to the Participants of the Plenary Session of the Pontifical Academy of Science, October 31, 1992, Vatican.va.

13. Pius XII, *Divino Afflante Spiritu*, September 30, 1943, Vatican.va, par. 3. Italics mine.

14. Leo XIII, *Providentissimus Deus*, November 18, 1893, Vatican.va, par. 20.

15. Joseph Ratzinger, "Biblical Interpretations in Conflict: On the Foundations and the Itinerary of Exegesis Today," *Opening up the Scriptures: Joseph Ratzinger and the Foundation of Biblical Interpretation,* ed. José Granados, Carlos Granados, and Luis Sánchez-Navarro (Grand Rapids, MI: Eerdmans, 2008), 1–29, and Joseph Ratzinger, "Exegesis and the Magisterium of the Church," in *Opening up the Scriptures*, 126–136.

16. Ratzinger, "Exegesis and the Magisterium of the Church," 133–134.

17. Joseph Ratzinger, *Faith and the Future* (Chicago: Franciscan Herald Press, 1971), 9.

18. See Joseph Ratzinger, "Zum Problem der Entmythologisierung des Neuen Testaments," *Religionsunterricht an Höheren Schulen* 3 (1960): 9–11.

19. Ratzinger, "Zum Problem," 11.

20. Ibid.

21. Pius XII, *Diviino Afflante Spiritu*, par. 33. Italics mine.

22. John Bright, *A History of Israel,* 4th ed. (Louisville, KY: Westminster John Knox Press, 2020), 80–110. Hereafter HOI. Bright has set out the broad outlines of the historical elements of the patriarchal narratives, the Exodus narrative, the desert narrative, and the conquest of Canaan narrative.

23. Ibid., 80–110.

24. For the historicity of Jesus' sayings and self-proclamation, see Joachim Jeremias, *New Testament Theology: The Proclamation of Jesus,* vol. 1 (London: SCM Press, 1971). For the historicity of Jesus' miracles, see John P. Meier, *A Marginal Jew: Rethinking the Historical Jesus, Volume 2: Mentor, Message, and Miracles* (New York: Doubleday, 1994). For the historicity of Jesus' resurrection and appearances, see N. T. Wright, *The Resurrection of the Son of God* (Minneapolis: Fortress Press, 2003), 451–870.

25. Richard Bauckham, *Jesus and the Eyewitnesses: The Gospels as Eyewitness Testimony,* 2nd ed. (Eerdmans: Grand Rapids, MI: 2017).

26. Ibid., 1–240.

27. Raymond E. Brown, Joseph A. Fitzmyer, and Roland Murphy, eds., *The New Jerome Biblical Commentary* (Englewood Cliffs, NJ: Prentice Hall, 1990), 4, hereafter NJBC.

28. Ibid., 4.

29. For a general introduction to prophetic literature, see Bruce Vawter, "Introduction to Prophetic Literature" in NJBC, 186–200. For a more in-depth interpretation of prophetic literature, see Gerhard von Rad, *Old Testament Theology, Vol. 2: The Theology of Israel's Prophetic Traditions* (Louisville, KY: Westminster John Knox Press, 1965).

30. For a general introduction to the psalms, see John S. Kselman and M. Barre, "Psalms," in NJBC, 523–552. For a more detailed and complex exegetical commentary of the psalms, see Mitchell Dahood, *Psalms,* 3 vols., in the Anchor Bible Series (originally published New York: Doubleday, 1966).

31. For a general introduction to Wisdom literature, see Roland Murphy, "Introduction to Wisdom Literature," in NJBC, 447–452. For a more in-depth assessment of wisdom literature, see James L. Crenshaw, *Old Testament Wisdom, Third Edition: An Introduction* (Louisville, KY: Westminster John Knox Press, 2010).

32. John Bright has identified some general events and the faith of Israel that came from them — see HOI, 81–90.

33. Ibid., chaps. 2–10.

34. See Richard Clifford and Roland Murphy, "Genesis," in NJBC, 8. The At-rahasis was written in about 1700 BC in ancient Akkad. The parallels between the Atrahasis and Genesis 2–9 are so remarkable that many scholars consider Genesis 2–9 to be an Israeli version of the Atrahasis. See Bernard F. Batto, *Slaying the Drag-on: Mythmaking in the Biblical Tradition* (Louisville, KY: Westminster John Knox Press, 1992), 51–52.

35. See Pius XII, *Divino Afflante Spiritu*, par. 3 and 33.

36. Clifford and Murphy, "Genesis," in NJBC, 10.

37. Ibid.

38. Ibid.

39. The Gilgamesh Epic and other ancient Mesopotamian texts refer to a devas-tating flood, which appears to point to a common historical source. From a geologi-cal point of view, there is evidence of such a flood around the Black Sea (near north-ern Turkey — north of the Upper Mesopotamian region from which the Atrahasis would have come), which seems to have occurred around 5000 BC (about 3,000 years before the patriarchs). An event of such huge proportions may well have been remembered and recounted for several thousand years. See James Trefil, "Evidence for a Flood," *Smithsonian Magazine*, April 1, 2000, https://www.smithsonianmag .com/science-nature/evidence-for-a-flood-102813115/.

40. The Yahwist is mostly responsible for the Genesis 6–9 narrative, but the Priestly Author has made some subsequent additions to it.

41. See Jeffery H. Tigay, *The Evolution of the Gilgamesh Epic* (Philadelphia: University of Pennsylvania Press, 1982), 217. Though the Yahwist could have been influenced by the flood story in the Gilgamesh Epic (rather than the Atrahasis), it should be noted that the Gilgamesh Epic flood story was probably taken from the Atrahasis and added to the eleventh tablet of Gilgamesh. Furthermore, the Yahwist was probably aware of the flood story in the Atrahasis because of his awareness of the other two stories from Atrahasis to which he responded in Genesis 2–3.

42. See Clifford and Murphy, "Genesis," in NJBC, 15.

43. See Michael Coogan, *A Brief Introduction to the Old Testament: The He-brew Bible in Its Context*, 4th ed. (Oxford: Oxford University Press, 2009), 55–60.

44. Herman Vanstiphout, *Epics of Sumerian Kings: The Matter of Aratta*, ed. Jerrold S. Cooper, Writings from the Ancient World no. 20 (Atlanta, GA: Society of Biblical Literature, 2003), available at the Brown University website, https:// www.brown.edu/Departments/Joukowsky_Institute/courses/materialworlds

/files/1308642.pdf.

Chapter 2: Questions Concerned with Evidence for God and the Soul from Contemporary Science, Medicine, and Philosophy

1. David Masci, "Scientists and Belief," Pew Research Center, November 5, 2009, https://www.pewforum.org/2009/11/05/scientists-and-belief/.

2. Ibid.

3. Kristin A. Robinson et al., "Religious and Spiritual Beliefs of Physicians," *Journal of Religion and Health* 56 (2017): 205–225, https://doi.org/10.1007/s10943-016-0233-8.

4. Bill Freeman, "Science or Miracle?; Holiday Season Survey Reveals Physicians' Views of Faith, Prayer and Miracles," WorldHealth.Net reporting survey by HCD Research and Louis Finkelstein Institute, December 22, 2004, https://www.worldhealth.net/news/science_or_miracle_holiday_season_survey/.

5. See Robert J. Spitzer, *Science at the Doorstep to God* (San Francisco, CA: Ignatius, 2023), Introduction, sec. 1. Hereafter SDG.

6. See Robert Kurland, "23 Famous Scientists Who Are Not Atheists," Magis Center, Juje 5, 2021, https://www.magiscenter.com/23-famous-scientists-who-are-not-atheists/.

7. Arthur Eddington, *The Nature of the Physical World* (Cambridge: Cambridge University Press, 1928), 327–328.

8. For additional information and references, see Spitzer, SDG, Introduction, sec. 2.

9. This will be a brief summary of three kinds of evidence for an intelligent Creator from contemporary science. For a full explanation with references, see SDG, chaps. 1 and 2.

10. Arvind Borde, Alan Guth, and Alexander Vilenkin, "Inflationary Spacetimes Are Incomplete in Past Directions," *Physical Review Letters* 90, no. 15 (2003), https://doi.org/10.1103/PhysRevLett.90.151301.

11. William Lane Craig and J. Sinclair, "The Kalam Cosmological Argument," in *The Blackwell Companion to Natural Theology*, ed. William Lane Craig and J. P. Moreland (Malden, MA: Wiley-Blackwell, 2009), 173–174.

12. Borde, Guth, and Vilenkin, "Inflationary Spacetimes Are Incomplete in Past Directions." For a detailed explanation, see SDG, chap. 1, sec. 2.

13. See Spitzer, SDG, chap. 1, sec. 3.

14. For a detailed explanation, Ibid., sec. 2.

15. See Sean Carroll's argument stated below in sec. 2. Sean Carroll, "Against Bounces," *Discover Magazine*, July 2, 2007, https://www.discovermagazine.com /the-sciences/against-bounces.

16. See Borde, Guth, and Vilenkin, "Inflationary Spacetimes Are Incomplete in Past Directions."

17. William Lane Craig, *The Kalam Cosmological Argument* (New York: Barnes and Noble, 1979), 158.

18. Lisa Grossman, "Why Physicists Can't Avoid a Creation Event," *New Scientist*, January 11, 2012, https://media.oiipdf.com/pdf/07177730-cc88-44d3-a9c6 -1456cfefd7a7.pdf.

19. Leonard Susskind, *The Black Hole War: My Battle with Stephen Hawking to Make the World Safe for Quantum Mechanics* (New York: Little, Brown and Company, 2008), 419.

20. Stephen Hawking and Thomas Hertog, "A Smooth Exit from Eternal Inflation?" *Journal of High Energy Physics* 147 (2018), https://doi.org/10.1007/ JHEP04(2018)147. See also Andre Pattenden, "Taming the Multiverse: Stephen Hawking's Final Theory about the Big Bang," University of Cambridge, May 2, 2018, https://www.cam.ac.uk/research/news/taming-the-multiverse-stephen-hawkings -final-theory-about-the-big-bang.

21. Hawking and Hertog, "A Smooth Exit from Eternal Inflation?," and Pattenden, "Taming the Multiverse."

22. Ibid.

23. Tom Banks, "Why I Don't Believe in Eternal Inflation," Sean Carroll, October 24, 2011, https://www.preposterousuniverse.com/blog/2011/10/24/guest-post -tom-banks-contra-eternal-inflation-2, and Tom Banks, "The Top 10500 Reasons Not to Believe in the Landscape," High Energy Physics-Theory, Cornell University, August 28, 2012, https://arxiv.org/abs/1208.5715.

24. Luke Barnes, "The Fine-Tuning of the Universe for Intelligent Life," *Publications of the Astronomical Society of Australia* 29, no. 4 (2012): 529–564, https:// arxiv.org/pdf/1112.4647.pdf. Robert Spitzer and James Sinclair, "Fine-Tuning and Indications of Transcendent Intelligence," in *Theism and Atheism: Philosophical Arguments in Opposition*, ed. Joseph Koterski and Graham Oppy (New York: Macmillan Reference Library, 2019), 349.

25. See Spitzer, SDG, chap. 1, sec. 4, for alternative views of "nothing" which are really "something," such as, a vacuum, a false vacuum fluctuation, a field with zero energy, and empty space. If physical reality itself came into existence, all of these other dimensions of physical reality would also have to come into existence along with it. They would not exist prior to physical reality itself. Hence, prior to the beginning, physical reality itself can only be absolutely *nothing*.

26. These examples are explained in detail in Spitzer, SDG, chap. 2, sec. 2.

27. See Roger Penrose, *The Emperor's New Mind: Concerning Computers, Minds, and the Laws of Physics* (Oxford University Press, 1989), 343–344.

28. Steven Weinberg, "Life in the Universe," *Scientific American* 271, no. 49 (October 1994), https://www.scientificamerican.com/article/life-in-the-universe/.

29. Ibid.

30. See Geraint F. Lewis and Luke A. Barnes, *A Fortunate Universe: Life in a Finely Tuned Cosmos* (Cambridge: Cambridge University Press, 2016), 97–101.

31. Spitzer, SDG, chap. 2 shows why these naturalistic explanations are either impossible, contrary to science, or exceedingly, exceedingly improbable. For a more detailed explanation of the implausibility of these naturalistic explanations, see Spitzer and Sinclair, "Fine-Tuning and Indications of Transcendent Intelligence."

32. See Spitzer, SDG, chap. 2.

33. For a more complex scientific explanation of this conclusion, see Spitzer and Sinclair, "Fine-Tuning and Indications of Transcendent Intelligence." This is also explained in detail in SDG, chap. 2, sec. 5.

34. Sir Fred Hoyle, "The Universe: Past and Present Reflections," in *Engineering & Science* (November 1981): 12.

35. Fully explained in Spitzer, SDG, chap. 3, sec. 2.

36. For an additional proof that the one uncaused, unrestricted Creator of everything else (God) must be an unrestricted act of thinking, see Spitzer, SDG, chap. 3, sec. 3.

37. See Sam Parnia et al., "Guidelines and Standards for the Study of Death and Recalled Experiences of Death — a Multidisciplinary Consensus Statement and Proposed Future Directions," *Annals of the New York Academy of Sciences* 1511, no. 1 (2022): 5–21, https://sonjalyubomirsky.com/files/2022/02/Parnia-et-al.-Shirazi-2022.pdf.

38. Emily Henderson, "Researchers Publish Consensus Statement for the Study of Recalled Experiences Surrounding Death", Life Sciences News, April 13, 2022,

https://www.news-medical.net/news/20220413/Researchers-publish-consensus -statement-for-the-study-of-recalled-experiences-surrounding-death.aspx.

39. See Sam Parnia et al., "AWARE—AWAreness during Resuscitation—A Prospective Study," *Journal of Resuscitation* 85, no. 12 (2014): 1799–1805, https://doi .org/10.1016/j.resuscitation.2014.09.004.

40. See Pim van Lommel et al. "Near-Death Experience in Survivors of Cardiac Arrest: A Prospective Study in the Netherlands," *The Lancet* 358, no. 9298 (2001): 2039–2045, https://doi.org/10.1016/S0140-6736(01)07100-8.

41. See Bruce Greyson, "Seeing Dead People Not Known to Have Died: 'Peak in Darien' Experiences," *AnthroSource* 35, no. 2 (2010): 159–171, http://onlinelibrary .wiley.com/doi/10.1111/j.1548-1409.2010.01064.x/abstract.

42. See Kenneth Ring and Sharon Cooper, *Mindsight: Near-Death and Out-of-Body Experiences in the Blind* (Palo Alto, CA: William James Center for Consciousness Studies, 1999).

43. See "Division of Perceptual Studies," University of Virginia School of Medicine, https://med.virginia.edu/perceptual-studies/.

44. See Kimberly Clark, "Clinical Interventions with Near-Death Experiencers," in *The Near-Death Experience: Problems, Prospects, Prospectives*, eds. B. Greyson and C. P. Flynn (Springfield, IL: Charles C. Thomas, 1984).

45. See Ring and Cooper, *Mindsight*, 122.

46. See Lynn Love, "Blind Man Near Death Experience," video, March 9, 2013, https://youtu.be/YA8L9W7KiOo.

47. Greyson, "Seeing Dead People Not Known to Have Died: 'Peak in Darien' Experiences." See also Emily Williams Kelly, "Near-Death Experiences with Reports of Meeting Deceased People," *Death Studies* 25 (2001): 229–249, https://med .virginia.edu/perceptual-studies/wp-content/uploads/sites/360/2017/01 /KEL13-NDEwithReports-of-Meeting-Deceased-People.pdf.

48. Van Lommel et al., "Near-Death Experience in Survivors of Cardiac Arrest: A Prospective Study in the Netherlands," 2039–2040.

49. For more information, see Spitzer, SDG, chap. 4, sec. 1.

50. These hypotheses are discussed in Spitzer, SDG, chap. 4, sec. 1.D.

51. Mario Beauregard, *Brain Wars: The Scientific Battle Over the Existence of the Mind and the Proof That Will Change the Way We Live* (New York: Harper One, 2012).

52. See Pim van Lommel, *Consciousness Beyond Life: The Science of the Near-*

Death Experience (New York: Harper One, 2010), 121–177.

53. See Sam Parnia, *Erasing Death: The Science That is Rewriting the Boundaries Between Life and Death* (New York: Harper One, 2014), 145–160.

54. Emily Williams Kelly, Bruce Greyson, and Edward F. Kelly, "Unusual Experiences Near Death and Related Phenomena," in Edward F. Kelly et al., *Irreducible Mind: Toward a Psychology for the 21st Century* (Lanham, MD: Rowman and Littlefield, 2009), 367–422.

55. Ibid.

56. Ibid.

57. See Parnia et al., "Guidelines and Standards for the Study of Death and Recalled Experiences of Death — a Multidisciplinary Consensus Statement and Proposed Future Directions."

58. A fuller explanation of these phenomena and the many medical studies confirming them can be found in Spitzer, SDG, chap. 4, secs. 2.A and 2.B.

59. John Lorber, "Is Your Brain Really Necessary?," in *Hydrocephalus im fru¨hen Kindesalter: Fortschritte der Grundlagenforschung, Diagnostik und Therapie*, ed. D. Voth. Stuttgart (Germany: Enke Verlag, 1983). Michael Nahm and Bruce Greyson, "Terminal Lucidity in Patients with Chronic Schizophrenia and Dementia: A Survey of the Literature," *Journal of Nervous and Mental Disease* 197, no. 12 (2009): 942–944.

60. See, for example, Thomas Aquinas, *Summa Theologiae*, I, qq. 84–88.

61. A full explanation of these studies can be found in Spitzer, SDG, chap. 5.

62. Bernard Lonergan, *Collected Works of Bernard Lonergan*, vol. 3, *Insight: A Study of Human Understanding*, ed. Frederic Crowe and Robert Doran (Toronto: University of Toronto Press, 1992), chap. 12, in particular 380–381.

63. David Chalmers, *The Conscious Mind: In Search of a Fundamental Theory* (New York: Oxford University Press, 1996), 94–123.

64. John Eccles, *Evolution of the Brain: Creation of the Self* (New York: Routledge, 1989), 179–227.

65. Robert Berwick and Noam Chomsky, *Why Only Us: Language and Evolution* (Cambridge, MA: MIT Press, 2017), 90.

66. These studies are explained in Spitzer, SDG, chap. 5, secs. 1 and 2.

67. Herbert S. Terrace, *Why Chimpanzees Can't Learn Language and Only Humans Can* (New York: Columbia University Press, 2019), 5–26.

68. Berwick and Chomsky, *Why Only Us*, 84–147. See also Noam Chomsky,

Language and Mind (New York: Harcourt Brace Jovanovich, 1972), 55–65.

69. Endel Tulving, "Episodic Memory and Autonoesis: Uniquely Human?" in *The Missing Link in Cognition: Origins of Self-Reflective Consciousness*, eds. Herbert S. Terrace and Janet Metcalfe (New York: Oxford University Press, 2005).

70. These kinds of transcendental awareness are explained in Spitzer, SDG, chap. 6, secs. 1–3.

71. See Rudolf Otto, *The Idea of the Holy: An Inquiry into the Non-Rational Factor in the Idea of the Divine and Its Relation to the Rational*, trans. John W. Harvey (New York: Oxford University Press, 1958), 6–31. Mircea Eliade, *The Sacred and the Profane: The Nature of Religion*, trans. Willard R. Trask (New York: Harcourt, 1959), chaps. 2 and 4.

72. See John Henry Newman, unpublished manuscript entitled "Proof of Theism," in *The Argument from Conscience to the Existence of God*, ed. Adrian Boekraad and Henry Tristram (London: Mill Hill, 1961).

73. Plato makes this argument in the *Symposium*, 172a–223d.

74. Plato was the first to articulate these five kinds of transcendental awareness — perfect truth (in the *Sophist*), perfect love (the *Symposium*), perfect goodness/justice (in the *Republic*), perfect beauty (the *Symposium*), perfect being (the *Sophist*), and perfect unity (the *Parmenides*). This was taken up by Saint Augustine, who recognized their significance for human freedom in *On the Freedom of the Will*. This argument was later developed by Thomas Aquinas in *Summa Theologiae*, I, q.83, then later developed by Bernard Lonergan in *Insight*, chap. 18, and Jacques Maritain in *Moral Philosophy*, chap. 13.

75. Bernard Lonergan, *Insight*, chap. 18.

76. Karl Rahner, *Spirit in the World*, ed. Johann Metz (New York: Continuum, 1994), 209–308. See also Karl Rahner, *Foundations of Christian Faith: An Introduction to the Idea of Christianity* (Herder & Herder, 1982), chap. 3, sec. 2.

77. Paul Ricoeur, *Freedom and Nature: The Voluntary and Involuntary* (Chicago: Northwestern University Press, 2007).

78. The capacity for free choice arising out of our *transcendental* self-consciousness, rational intellection, religious experience, conscience, and awareness of perfect truth, goodness, love, beauty, and being/home is explained in Spitzer, SDG, chap. 6, sec. 5.

Chapter 3: Questions Concerned with the Relationship Between Science and the Bible

1. See Eric Chaisson, "First Few Minutes," Cosmic Evolution, https://lweb.cfa .harvard.edu/~ejchaisson/cosmic_evolution/docs/fr_1/fr_1_part3.html. See also M. Tanabashi "Big-Bang Cosmology," revised September 2017 by Keith A. Olive and John A. Peacock, https://pdg.lbl.gov/2018/reviews/rpp2018-rev-bbang-cosmology .pdf, 21.4.1.

2. For a more detailed account see Spitzer, SDG, chap. 1, sec. 1.

3. Michael Polanyi, "Life's Irreducible Structure," *Science* 160, no. 3834 (1968): 1308–1309. Polanyi is a world-famous chemist and philosopher.

4. See M. S. Dodd et al., "Evidence for Early Life in Earth's Oldest Hydrothermal Vent Precipitates," *Nature* 543, no. 7643 (2017): 60–64, https://eprints.whiterose .ac.uk/112179/1/ppnature21377_Dodd.

5. Dodd et al., "Evidence for Early Life in Earth's Oldest Hydrothermal Vent Precipitates."

6. A brief scientific explanation of evolution is provided below in OT#15.

7. See Michael Marshall, "Timeline: The Evolution of Life," *New Scientist*, July 14, 2009, https://www.newscientist.com/article/dn17453-timeline-the-evolution -of-life/. All other stages of evolution below are taken from this *New Scientist* article.

8. See Kieran McNulty, "Paleontology and Primate Evolution," Nature Education, https://www.nature.com/scitable/knowledge/paleontology-and-primate -evolution-135304123/.

9. See Herman Pontzer, "Overview of Hominin Evolution," Nature Education, https://www.nature.com/scitable/knowledge/library/overview-of-hominin -evolution-89010983/.

10. See Polanyi, "Life's Irreducible Structure," 1308–1309.

11. Thomas Nagel, *Mind & Cosmos: Why the Materialist Neo-Darwinian Conception of Nature Is Almost Certainly False* (New York: Oxford University Press, 2012).

12. "Human Evolution Interactive Timeline," Smithsonian National Museum of Natural History, https://humanorigins.si.edu/evidence/human-evolution -interactive-timeline. All of the other stages of human evolution mentioned below are taken from this article.

13. Nagel, *Mind & Cosmos*.

14. Polanyi, "Life's Irreducible Structure," 1308–1312, and Michael Polanyi

"Transcendence and Self-Transcendence," *Soundings* 53, no. 1 (1970): 88–94.

15. Polanyi, "Life's Irreducible Structure," 1308–1309.

16. Ibid., 1309.

17. Ibid., 1311–1312.

18. Ibid., 1312.

19. Ibid., 1308–1309.

20. See Nagel, *Mind & Cosmos*.

21. Masci, "Scientists and Belief." See above, OT#5.

22. Pius XII, *Humani Generis*, August 12, 1950, Vatican.va, par. 36.

23. John Paul II, "Message to the Papal Academy of Science on Evolution," October 22, 1996, https://www.ewtn.com/catholicism/library/message-to-the -pontifical-academy-of-science-on-evolution-8825, par. 4.

24. Spitzer, SDG, chap. 6, sec. 5.

25. Ibid., chaps. 5–6.

26. See OT#11 and Spitzer, SDG, chap. 4. See also Spitzer, *The Soul's Upward Yearning: Clues to Our Transcendent Nature from Experience and Reason* (San Francisco: Ignatius, 2015), chap. 5.

27. See Eccles, *Evolution of the Brain: Creation of the Self*, 195–199.

28. Ibid., 121–178.

29. See also Spitzer, SDG, chap. 5, secs, 1.B and 2.C.

30. See "Acceptance of Evolution by Religious Groups," Wikipedia, https:// en.wikipedia.org/wiki/Acceptance_of_evolution_by_religious_groups.

31. See "Acceptance of Evolution by Religious Groups" and Eugenie C. Scott, "Antievolution and Creationism in the United States," *Annual Review of Anthropology* 26 (October 1997): 263–289.

32. Francis Collins, *The Language of God: A Scientist Presents Evidence for Belief* (New York: Free Press, 2007), 200. It should be noted that Collins does believe that God interacts with human beings both interiorly and providentially, particularly through conscience and the moral law, as well as through spiritual yearning and satisfaction.

33. Pierre Teilhard de Chardin, *The Phenomenon of Man* (New York: Harper Perennial, 2008). See also Pierre Teilhard de Chardin, *The Divine Milieu* (New York: Harper Perennial, 2001).

34. Vincent Smiles, "Transcendent Mind, Emergent Universe in the Thought of Michael Polanyi," *Science & Religion*, digitalcommons.csbsju.edu/cgi/viewcontent

.cgi?article=1101&context=theology_pubs.

35. Bernard Lonergan, *Insight*, 154–157, 288–293, and chaps. 8 and 19.

36. Don Vaughan, "Human Ancestors," *Britannica*, https://www.britannica.com/list/human-ancestors.

37. Ewen Callaway, "Genetic Adam and Eve Did Not Live Too Far Apart in Time," *Nature* (August 2013), https://doi.org/10.1038/nature.2013.13478.

38. Callaway, "Genetic Adam and Eve Did Not Live Too Far Apart in Time."

39. See Berwick and Chomsky, *Why Only Us*, 164–166.

40. Ibid.

41. Ibid., 90.

42. See Spitzer, SDG, chap. 5, sec. 1.B.

43. Nick Longrich, "Evolution's 'Great Leap Forward': When Did Humans Cross the Intelligence Rubicon?" Genetic Literacy Project, November 4, 2020, https://geneticliteracyproject.org/2020/11/04/evolutions-great-leap-forward-when-did-humans-cross-the-intelligence-rubicon/.

44. See Berwick and Chomsky, *Why Only Us*, 164–166.

45. Ibid., 90.

46. See Georges Ifrah, *The Universal History of Numbers: From Prehistory to the Invention of the Computer*, trans. David Bellos et al. (John Wiley & Sons, Inc., 2000), 64–67. A complex triple column tallying bone — the Ishango bone — probably originated 25,000 years ago. Scott Williams, "Ishango Bone," Mathematicians of the African Diaspora, http://www.math.buffalo.edu/mad/Ancient-Africa/ishango.html.

47. Longrich, "Evolution's 'Great Leap Forward.'"

48. Jill Cook, "The Lion-Man: An Ice Age Masterpiece," The British Museum, October 10, 2017, https://www.britishmuseum.org/blog/lion-man-ice-age-masterpiece. Jörg Orschiedt, "The Late Upper Paleolithic and Earliest Mesolithic Evidence of Burials in Europe," July 16, 2018, The Royal Society, https://royalsocietypublishing.org/doi/10.1098/rstb.2017.0264.

49. Andrew Curry, "This 11,000-Year-Old Statue Unearthed in Siberia May Reveal Ancient Views of Taboos and Demons: Gigantic Wooden Statue Is among World's Oldest Monumental Art," American Association for the Advancement of Science, April 25, 2018, https://www.science.org/content/article/11000-year-old-statue-unearthed-siberia-may-reveal-ancient-views-taboos-and-demons.

50. Jo Marchant, "A Journey to the Oldest Cave Paintings in the World: The

Discovery in a Remote Part of Indonesia Has Scholars Rethinking the Origins of Art — and of Humanity," *Smithsonian Magazine*, January 2016, https://www .smithsonianmag.com/history/journey-oldest-cave-paintings-world-180957685/.

51. James Owen, "Bone Flute Is Oldest Instrument, Study Says," *National Geographic*, June 24, 2009, https://www.nationalgeographic.com/culture/article /bone-flute-is-oldest-instrument--study-says.

52. Paul Mellars, "Why Did Modern Human Populations Disperse from Africa *ca*. 60,000 Years Ago? A New Model," *Proceedings of the National Academy of Sciences of the USA* 103, no. 25 (2006), https://doi.org/10.1073/pnas.0510792103.

53. Ker Than, "Humans Were in the Arctic 10,000 Years Earlier Than Thought," *Smithsonian Magazine*, January 14, 2016, https://www.smithsonianmag.com /science-nature/humans-were-arctic-10000-years-earlier-thought-180957819/.

54. See Gustavo Politis et al., "The Arrival of *Homo Sapiens* into the Southern Cone at 14,000 Years Ago," *Plos One* 11, no. 9 (2016), https://doi.org/10.1371/journal .pone.0162870.

55. For additional explanation see Spitzer, SDG, chaps. 5–6.

56. See Kenneth Samples, "What Does It Mean to be Made in the Image of God?" Reasons to Believe, September 5, 2017, https://reasons.org/explore/blogs /reflections/what-does-it-mean-to-be-made-in-the-image-of-god.

57. See CCC 390: "The account of the fall in *Genesis* 3 uses figurative language, but affirms a primeval event, a deed that took place *at the beginning of the history of man*." See also Pius XII, *Divino Afflante Spiritu*, par. 33.

58. See Pius XII, *Divino Afflante Spiritu*, par. 3.

59. This is affirmed by the Dogmatic Constitution on the Church of Vatican II. See *Lumen Gentium*, sec. 16.

60. Pius XII, *Humani Generis*, par. 37.

61. Berwick and Chomsky, *Why Only Us*, 164–166.

Chapter 4: Questions Concerned with the Historicity of the Old Testament

1. Bright, HOI, 84.

2. Ibid., 75.

3. Ibid., 77.

4. Ibid., 82.

5. Ibid., 77.

6. Ibid., 81.

7. Ibid., 83–85.

8. Ibid., 84.

9. Ibid.

10. Ibid.

11. Jean-Pierre Isbouts, "We May Now Know Which Egyptian Pharaoh Challenged Moses," *National Geographic*, December 28, 2018, https://www .nationalgeographic.com/culture/article/pharaoh-king-punished-god.

12. See Clifford and Murphy, "Genesis," in NJBC, 18.

13. Bright, HOI, 87.

14. Ibid., 86–88.

15. Ibid., 105–130.

16. Ibid., 25.

17. Ibid., 103.

18. Ibid., 25.

19. Ibid.

20. Ibid., 104.

21. Biblical Archaeology Society Staff, "The Exodus: Fact or Fiction?" Biblical Archaeology Society, April 6, 2023, https://www.biblicalarchaeology.org/daily /biblical-topics/exodus/exodus-fact-or-fiction/.

22. Ibid.

23. Bright, HOI, 104.

24. Ibid., 103.

25. Ibid., 104.

26. Clifford, "Exodus," in NJBC, 49.

27. Bright, HOI, 106.

28. The Midianites *may* have worshiped a god called *Yahweh*, and Moses' father-in-law, Jethro, may have worshiped him as well. However, "Mosaic Yahwism" into which Moses (speaking on behalf of Yahweh) integrated election, the covenant, and commandments of the law, was quite unique. See Bright, HOI, 107.

29. Ibid., 107.

30. Ibid., 124.

31. Ibid., 123.

32. Ibid., 122.

33. Ibid., 123.

34. Ibid., 107.

35. Ibid.

36. Ibid., 130.

37. Ibid.

38. Clifford, "Exodus," in NJBC, 52.

39. Bright, HOI, 113.

40. Ibid., 114.

41. Ibid., 113–115.

42. Eero Junkkaala, *Three Conquests of Canaan: A Comparative Study of Two Egyptian Military Campaigns and Joshua 10–12 in the Light of Recent Archaeological Evidence* (Finland: Åbo Akademi University Press, 2006), https://core.ac.uk/download/pdf/39937804.pdf, 47–61.

43. Junkkaala, *Three Conquests of Canaan*, 22.

44. Ibid., 33.

45. Bright, HOI, 115.

46. Ibid.

47. Ibid.

48. Ibid.

49. Ibid.

50. Ibid.

51. Ibid., 115–116.

52. Junkkaala, *Three Conquests of Canaan*, 227–252.

53. Bright, HOI, 116.

54. Ibid., 115–117.

55. Ibid., 116.

56. Ibid.

57. Ibid., 141.

58. Ibid.

59. Ibid., 142.

60. Ibid., 143.

61. Ibid., 143–145.

Chapter 5: Questions Concerned with the Development of Morality, the Historicity of Miracles, and the Inspiration of Prophesy in the Old Testament

1. For this and the following paragraph, see Ratzinger, "Zum Problem," 9–11.

2. Pontifical Biblical Commission, *The Bible and Morality: Biblical Roots of Christian Conduct*, May 11, 2008, Vatican.va.

3. Ibid., par. 120–121.

4. Ibid., par. 121.

5. See Psalms 5, 6, 11, 12, 35, 37, 40, 52, 54, 56, 57, 58, 59, 69, 79, 83, 94, 109, 137, 139 and 143.

6. The idea of "justice" develops considerably in the Old Testament, reaching its fullest expression in Jesus' preaching. See John L. McKenzie, *Dictionary of the Bible* (New York: Macmillan, 1965), 739–743.

7. Julius H. Greenstone, "Polygamy," *Jewish Encyclopedia*, https://www.jewishencyclopedia.com/articles/12260-polygamy.

8. Dt 12:31; 18:10; Lv 18:21; 20:2–5; 2 Kgs 3:27; 16:3; 21:6; Jer 7:31; 32:35; Ez 20:25–26; Ps 106:37–41.

9. Deuteronomy 12:29–31 preserves a tradition in which Israelite leaders admonished the Israelites at the time of the conquest to refrain from adopting Canaanite customs, the worst of which was sacrificing their children by burning them. Since this was considered the exemplar of the debased nature of Canaanite religion, the Yahwist would have known how contrary it was to the will and law of Yahweh. See Joe Heschmeyer, "How Should We Understand Old Testament Human Sacrifice?" Word on Fire, February 18, 2019, https://www.wordonfire.org/articles/how-should-we-understand-old-testament-human-sacrifice/.

10. Gn 4:9–15; 9:6; Lv 24:17; Ex 20:13; 21:12; Nm 35:30–31.

11. Mt 5:21–22, 28–39.

12. Certain verses in Pss 5, 11, 12, 35, 37, 40, 52, 54, 56, 57, 58, 59, 69, 79, 83, 94, 109, 137, 139, 143.

13. Ratzinger, "Zum Problem," 9–11.

14. John S. Marr and Curtis D. Malloy, "An Epidemiological Analysis of the Ten Plagues of Egypt," *Caduceus* 12, no. 1 (1996):10. See also H. M. Duncan Hoyte, "The Plagues of Egypt: What Killed the Animals and the First Born?," *Medical Journal of Australia* 158, no. 10 (1993):706–708.

15. See Marr and Malloy, "An Epidemiological Analysis of the Ten Plagues." See

also Anne Raver, "Biblical Plagues: A Novel Theory," *The New York Times,* April 4, 1996, https://www.nytimes.com/1996/04/04/garden/biblical-plagues-a-novel-theory.html.

16. Olaf Alfred Toffteen, *The Historic Exodus* (Chicago: University of Chicago Press, 1909), 159, 162, and 164.

17. See Clifford, "Exodus," in NJBC, 49.

18. According to NJBC (49–50), the Priestly Author's account includes the detail that the Egyptian soldiers drowned in their pursuit of the Israelites. However, the Yahwist — the earlier author — simply states that God pushed back the waters, allowing the Israelites to escape, then letting the waters return to their normal level and apparently prohibiting the Egyptians from crossing. The Priestly Author wrote much later (during and after the Exile in the mid-500s BC), long after the Yahwist (writing five hundred years earlier), who was much closer to the events being narrated.

19. Anna Diamond, "What Would Happen if the Earth Stopped Rotating?" *Smithsonian Magazine,* October 2018, https://www.smithsonianmag.com/history/what-happen-earth-stopped-rotating-180970312/.

20. Kevin Baird, "Oldest Recorded Solar Eclipse Helps Date the Egyptian Pharaohs," University of Cambridge, https://www.cam.ac.uk/research/news/oldest-recorded-solar-eclipse-helps-date-the-egyptian-pharaohs. See also Colin Humphreys and Graeme Waddington, "Solar Eclipse of 1207 BC Helps to Date Pharaohs," *Astronomy & Geophysics* 58, no. 5 (October 2017), https://doi.org/10.1093/astrogeo/atx178.

21. Strong's *Exhaustive Concordance of the Bible,* 1826a, https://biblehub.com/lexicon/joshua/10-12.htm.

22. See Stanley Jaki, *God and the Sun at Fatima* (Royal Oak, MI: Real View Books, 1999), 338–339.

23. Louis Hartman and Alexander Di Lella, "Daniel," in NJBC, 407–408.

24. Hartman and Di Lella, "Daniel," in NJBC, 408.

25. See Hartman and Di Lella, "Daniel," in NJBC, 408.

26. Pius XII, *Divino Afflante Spiritu,* par. 33.

27. Anthony Ceresko, "Jonah," in NJBC, 580.

28. Jerome Walsh and Christopher Begg, "1–2 Kings," in NJBC, 160.

29. Ibid.

30. Ibid.

31. Bruce Vawter, "Introduction to Prophetic Literature," in NJBC, 191–192, 196–197.

32. Ibid., 192.

33. Ibid., 196.

34. Ibid., 195.

35. Ibid.

36. David J. Gibson, *The Chronology of Jeremiah (and the Lachish Letters)* (CanBooks 2004, 2019), Nabatea.net, https://nabataea.net/explore/biblical _studies/biblicalhistory/the-chronology-of-jeremiah-and-the-lachish-letters/.

37. Pontifical Biblical Commission, "Document on the Interpretation of the Bible in the Church," in *The Scripture Documents: An Anthology of Official Catholic Teachings*, ed. and trans. by Dean P. Béchard (Collegeville, MN: Liturgical Press, 2002), 244–317.

38. Pontifical Biblical Commission, *The Interpretation of the Bible in the Church*, April 23, 1993, https://www.catholic-resources.org/ChurchDocs/PBC _Interp-FullText.htm, sec. 2.B.2.

39. Pontifical Biblical Commission, *The Interpretation of the Bible in the Church*, sec. 2.B.2.

40. Ibid.

41. Joseph Jensen and William Irwin, "Isaiah 1–39" in NJBC, 235.

42. A. Houtman, "Description of *History and Origin of Targum Jonathan*," Protestant Theological University, Kampen, 2002–2006, http://www.targum.nl/pdf /History%20and%20Origin%20of%20Targum%20Jonathan.pdf.

43. A full Aramaic text and English translation of the prophets in Targum Jonathan can be obtained at Sefaria.org, https://www.sefaria.org/Targum_Jonathan _on_Isaiah.9.5.

44. Houtman, "Description of *History and Origin of Targum Jonathan*."

45. Jonathan ben Uziel, "Targum Jonathan Ben UzielL The Chaldee Paraphrase on the Prophet Isaiah," trans. Rev. C. W. H. Pauli, 1871, Judeo-Christian Research, http://juchre.org/targums/isaiah/benisa.htm#42.

46. Carroll Stuhmueller, "Deutero-Isaiah," in NJBC, 331.

47. "Psalm 22 — Is It Messianic?," The Messiah Factor, Tony Pearce, https:// messiahfactor.com/psalm-22/.

48. Although there is controversy about whether *aryeh* should be translated as "pierced," there can be little doubt that the pre-Christian Septuagint translators

thought it had this meaning (*oruxan*). See "Psalm 22 — Is It Messianic?"

49. Ratzinger, "Exegesis and the Magisterium of the Church," 133–134.

PART TWO: QUESTIONS ABOUT
THE NEW TESTAMENT

Chapter 6: The Historicity of the Gospels

1. Cornelius Tacitus, *Annals*, in "The Annals of Tacitus," Early Christian Writings, http://www.earlychristianwritings.com/text/annals.html, bk. 15, chap. 44.

2. Peter Kirby, "Cornelius Tacitus," Early Christian Writings, 2014, http://www.earlychristianwritings.com/tacitus.html.

3. Luke Timothy Johnson, *The Gospel of Luke*, vol. 3. of the *Sacra Pagina* series, ed. Daniel J. Harrington, SJ (Collegeville, MN: Liturgical Press, 1991), 113–114.

4. Raymond Brown, *An Introduction to New Testament Christology* (New York: Paulist Press, 1994), 373–376.

5. Meier, *A Marginal Jew, Volume 2*, 592–593.

6. Flavius Josephus, *Jewish Antiquities*, ed. and trans. Louis H. Feldman, Loeb Classical Library (Cambridge, MA: Harvard University Press, 1965), 18:3.3. The ellipsis in this text is in place of a deletion of a later Christian interpolation as determined by John P. Meier, Luke Timothy Johnson, and Raymond Brown. See the references to these scholars immediately above.

7. Meier, *A Marginal Jew, Volume 2*, 592–593.

8. Peter Schäfer, *Jesus in the Talmud* (Princeton, NJ: Princeton University Press, 2007), 18–19.

9. Ibid.

10. Gerd Theissen and A. Merz, *The Historical Jesus: A Comprehensive Guide*, trans. John Bowden (London: SCM, 1998), 102–104.

11. Samuel Byrskog, *Story as History — History as Story: The Gospel Tradition in the Context of Ancient Oral History* (Philadelphia: Coronet Books, 2001).

12. Birger Gerhardsson, *The Reliability of the Gospel Tradition* (Grand Rapids, MI: Baker Academics, 2001). See also Birger Gerhardsson, *Memory and Manuscript with Tradition and Transmission in Early Christianity* (Grand Rapids, MI: Eerdmans, 1998).

13. Martin Hengel, *The Four Gospels and the One Gospel of Jesus Christ*, trans. John Bowden (London: SCM Press, 2000). Martin Hengel and Anna Maria

Schwemer, *Paul Between Damascus and Antioch*, trans John Bowden (London: SCM Press, 1997).

14. Kenneth Bailey, "Informal Controlled Oral Tradition and the Synoptic Gospels," *Asia Journal of Theology* 5 (1991): 34–51.

15. James Dunn, *Christianity in the Making, vol. 1: Jesus Remembered* (Grand Rapids, MI: Eerdmans, 2003).

16. Jan Vansina, *Oral Tradition as History* (Madison, WI: University of Wisconsin Press, 1985).

17. Gerd Theissen and Dagmar Winter, *The Quest of the Plausible Jesus: The Question of Criteria*, trans. M. Eugene Boring (Louisville, KY: Westminster John Knox, 2002). See also Theissen and Merz, *The Historical Jesus: A Comprehensive Guide.*

18. Grant Stanton, *Jesus of Nazareth in New Testament Preaching*, Society for New Testament Studies Monograph Series, 27 (Cambridge: Cambridge University Press, 1974).

19. E. P. Sanders, *The Historical Figure of Jesus* (London: Allen Lane [Penguin], 1993).

20. N. T. Wright, *The Challenge of Jesus* (London: SPCK Publishing, 2000). See also N. T. Wright, *Jesus and the Victory of God*, Christian Origins and the Question of God 2 (Minneapolis, MN: Fortress Press, 1997).

21. John P. Meier, *A Marginal Jew: Rethinking the Historical Jesus, Volume 1: The Roots of the Problem and the Person* (New York: Doubleday, 1991); Meier, *A Marginal Jew, Volume 2*; and John P. Meier, "The Present State of the 'Third Quest' for the Historical Jesus: Loss and Gain," *Biblica* 80, no. 4 (1999): 459–487, https://www.jstor.org/stable/42614221.

22. Vincent Taylor, *The Formation of the Gospel Tradition* (London: Macmillan, 1933), 41.

23. Bauckham, *Jesus and the Eyewitnesses*, 5.

24. David Wenham, "Jesus and the Eyewitnesses: The Gospels as Eyewitness Testimony," *Themelios* 33, no. 1, https://www.thegospelcoalition.org/themelios/review/jesus-and-the-eyewitnesses-the-gospels-as-eyewitness-testimony/.

25. Felix Just, SJ, "The New Testament Canon," Catholic-Resources.org, https://catholic-resources.org/Bible/NT_Canon.htm.

26. Ibid. For further explanation of this, see Raymond E. Brown and Raymond F. Collins, "Canonicity," in NJBC, 1044.

27. See Brown and Collins, "Canonicity," in NJBC, 1046. See also Bauckham, *Jesus and the Eyewitnesses*, 415.

28. See Bauckham, *Jesus and the Eyewitnesses*, 155–182.

29. This quote from Papias was originally written in his work *Exposition of the Sayings of the Lord*. Unfortunately, this work is no longer extant. However, Eusebius saved the fragment quoted in the text in his later work *Ecclesiastical History*, bk. 2, chap. 15; bk. 3, chap. 30; and bk. 6, chap. 14. The translation of *Ecclesiastical History* is taken from Bauckham, *Jesus and the Eyewitnesses*, 203.

30. Justin Martyr, *Dialogue with Trypho*, chap. 106.

31. Irenaeus, *Against Heresies*, bk. 3, chap. 1.

32. Clement of Alexandria, *Ecclesiastical History*, bk. 2, chap. 15.

33. Eusebius, *Ecclesiastical History* 3.39.3–4.

34. See Bauckham, *Jesus and the Eyewitnesses*, p. 158.

35. See Bauckham's explanation of John and Mark in ibid., 69 and 206.

36. Ibid., 206.

37. Robert J. Karris, "The Gospel According to Luke," in NJBC, 675.

38. Gerhardsson, *The Reliability of the Gospel Tradition*.

39. Harald Riesenfeld, "The Gospel Tradition and Its Beginnings," in *The Gospel Tradition* (Oxford: Blackwell 1970), 1–29.

40. Matthias, who was designated to replace Judas Iscariot, had to be an official witness, meaning he had to be a part of the company who surrounded Jesus "from the beginning." See Acts 1:21–26. This is precisely the criterion for "eyewitness" that Luke uses in the prologue of his Gospel in his dedication to Theophilus in Luke 1:3.

41. Bauckham, *Jesus and the Eyewitnesses*, 94.

42. Ibid., 93.

43. Ibid.

44. Ibid., 93–94.

45. Ibid.

46. Ibid.

47. Ibid., 99.

48. Ibid., 39.

49. Ibid.

50. Ibid., 39–40.

51. Ibid., 48–49.

52. Ibid., 48. See also Birger Gerhardsson, "Mark and the Female Witnesses"

(Philadelphia: University of Pennsylvania the University Museum, 1989).

53. Bauckham, *Jesus and the Eyewitnesses*, 50–52.

54. See Brown and Collins, "Canonicity," in NJBC, 1046. See also Bauckham, *Jesus and the Eyewitnesses*, 415.

55. Just, "The New Testament Canon." For further explanation of this, see Brown and Collins, "Canonicity," in NJBC, 1044.

56. See Bauckham, *Jesus and the Eyewitnesses*, chaps. 14–16, 358–437.

57. Ibid., 129, 405–409.

58. Ibid., 129.

59. Ibid.

60. Ibid., 36–38.

61. Brown and Collins, "Canonicity," in NJBC, 1046. See also Bauckham, *Jesus and the Eyewitnesses*, 415. See also Pheme Perkins, "The Gospel According to John," in NJBC, 946–947.

62. Perkins, "The Gospel According to John," in NJBC, 947.

63. Bauckham, *Jesus and the Eyewitnesses*, 415.

64. See, for example, J. A. T. Robinson, *The Priority of John*, ed. J. F. Coakley (London: SCM, 1985), 93–122 and D. A. Carson, *The Gospel According to John* (Grand Rapids, MI: Eerdmans, 1991), 68–81.

65. Bauckham, *Jesus and the Eyewitnesses*, 422.

66. Ibid., 358.

67. Perkins, "The Gospel According to John," in NJBC, 945–946.

68. Dunn, *Jesus Remembered*, 192–210.

69. Robert J. Karris, "The Gospel According to Luke," in NJBC, 675.

70. Ibid.

71. Ibid., 675–676.

72. Bauckham, *Jesus and the Eyewitnesses*, 120–121.

73. For additional themes, see John Navone, *Themes of St. Luke* (Rome: Gregorian University Press, 1970).

74. See Bauckham, *Jesus and the Eyewitnesses*, 37.

75. Ibid., 3–11, 23–25, 117–119, 384–410, 472–491.

76. Ibid., 264–277.

77. Ibid., 112.

78. Ibid., 302.

79. Papias, being quoted by Eusebius in *Ecclesiastical History*, 3.39.16. Papias

implies that John the Elder is his source for this information. See Bauckham, *Jesus and the Eyewitnesses*, 203.

80. Bauckham, *Jesus and the Eyewitnesses*, 224.

81. Ibid.

82. Benedict Viviano, "The Gospel According to Matthew," in NJBC, 630–631.

83. Ibid.

84. Ibid., 631.

85. Ibid.

86. Ibid. Caesarea Maritima was formerly known as Caesarea Palestinae — a cultural capital of Palestine for the Romans and a central city of Christianity.

87. Ibid.

88. Ibid., 632.

89. Ibid.

90. Ibid.

91. Ibid.

92. Karris, "Gospel According to Luke," in NJBC, 676.

93. Martin Dibelius, *From Tradition to Gospel*, trans. B. L. Woolf (London: Ivor Nicholson and Watson, 1934). See also Rudolf Bultmann, *The History of the Synoptic Tradition*, trans. J. Marsh, 2nd ed. (Oxford: Blackwell, 1968), and Bauckham, *Jesus and the Eyewitnesses*, 263.

94. Gerhardsson, *The Reliability of the Gospel Tradition*, 40 and Bauckham, *Jesus and the Eyewitnesses*, 11.

95. James Dunn, "Altering the Default Setting: Re-Envisaging the Early Transmission of the Jesus Tradition," *New Testament Studies* 49, no. 2 (2003): 144–145; Dunn, *Jesus Remembered*, 194–195, 248–249; Bauckham, *Jesus and the Eyewitnesses*, 263.

96. Bailey, "Informal Controlled Oral Tradition and the Synoptic Gospels," 34–51; Bauckham, *Jesus and the Eyewitnesses*, 263.

97. Dunn, "Altering the Default Setting: Re-Envisaging the Early Transmission of the Jesus Tradition," 144–45; Bauckham, *Jesus and the Eyewitnesses*, 263.

98. Bauckham, *Jesus and the Eyewitnesses*, 240–249, 251–262.

99. Gerhardsson, *The Reliability of the Gospel Tradition*, 50–80; Bauckham, *Jesus and the Eyewitnesses*, 114–154.

100. Bailey, "Informal Controlled Oral Tradition and the Synoptic Gospels," 34–51.

101. Ibid.

102. Dunn, "Altering the Default Setting: Re-Envisaging the Early Transmission of the Jesus Tradition," 144–145.

103. Ibid.

104. Gerhardsson, *Memory and Manuscript*, 202; Bauckham, *Jesus and the Eyewitnesses*, 262–264.

105. Bauckham, *Jesus and the Eyewitnesses*, 252–262.

106. Ibid.

107. Ibid.

108. Ibid.

109. Ibid., 93–95, 262–263.

110. Ibid., 251–252, 279–281.

111. Ibid., 252–262.

112. "The Infancy Gospel of Thomas" in Andrew Bernhard, *Other Early Christian Gospels: A Critical Edition of the Surviving Greek Manuscripts* (London: T&T Clark, 2006), chaps. 4 and 5.

113. "One might add, for good measure, the followers not only of John the Baptist but of Judas the Galilean, Simon, Athronges, Eleazar ben Deinaus and Alexander, Menahem, Simon bar Giora, and bar-Kochba himself. Faced with the defeat of their leader, followers of such figures would either be rounded up as well or melt away into the undergrowth." Wright, *Jesus and the Victory of God*, 110.

114. E. P. Sanders, *Jesus and Judaism* (Philadelphia: Fortress, 1985), 240.

115. Wright, *Jesus and the Victory of God*, 109–111.

116. Meier, *A Marginal Jew: Volume 2*, 623.

117. Ibid.

118. Joachim Jeremias, *New Testament Theology*, vol. 1, *The Proclamation of Jesus* (New York: Scribner, 1971); Joachim Jeremias, "The Problem of the Historical Jesus," in *In Search of the Historical Jesus*, ed. Harvey K. McArthur (London: Scribner, 1969); Joachim Jeremias, *The Parables of Jesus* (London: SCM Press, 1972).

119. Sanders, *The Historical Figure of Jesus*.

120. Wright, *Jesus and the Victory of God*; Wright, *The Resurrection of the Son of God*.

121. Meier, *A Marginal Jew*, vols. 1–4.

122. Jeremias, "The Problem of the Historical Jesus," 139–140.

123. Béda Rigaux, "L'historicité de Jésus devant l'exégese récente," *Revue Bib-*

lique 68 (1958):481–522.

124. René Latourelle, *Finding Jesus Through the Gospels: History and Herme-neutics* (New York: Alba House 1979), 227; Joachim Jeremias, *Jerusalem in the Time of Jesus* (Philadelphia: Fortress Press, 1962).

125. Bauckham, *Jesus and the Eyewitnesses*, 39–92.

126. Tal Ilan, *Lexicon of Jewish Names in Late Antiquity: Part I: Palestine 330 BCE–200 CE* (Tübingen: Mohr Siebeck, 2002).

127. Ibid.

128. Ibid., 74.

129. Brown, *An Introduction to New Testament Christology*, 60–70; Meier, *A Marginal Jew: Volume 2*, 450–553.

130. McKenzie, *Dictionary of the Bible*, 1; Jeremias, *New Testament Theology*, 64–65.

131. Jeremias, *New Testament Theology*, 252–254.

132. Ibid.

133. Ibid.

134. Wright, *The Resurrection of the Son of God*, 401–584.

Chapter 7: The Life and Miracles of Jesus: History and Science

1. Brown, *An Introduction to New Testament Christology*, 61–64.

2. Meier, *A Marginal Jew: Volume 2*, 650–870.

3. Ibid..

4. Ibid., 647–648.

5. Ibid., 648.

6. Ibid., 678.

7. Ibid.

8. Ibid., 780–797.

9. Ibid., 795.

10. For a full explanation of these phenomena, see Spitzer, SDC, chap. 6, and Robert Spitzer, *Christ versus Satan in Our Daily Lives: The Cosmic Struggle between Good and Evil* (San Francisco: Ignatius, 2020), appendix.

11. See "The Medical Bureau of the Sanctuary," Lourdes Sanctuaire, https://www.lourdes-france.org/en/medical-bureau-sanctuary/.

12. The seven thousand recorded cures have varying degrees of tests and records

to establish scientific inexplicability. According to Dr. Michael Lasalle of the Lourdes Medical Bureau, 2,500 of these cures have sufficient tests and records to be classified as "medically inexplicable." This does not mean that the other 4,500 cures are scientifically explicable, but only that the nature, testing, and records leave the possibility open for some unknown scientific explanation. See personal communication of Dr. Lasalle to Paul Glynn in June 1997 in Paul Glynn, *Healing Fire of Christ: Reflections on Modern Miracles* (San Francisco: Ignatius, 2003), 73.

13. This number was disclosed by Dr. Alessandro de Franciscis, current president of the Lourdes Office of Medical Observations, in an interview given to Fr. Seán Connolly. Fr. Seán Connolly, "70th Miracle of Lourdes Affirmed by the Church," The Catholic World Report, February 13, 2018, https://www.catholicworldreport .com/2018/02/13/70th-miracle-of-lourdes-affirmed-by-the-church/.

14. See Bernard François, E. Sternberg, and E. Fee, "The Lourdes Medical Cures Revisited," *Journal of the History of Medicine and Allied Sciences* 69, no. 1 (January 2014): 159, https://doi.org/10.1093/jhmas/jrs041.

15. François, Sternberg, and Lee, "The Lourdes Medical Cures Revisited," 159. For a description of the many steps in recording a cure with the Lourdes Medical Bureau, and a history of the development of the medical bureau, see John Dowling, "Lourdes Cures and Their Medical Assessment," *Journal of the Royal Society of Medicine* 77 (August 1984): 634–638, https://journals.sagepub.com/doi/ pdf/10.1177/014107688407700803.

16. For a fuller explanation and case studies, see Spitzer, SDC, chap. 6.

17. See Spitzer, *Christ versus Satan in Our Daily Lives*, appendix (sec. 2).

18. Michael Lipka and Tim Townsend, "Papal Saints: Once a Given, Now Extremely Rare," Pew Research Center, April 24, 2014, https://www.pewresearch .org/fact-tank/2014/04/24/papal-saints-once-a-given-now-extremely-rare.

19. "Pope Benedict XVI Beatified 870 People, Canonized 45 Saints and Made a Female Saint a Doctor of the Church — See Who They Are!" Catholic World News, January 3, 2023, http://www.catholicnewsworld.com/2023/01/pope -benedict-xvi-beatified-870-people.html.

20. Pope Francis also canonized 813 martyrs as a single group, but each one of these individuals did not have a separate scientific panel to validate miracles through his or her intercession. The intercession of the group was responsible for the miraculous occurrence. See "List of Saints Canonized by Pope Francis," Wikipedia, https://en.wikipedia.org/wiki/List_of_saints_canonized_by_Pope_Francis.

21. See Kathleen Manning, "How Many Saints Are There?" *U.S. Catholic*, October 31, 2013, https://uscatholic.org/articles/201310/how-many-saints-are-there/.

22. Brown, *An Introduction to New Testament Christology*, 90.

23. Wright, *Jesus and the Victory of God*, 551.

24. McKenzie, *Dictionary of the Bible*, 480.

25. See Wright, *Jesus and the Victory of God*, 463–464.

26. Ibid. Italics mine.

27. Ibid.

28. See Jeremias, *New Testament Theology*, 64.

29. Ibid., 65.

30. Ibid., 64–65.

31. John L. McKenzie, in *The Jerome Biblical Commentary*, vol. 2, ed. Raymond Brown, Joseph A. Fitzmeyer, and Roland E. Murphy (Englewood Cliffs, NJ: Prentice-Hall, 1968), 83.

32. Ibid.

33. Ibid.

34. See Wright, *Jesus and the Victory of God*, 463–464.

35. Ibid., 497–501.

36. Ibid., 551.

37. See Fr. Robert Spitzer, *The Moral Wisdom of the Catholic Church: A Defense of Her Controversial Moral Teachings* (San Francisco: Ignatius, 2022), 371–373.

38. Ibid., 377–384.

39. *Agapē* was a little-used Greek word, which the Christians intentionally chose to express Jesus' unique view of love. This helped them to distinguish it from other popular views of love in the culture — *storgē* (feelings of affection), *philia* (friendship — love based on reciprocity), and *eros* (sexual love). See C. S. Lewis, *The Four Loves* (New York: Harcourt Brace, 1960).

40. These four passages are explained in Robert Spitzer, *Escape from Evil's Darkness: The Light of Christ in the Church, Spiritual Conversion, and Moral Conversion* (San Francisco: Ignatius, 2021), 296–373.

41. These four passages are explained in Robert Spitzer, *God So Loved the World: Clues to Our Transcendent Destiny from the Revelation of Jesus* (San Francisco: Ignatius, 2016), 74–87.

42. These four passages are explained in Spitzer, *God So Loved the World*, 107–141.

43. See Spitzer, *The Moral Wisdom of the Catholic Church*, 369–398.

44. See "Preparing for the 'Year of Creation,'" *Vermont Catholic*, Winter 2016–2017, http://www.onlinedigeditions.com/publication/index.php?i=365491.

45. "Catholic Hospitals Comprise One Quarter of World's Healthcare, Council Reports," Catholic News Agency, February 10, 2010, https://www.catholicnewsagency.com/news/catholic_hospitals_represent_26_percent_of_worlds_health_facilities_reports_pontifical_council.

46. See "Vatican — Catholic Church Statistics 2018," *Agenzia Fides*, October 20, 2018, http://www.cccb.ca/site/images/stories/pdf/Dossier_Statistics_2018_FIDES_ENG.pdf.

47. See Spitzer, *God So Loved the World*, chap. 7, sec. 2.

48. Lk 12:12; 24:49; Acts 2:38; 4:8, 31; 6:8; 7:55, 9:17; 11:24; 13:2, 52; 15:28; 19:2; 20:28.

49. Acts 13:2; 15:28; 20:28.

50. See Spitzer, *Moral Wisdom of the Catholic Church*, chaps. 1–4. I give over one hundred secular, medical, psychiatric, and university studies showing that Jesus' moral teaching as interpreted by the Catholic Church leads to significantly better spiritual, emotional, relational, and marital health.

51. We have Jesus' direct words in the Gospels to institute baptism, which includes confirmation (see Mt 28:19), the holy Eucharist (Lk 22:19–20; Mt 26:26–28; and Mk 14:22–24), and reconciliation (Jn 20:22–23). Though we do not have His direct words of institution for marriage, holy orders, or the Sacrament of the Sick, the sacramentality of marriage is clear from His teaching on the sacredness, exclusivity, and permanence of marriage as the will of the Creator (see Mt 19:4–6), as well as evidence of holy orders (the laying on of hands) in the Pauline Letters (e.g., 1 Tm 4:13–14 and 2 Tm 1:6). We also have evidence of the Sacrament of the Sick from the Letter of James (Jas 5:14). See Spitzer, *Escape from Evil's Darkness*, chap. 2.

52. See Robert Spitzer, *Big Book — Volume 9: The Sacraments, Part 1 — The Sacred Eucharistic Liturgy* and *Volume 10: The Sacraments, Part 2 — Baptism, Confirmation, Reconciliation, Orders, and the Sacrament of the Sick*, Magis Center, https://www.magiscenter.com/catechism-resource-book.

53. The first line of Psalm 22 (which is very probably Jesus' final proclamation before His death on the cross) refers to the whole psalm. The last verses of the psalm make it clear that the self-sacrifice of the victim in the psalm is *for everyone for all time* — from the creation of the world to its end. See Ps 22:29–31. See also Spitzer,

God So Loved the World, 123–142.

54. See Spitzer, *Christ versus Satan in Our Daily Lives*, 89–133.

55. Spitzer, *Christ versus Satan in Our Daily Lives*, 106–118, and chaps. 5 and 6.

Chapter 8: The Passion of Jesus and the Eucharist: History and Science

1. Tacitus, *Annals*, bk. 15, chap. 44.

2. Josephus, *Jewish Antiquities*, 18:3.3.

3. Schäfer, *Jesus in the Talmud*, 18–19.

4. See Bauckham, *Jesus and the Eyewitnesses*, 49–51.

5. A detailed explanation of the scientific research and scientific studies and journals in which they are reported is given in Spitzer, SDC, chap. 3.

6. Ibid., sec. 2.A.

7. Ibid., sec. 3.

8. For scientific/medical certification, ibid.

9. For scientific/medical references, ibid., sec. 4.A.

10. For scientific/medical references, ibid., sec. 4.B.

11. For scientific/medical references, ibid., sec. 4.C.

12. For the scientific/medical references, ibid., sec. 4.E.

13. For the scientific/medical references, ibid., sec. 4.D.

14. See McKenzie, *Dictionary of the Bible*, 757.

15. Ibid., 99.

16. Ibid., 755–758.

17. Ibid., 155–156.

18. According to Bruce Vawter, "The prophetic word lives a life of its own once it has emanated from the prophet." Vawter, "Introduction to Prophetic Literature," in NJBC, 200.

19. See Johannes Betz, "Eucharist," in *Sacramentum Mundi: An Encyclopedia of Theology*, vol. 2, ed. Karl Rahner (London: Burns & Oates, 1968–1970), 260–261. See also Joachim Jeremias, *The Eucharistic Words of Jesus* (London: SCM Press, 1966), 223–224. For an explanation of the ancient Jewish view of the collapse of time in the reenactment of the Passover, see von Rad, *Old Testament Theology*, 104–108. For studies concerned with "collapsible sacred time" in other ancient cultures, see Eliade, *The Sacred and the Profane*, 40–45. See also Mircea Eliade, *The Myth of the Eternal Return: Or, Cosmos and History*, trans. Willard R. Trask (Princeton: Princ-

eton University Press, 1971), the entire volume.

20. See Vawter, "Introduction to Prophetic Literature," in NJBC, 199–200.

21. Betz, "Eucharist," 260.

22. See Eliade, *The Myth of the Eternal Return.* See also Mircea Eliade, *Myths, Dreams, and Mysteries,* trans. Philip Mairet (NY: Harper and Row, 1975).

23. Eliade, *The Myth of the Eternal Return.* See also Eliade, *The Sacred and the Profane,* 92–96 and 201–203.

24. See von Rad, *Old Testament Theology,* 104–108.

25. See *Didache,* 10:7, "Charge the prophets to hold Eucharist as they will." Also, in *Didache* 11, a set of rules is given to distinguish true apostles and prophets from false apostles and prophets, with the implication being that there were itinerant apostles and prophets who had to be tested before they would be allowed to celebrate the Eucharist and instruct the faithful.

26. Betz, "Eucharist," 260.

27. As the Church evolved, the "prophets" (who were set aside to do the Eucharistic remembrance) were known as *presbyters* ("elders") because they also were leaders in local parishes and regions. Prophets and presbyters were later called *priests* because the separation of the Christian Church from the Synagogue enabled "priest" to be used without confusion with the Jewish priesthood. The term *priest* once again put the emphasis on Jesus' Eucharistic *sacrifice,* which embraces both the Person and salvific action intrinsic to His crucifixion and Last Supper. By the late second century, the terms *priest* and *sacrifice* are used and recognized. See Irenaeus, *Against Heresies,* bk. 4, chap. 8, par. 3.

28. See Henri Bergson, *Time and Free Will: An Essay on the Immediate Data of Consciousness* (Mineola, NY: Dover, 2001), 90–121. See also, Robert Spitzer, *New Proofs for the Existence of God: Contributions of Contemporary Physics and Philosophy* (Grand Rapids, MI: Eerdmans, 2010), 183–196.

29. Ignatius of Antioch, Letter to the Romans, 7:3.

30. Thomas Aquinas, *De Venerabili Sacramento Altaris nec non de Exposition Missae,* https://www.worldcat.org/title/de-venerabili-sacramento-altaris-nec -non-de-expositione-missae-ex-operibus-d-thomae-aquinatis-excerptus/oclc /26191510.

31. The scientific research and publications in this unit can be found in Spitzer, SDC, chap. 4.

32. The scientific studies and references for Buenos Aires can be found in

Spitzer, SDC, chap. 4, sec. 4.

33. For a list of all the individual physicians, geneticists, and laboratories, see Spitzer, SDC, chap. 8.

34. Ricardo Castañón Gomez, *Cronica de un Milagroro Eucaristico: Esplendor en Tixtla Chilpancingo,* trans. English Coaching (Fiverr), Kindle edition (Mexico: Grupo Internacional Para La Paz, 2014).

35. The scientific studies and references on the Sokolka Host can be found in Spitzer, SDC, chap. 4, sec. 3.

Chapter 9: The Resurrection, Holy Spirit, and Catholic Church: History and Science

1. Gary Habermas, "Mapping the Recent Trend toward the Bodily Resurrection Appearances of Jesus in Light of Other Prominent Critical Positions," in *The Resurrection of Jesus: John Dominic Crossan and N.T. Wright in Dialogue,* ed. Robert B. Stewart (Minneapolis, MN: Fortress Press, 2006), 74–89.

2. Habermas, "Mapping the Recent Trend toward the Bodily Resurrection Appearances of Jesus in Light of Other Prominent Critical Positions," 79, italics mine.

3. See Karl Rahner, "Ho Theos in the New Testament" in *Theological Investigations, Vol. I: God, Christ, Mary, and Grace* (London: Darton, Longman & Todd, 1963).

4. Deena Kopyto, "Women's Testimony and Talmudic Reasoning," *Kedma: Penn's Journal on Jewish Thought, Jewish Culture, and Israel* 2, no. 2 (2018), https://repository.upenn.edu/kedma/vol2/iss2/8/.

5. Wright, *Jesus and the Victory of God,* 110.

6. Ibid.

7. Ibid., 109–111. See also Meier, *A Marginal Jew: Volume 2,* 623.

8. See Wright, *Jesus and the Victory of God,* 109–111. See also Meier, *A Marginal Jew: Volume 2,* 623.

9. Wright, *The Resurrection of the Son of God,* 401–584.

10. The scientific studies and references substantiating the information in this unit can be found in Spitzer, SDC, chap. 3, sec. 5.

11. In a comprehensive paper that tested all of these possibilities, physicists John Jackson, Eric Jumper, and William Ercoline tested all eight major possibilities using laboratory conditions to replicate a non-radiation means of duplicating the image on the Shroud. They compared the results of the above attempts with the macro-

scopic and microscopic features of the Shroud image and argued that none of the techniques tested can simultaneously reproduce its main features, from the 3-D property to the coloration depth, to the resolution of the spatial details. They concluded from this that it could not be the work of an artist or a forger. See J. Jackson, E. Jumper, and W. Ercoline, "Correlation of Image Intensity on the Turin Shroud with the 3-D Structure of a Human Body Shape," *Applied Optics* 23, no. 14 (1984): 2244–2270, https://doi.org/10.1364/AO.23.002244.

12. See Spitzer, SDC, chap. 3, sec. 5.B.

13. For a summary of this hypothesis and its explanation of twenty-five enigmas, see Spitzer, SDC, chap. 3, sec. 5.

14. For all of the scientific studies and references concerned with the particle radiation hypothesis, see Spitzer, SDC, chap. 3, secs. 5.A through 5.D. For additional explanation, see Mark Antonacci, "Particle Radiation from the Body Could Explain the Shroud's Images and Its Carbon Dating," *Scientific Research and Essays* 7, no. 29 (July 30, 2012): 2613–2623, https://academicjournals.org/article/article1380798649_Antonacci.pdf.

15. These are summarized in Spitzer, SDC, chap. 3, sec. 5.B.

16. The enigmas not addressed here are explained in Mark Antonacci's article (cited above) and summarized in Spitzer, SDC, chap. 3, sec. 5.B–C.

17. Wright, *Jesus and the Victory of God*, 109–111.

18. Meier, *A Marginal Jew: Volume 2*, 623.

19. Wright, *Jesus and the Victory of God*, 109–111.

20. See Robert Spitzer, *Five Pillars of the Spiritual Life: A Practical Guide to Prayer for Active People* (San Francisco: Ignatius, 2008), chaps. 4 through 5. See also Spitzer, *Escape from Evil's Darkness*, chaps. 2 through 3.

21. The phrase "power from on high" is an early Church reference to the Holy Spirit. See Carroll Stuhlmuller, "The Gospel According to Luke," in *The Jerome Biblical Commentary*, vol. 2, 163.

22. See Bruce Vawter, "The Gospel According to John," in *The Jerome Biblical Commentary*, vol. 2, 464.

23. Ibid. Vawter shows that Jesus' statement to Mary Magdalene that He is not yet ascended but will soon ascend to the Father (Jn 20:17) has now been fulfilled when He gives the Holy Spirit to the apostles. Thus, Jesus gives the Spirit to His apostles after His ascension.

24. See the more complete list in James Dunn, *Jesus and the Spirit: A Study of*

the Religious and Charismatic Experience of Jesus and the First Christians as Reflected in the New Testament (Philadelphia: The Westminster Press, 1975), 163–170.

25. See Rom 15:19; 1 Cor 12:10, 28; 2 Cor 12:12; Gal 3:5; Heb 2:4. See also Dunn, *Jesus and the Spirit*, 163.

26. Craig Keener, *Miracles Today: The Supernatural Work of God in the Modern World* (Grand Rapids, MI: Baker Academic, 2021).

27. See CCC 688, 768, 799–801, 890, 951, 1508 (charism of healing), and 2035.

28. Briege McKenna, *Miracles Do Happen: God Can Do the Impossible* (Cincinnati: Servant, 2002). See also her website, http://www.sisterbriege.com/.

29. Richard McAlear, *The Power of Healing Prayer* (Huntington, IN: OSV, 2013). See also his website, https://www.frmac.org/.

30. Lawrence Carew, *Healer of Hearts, Healer of Minds* (Community of the Cross Publications, 1989).

31. See the articles about his healing ministry, "Burden of Light," Beliefnet, https://www.beliefnet.com/faiths/faith-tools/meditation/2002/05/burden-of-light.aspx.

32. See Robert Spitzer, *Finding True Happiness: Satisfying Our Restless Hearts* (San Francisco: Ignatius, 2015), 222–236.

33. See Spitzer, *Five Pillars of the Spiritual Life*, chap. 5, and Spitzer, *Christ versus Satan in Our Daily Lives*, 246–259.

34. Ignatius of Loyola, "Rules for Perceiving and Knowing in Some Manner the Different Movements Which Are Caused in the Soul," Internet Sacred Text Archive, https://www.sacred-texts.com/chr/seil/seil78.htm and "Rules for the Same Effect with Greater Discernment of Spirits," Internet Sacred Text Archive, https://www.sacred-texts.com/chr/seil/seil79.htm. Those who are unfamiliar with these rules of Saint Ignatius will want to consult one of these books or websites: Timothy Gallagher, *The Discernment of Spirits: An Ignatian Guide for Everyday Living* (San Francisco: Ignatius, 2005). For an introduction to discernment, see the following video, "Father Timothy Gallagher on Discernment," Augustine Institute, https://show.augustineinstitute.org/post/father-timothy-gallagher-on-discernment. See also Spitzer, *Christ versus Satan in Our Daily Lives*, chap. 4.

35. See Spitzer, *Five Pillars of the Spiritual Life*, chap. 4, and Spitzer, *Christ versus Satan in Our Daily Lives*, 46–62.

36. See Spitzer, *Escape from Evil's Darkness*, chaps. 4 through 6.

37. Joachim Jeremias, *Heiligengräber in Jesu Umwelt* (Göttingen: Vandenhoeck

und Ruprecht, 1958).

38. These *kerygmas* (brief creedal proclamations) are the very earliest extant writings we have (dating to around AD 34–35, immediately after the Resurrection). They were initially elucidated for the English world by C. H. Dodd in his seminal work, *The Apostolic Preaching and Its Developments* (New York: Harper and Brothers, 1962).

39. Acts 2:14–39; 3:13–26; 4:10–12; 5:30–32; 10:36–43; 13:17–41; 1 Thes 1:10; 1 Cor 15:1–7; and Rom 8:34.

40. See also NT#7.

41. Wright, *Jesus and the Victory of God*, 551.

42. See NT#13 and NT#14.

43. Wright, *Jesus and the Victory of God*, 109–111. See also Meier, *A Marginal Jew, Volume 2*, 623.

44. See NT#5.

45. See NT#15.

46. See NT#8 through NT#11.

47. According to the 2010 comprehensive Pew survey, 84 percent of the world's population (5.8 billion out of 6.9 billion) is religiously affiliated and belongs to a particular religious group or community. See "The Global Religious Landscape," Pew Research Center, December 18, 2012, https://www.pewforum.org/2012/12/18/global-religious-landscape-exec/.

48. See Mircea Eliade's description of what happens to human beings when they become irreligious or non-religious — the loss of ultimate meaning, direction, fulfillment, and dignity, in *The Sacred and the Profane*, 163–211.

49. See Kanita Dervic et al., "Religious Affiliation and Suicide Attempt," *The American Journal of Psychiatry* 161, no. 12 (December 2004): 2303–2308, https://ajp.psychiatryonline.org/doi/full/10.1176/appi.ajp.161.12.2303. See also Harold Koenig, "Research on Religion, Spirituality and Mental Health: A Review," *Canadian Journal of Psychiatry* 54, no. 5 (May 2009): 283–291, and also Harold Koenig, "Religion, Spirituality, and Health: a Review and Update," *Advances in Mind-Body Medicine* 29, no. 3 (Summer 2015): 19–26. See also Raphael Bonelli et al., "Religious and Spiritual Factors in Depression: Review and Integration of the Research," *Depression and Research Treatment* (2012). See also Stefano Lassi and Daniele Mugnaini, "Role of Religion and Spirituality on Mental Health and Resilience: There Is Enough Evidence," *International Journal of Emergency Mental Health and Human*

Resilience (2015). See also Corina Ronenberg et al., "The Protective Effects of Religiosity on Depression: A 2-Year Prospective Study," *The Gerontologist* 56, no. 3 (June 2016): 421–431.

50. See Dervic et al., "Religious Affiliation and Suicide Attempt," 2303–2308.

51. Saint Augustine, *Confessions*, bk. 1, chap. 1.

52. See Stephen Beale, "Just How Many Protestant Denominations Are There?" *National Catholic Register,* October 31, 2017, https://www.ncregister.com/blog /just-how-many-protestant-denominations-are-there.

53. See W. D. Davies and Dale C. Allison, *International Critical Commentary, Volume 2: Matthew 8–18* (New York: T& T Clark, 1991), 622–624.

54. Ibid.

55. Ibid.

56. For a more complete study of the Aramaic background to both Matthew 16:17–19 and Galatians 1 and 2, see Davies and Allison, *International Critical Commentary, Volume 2: Matthew 8–18*, 626–629.

57. Davies and Allison, *International Critical Commentary, Volume 2: Matthew 8–18*, 626–629.

58. Ibid.

59. Ibid., 610.

60. Ibid., 610–611.

61. Ibid.

62. See, for example, McKenzie, *Dictionary of the Bible*, 663–664.

63. Viviano, "The Gospel According to Matthew," in NJBC, 630.

64. For other similar uses of "keys" in Old Testament political contexts, see Timothy Gray, *Peter — Keys to Following Jesus* (San Francisco: Ignatius and Augustine Institute, 2016), 70–76.

65. Ibid.

66. See Jeremias, *New Testament Theology*, 252–254.

67. Jeremias indicates that Jesus' virtually exclusive use of the emphatic *ego* is used as a solemn command to expel demons, make modifications to the law, to make a new law, and to mission His disciples. This expression translates Jesus' unique Aramaic expression, "Amen, I say to you." See Jeremias, *New Testament Theology*, 252–254.

68. Jeremias notes in this regard, "In the literature of Palestinian Judaism *no evidence has yet been found* of 'my Father' being used by an individual as an address

to God. … It is quite unusual that Jesus should have addressed God as 'my Father'; it is even more so that he should have used the Aramaic form '*Abba*.'" Jeremias, *New Testament Theology*, 64. Though a few rare references of *pater mou* and *Abba* have been found since Jeremias's claim, it is still exceedingly rare and is therefore a good indicator of the *ipsissima verba* ("the very words" of Jesus).

69. Frank Leslie Cross and Elizabeth A. Livingstone, eds. "Clement of Rome, St," in *The Oxford Dictionary of the Christian Church*, 3rd rev. ed. (Oxford University Press, 2005), 363.

70. Clement of Rome, First Epistle to the Corinthians, https://www.ewtn.com /catholicism/library/first-epistle-to-the-corinthians-12498, 59, 63,. Italics mine.

71. Charles Belmonte, "Letter of St Ignatius of Antioch to the Romans," in *Faith Seeking Understanding*, 2 vols. (Quezon City, Philippines: Cobrin, 2012), http:// fsubelmonte.weebly.com/letter-of-st-ignatius-of-antioch-to-the-romans.html.

72. Arnold Toynbee, "Christianity and Civilization," in *Civilization on Trial* (Oxford: Oxford University Press, 1948), Myriobiblos, http://www.myriobiblos .gr/texts/english/toynbee.html.

About the Author

Fr. Robert J. Spitzer, SJ, Ph.D is a Catholic priest in the Jesuit order and president of the Spitzer-Magis Institute of Reason and Faith (www.magiscenter.com). Father Spitzer is also the president, master of ceremonies, and speaker at the Napa Institute. He was president of Gonzaga University from 1998 to 2009. He currently hosts a weekly EWTN television program, *Father Spitzer's Universe*, and has made multiple media appearances, including *Larry King Live* (debating Stephen Hawking, Leonard Mlodinow, and Deepak Chopra on God and modern physics), the *Today Show* (debating on the topic of physician-assisted suicide), The History Channel in *God and The Universe*, and a multiple-part PBS series, *Closer to the Truth*. He has also appeared on dozens of nationally syndicated radio programs.

His academic specialties are philosophy of science, particularly space-time theory and transcendent implications of contemporary big bang cosmology; metaphysics, particularly the theory of time and philosophy of God; and biblical apologetics concerned with science, reason, and faith. He founded five major national institutes: 1) The Spitzer-Magis Institute, 2) the Spitzer Center, 3) Colleagues in Jesuit Business Education, 4) Healing the Culture, and 5) University Faculty for Life. He is the author of fifteen books, including *New Proofs for the Existence of God: Contributions of Contemporary Physics and Philosophy* (Eerdmans, 2010), for which he won the Catholic Press Association's Award for best book in faith and science.